CW01073077

PSYCHOLOGY SURVEY
No. 2

Other works by Professor Connolly

MECHANISMS OF MOTOR SKILL DEVELOPMENT, Academic
  Press
THE GROWTH OF COMPETENCE, Edited with Professor
  J. S. Bruner, Academic Press

Note on Series

The first volume of the *Psychology Survey* series was
published under the editorship of Professor Brian M.
Foss. A list of the chapters and their authors is provided
at the end of this book.

Psychology Survey
No. 2

edited by
KEVIN CONNOLLY
Professor of Psychology, Sheffield University

London
GEORGE ALLEN & UNWIN
Boston   Sydney

First published in 1979

GEORGE ALLEN & UNWIN LTD
40 Museum Street, London WC1A 1LU

© George Allen & Unwin (Publishers) Ltd, 1979

British Library Cataloguing in Publication Data

Psychology survey
  No. 2
  1. Psychology
  I. Connolly, Kevin
  150   BF121   78–41039

  ISBN 0–04–150068–7
  ISBN 0–04–150069–5 Pbk

Typeset in 10 on 12 point Times by Northampton Phototypesetters Ltd
and printed in Great Britain by
Billing & Sons Limited, Guildford, London and Worcester

Foreword

Ebbinghaus once commented of psychology that it has 'a long past, but only a short history'. Although the scientific history of the subject may be relatively short, about a hundred years, its growth and diversification over the last twenty-five years has been enormous. We not only have new theories and vast amounts of new data, but whole new fields of study, especially on the boundaries with other sciences. New ways of thinking about behaviour and mental life, along with the implications and applications of psychological science, make the subject fascinating to anyone who is intellectually curious. But such is the 'explosion' in psychology that beating the boundaries of the subject, and trying to keep abreast of major new developments, is a daunting task not only for the student but also for the professor.

Only about twenty years ago I remember colleagues saying that as fast as new material came into psychology old material went out. Old material still goes out, of course, but it certainly is no longer a balanced flow. How we cope with the accretion of new facts, new ideas and new approaches is a very real problem for all seriously interested in the subject. Narrowly defined degree courses for students, or looking only at one's own 'cabbage patch' in the case of the researcher, is certainly not the answer because it will be self-defeating. Knowing more and more about less and less has a nasty habit of becoming less and less about less and less. Different aspects of psychology are in varying degrees interdependent, new ways of looking at problems both conceptually and empirically have often far reaching implications in seemingly distant areas of the subject. An example is provided by the development of behaviour genetics over the last twenty years, or by artificial intelligence over the last ten years.

This series of books is an attempt at finding a means of keeping abreast of new ideas and important new data. Whilst the primary target readership is the student reading for a degree in psychology, there can be few teachers and researchers who do not find some of the chapters valuable in bringing them up to date with topics outside their own speciality. No topic is dealt with exhaustively or finally, for that could not be so. How long each contribution lasts as an adequate indication of the 'state of the art' in that bit of the subject will depend upon the quality of the chapter and upon the rate of progress in the area. Inevitably this will differ. Those topics which are attracting a lot of research effort, or where important advances are made, will require to be reviewed more often than less currently fashionable problems.

Psychology has become a generic term, and nesting under it there are a great number of more specialist sub-disciplines and inter-disciplines; social psychology, sensory psychology, psycho-pharmacology, developmental psychology, behaviour genetics, artificial intelligence, neurobiology, engineering psychology, psycholinguistics and so on. We hope that this series of books will provide a means whereby the student, the professor, the specialist researcher in one area, and the intellectually curious from other disciplines or no discipline can gain a grasp of the rapid and exciting growth of the subject. This is a grand ideal, but we believe that at the rate of about fifteen chapters a year a sound conspectus will be built up, maintained and up-dated. Although there are times when many of us who make our living in psychology feel jaded and disappointed with progress, a glance across the great patchwork is usually very heartening. There can be little doubt that the genus psychology is going to have profound effects upon our intellectual, cultural and social life over the next half-century.

My choice of topics and authors for this volume reflects several things. A number of the topics treated interest *me* very much and I believe that recent developments here should be made more widely known. Other topics I selected because of my own ignorance – I wanted to know what was going on there. Also I have sought to provide some-thing of a balance and certainly some variety. The authors are all actively engaged in research in the field about which they have written and each of them has made a significant contribution in their field. I am grateful to them for 'entering the lists' and taking up the challenge of communicating the state of their art, be it primarily to the undergraduate or more widely.

My thanks go to a number of people. To Mrs. Audrey Rixham for dealing with a great deal of correspondence about the project. To Mrs. Brenda Marshall for astute and sensitive sub-editing and to Brian Foss, Stuart Sutherland and Malcolm Jeeves for their sharp and honest criticism of the final manuscripts. I have especially enjoyed working with John Churchill, a bold and enthusiastic publisher.

KEVIN CONNOLLY
Sheffield

Contents

buzzing activity level – quantifying of shaking behaviour – double mutants – gene dosage – neurological basis of leg-shaking – studies on mosaic flies – kinetogenic response of hyperkinetic flies – combination of HK^1 with other behavioural mutants – summary – *envoi*.

Chapter 1

Personality Appraisal

D. B. BROMLEY

INTRODUCTION

The use of the term 'personality' can be illustrated by mentioning some of the subordinate concepts which contribute to the meaning of this obscure and abstract idea. For example, when we form an impression of someone's personality we may refer to his traits, motives, attitudes, abilities, beliefs and values, and to his characteristic thoughts, feelings and desires. In so doing, we are not referring directly to the person's overt behaviour, but to certain covert or inner dispositions and mental states which seem to underlie his behaviour. We cannot observe these inward processes directly, so we have to infer them from what the person does and does not do, from what he says and does not say, and from his demeanour, in the context of the situation in which that person is placed.

Thus, our commonsense views about understanding other people are not as simple as we might suppose, and it is not easy to resolve some of the apparent contradictions in personality appraisal. For example, how can you know what a person is thinking or feeling when all you can observe is what he says and does? How can you know his inward inclinations, beliefs, attitudes, abilities and values when all that you can observe are his outward actions? The dilemma we face in justifying our knowledge of other people is of course a philosophical dilemma – see Ryle (1954). We can, if we wish, accept a simple commonsense solution, or we can reject it and be thoroughly sceptical about our knowledge of other minds. This philosophical dilemma has given rise to two contrasting approaches to the problem of personal adjustment. First, the psychodynamic approach attempts to assess and, where appropriate, change a person's psychological make-up by dealing as directly as possible with his thoughts, feelings and desires, e.g. by psychological counselling. Second, the behaviouristic approach attempts to assess and, where appropriate, change a person's behaviour or performance directly with little or no reference to dispositional or mentalistic processes, e.g. by modifying the pleasurable or painful consequences of his behaviour. The history of personality study in recent times has been the story of the conflict between these contrasting approaches and of attempts to reconcile them.

The study of personality has not yet given rise to a systematic and firm body of knowledge. It is, rather, a loose aggregation of concepts, methods and findings connected with the study of individual differences and personal adjustment – see Holt (1969) for a useful, brief introduction and Mischel (1976) for a more extended treatment. No attempt will be made to provide an historical perspective – see Burnham (1968) and McReynolds (1975) or to review the entire area – see Sarason and Smith (1971) and Carlson (1975). This chapter is confined to basic issues and offers alternatives to the traditional approaches to personality.

PERSONALITY MEASUREMENT

It is usual to distinguish three kinds of evidence relevant to personality measurement. First, there are data derived from observers' judgements of individuals in their natural behaviour settings – at work, school, home or play. For the purpose of personality measurement, these have usually taken the form of adjective check-lists, rating scales and the sorting of standardized statements. Second, there are data derived from self-reports by subjects. These usually take the form of self-ratings or responses to personality questionnaires. Third, there are data derived from objective tests and laboratory procedures, such as the accuracy of the individual's spatial orientation or the frequency and duration of his rest pauses when working. There is a considerable literature on the problems and methods of personality measurement; the more recent publications include the following: Kleinmuntz (1967), Eysenck and Eysenck (1969), Goodstein and Lanyon (1971), Fiske (1971), Butcher (1972) and Cattell and Dreger (1977).

The mental measurement movement, with its considerable advances in the theory and practice of intelligence testing for both children and adults in the earlier decades of this century paved the way for the personality measurement movement. It must have seemed that all that was required were the resources to implement the obvious research into test construction and validation. By about 1960, however, it was clear that the successes that had attended the measurement of intelligence were not to be so easily achieved in the measurement of personality.

It should be noticed that intelligence tests fall into the category of objective measures. Personality tests, by contrast, include those based on self-reports, expressive reactions and subjective assessments by observers. Whereas an intelligence test requires a person to *exercise* his intelligence by thinking quickly, discerning complex relationships and solving problems, a personality test may not require a person to *exercise* his non-intellectual characteristics. He does not have to exercise his introversion, emotional stability or optimism in response to a questionnaire or self-rating scale. He simply has to say what he thinks or judge how he tends to react in certain sorts of situation. This is why some tests are called 'self-report' measures. Objective tests and laboratory procedures are better in this respect, but suffer from other disadvantages. Psychometric tests generally have not been altogether convincing as indices of stable personality variables.

The personality measurement movement flourished until Mischel (1968) published his now well-known criticisms. These amounted to a root and branch attack on the whole system of concepts, methods and findings that had evolved up to that time. Mischel did not dispute the reasonableness of the assumptions underlying personality measurement, but in his view these assumptions were not justified by the relevant empirical evidence. He cited numerous examples of studies which failed to support the claim that tests were valid measures of personality, that test scores could be used to predict behaviour or that scores were consistent over time. It had been shown that scores on self-report measures and other personality tests were not very robust, in the sense of depending mainly on the latent disposition they were intended to measure. Instead they turned out to be sensitive to all kinds of methodological distortions known as response sets, such as the social desirability of multiple-choice answers to questions or the differential effects of questions phrased positively or negatively; they were sensitive to fatigue, practice effects and the attitude of the subject to the test situation; they were affected by his tendency to agree or disagree, or to lie and fake his responses, by his openness or evasiveness, by his tendency to respond in a neutral or in an extreme fashion when using rating scales, and by the extent of his interest, co-operativeness, carelessness and so on.

The discovery that personality tests were prone to such methodological artefacts naturally led to comparisons between, and attempts to improve, them. The effects of adopting one method of appraisal rather than another can be illustrated by comparing anxiety as measured by self-report items in a questionnaire with anxiety as measured by keeping a diary. The two methods may not agree: a person may believe that he is more (or less) anxious than his daily reactions indicate. Another illustration would be a person who displays anxiety in the face of threats to self-esteem, e.g. examinations, but not in the face of physical pain, e.g. dental treatment; hence, if a questionnaire includes too few items that sample his kind of anxiety (or includes too many), it will give a biased estimate of his anxiety and fail to assess him relative to other people, because the test (the measuring instrument) may not be equally applicable to all cases.

One attempt to deal with this array of difficulties in personality measurement has been to regard them as perturbations and to assimilate them into a complex, multivariate, statistical approach. This approach – see Cattell and Dreger (1977) – follows a natural science paradigm, i.e. one modelled on physics, chemistry and mathematics. Cattell likens his mathematical portrayals of personality to astronomical phenomena; and for him, perturbations in personality measurement have the same value as do perturbations in astrophysics, they provide empirical data against which theoretical expectations can be tested.

The criticisms by Mischel (1968) and many others have not gone unanswered. Block (1977), for example, asserts that 'perhaps 90 per cent of the studies . . . in personality research . . . are methodologically inadequate, without conceptual implication and even foolish.' (p. 39). But he goes on to argue that Mischel's criticisms are based on selected evidence and that a closer examination of some of the higher quality research reveals evidence which supports the traditional psychometric approach to personality. He reports that some of the well-established self-report measures – such as the MMPI, the CPI and the 16PF test – of personality are functionally similar in that they seem to be assessing similar sets of personality characteristics. He also cites a study of his own – see Block (1971) – based on repeated measures on a large sample of children and adults by means of a procedure which enables independent investigators to make standardized judgements about people, using the same or different evidence.

On the basis of his investigations, Block claims that a substantial number of personality variables – for example compliance, lack of self-control – are consistent over time. The persons he studied were judged by independent observers to manifest similar personal characteristics at different ages: from junior school, through senior school, to adult life. This may not sound like a revolutionary discovery; but it is, in fact, remarkably difficult to give a scientific demonstration of this apparently simple commonsense notion.

Both Mischel (1968) and Block (1977) agree in finding that data derived from objective tests and laboratory procedures do not succeed well in distinguishing between different kinds of personality characteristics and do not reveal much consistency in individual behaviour. The reliability and consistency of responses to objective tests, however, will usually increase if the number of trials is increased. Mischel and Block disagree, however, about the interpretation to be put on the data derived from observers' judgements and self-reports. Mischel's lack of confidence in all three kinds of data led him to prefer behavioural assessment over personality assessment. He seems to have abandoned the search for general traits which characterize a person in a wide range of situations and over long periods of time. He prefers instead to study the complexities and variations in individual adjustment in different situations.

Investigations summarized by Mischel (1968) seem to demonstrate that, given the same basic information about people, psychologists were *no better* than, and sometimes *less* accurate in their predictions about, the subsequent behaviour of these people than were non-psychologists. Similarly, some experiments have shown that training in psychological assessment confers no distinct advantage, since judgement after training is little or no better than judgement based on base-rate expectations and common knowledge. There have been many demonstrations that predictions about people based on relatively simple actuarial (statistical) procedures are usually more accurate than predictions based on complex clinical (psychological) procedures – see Meehl (1954) and Sawyer (1966).

One should not take investigations like these at their face value, of course, or draw conclusions from them in a simple-minded way. Nevertheless, they do give cause for concern; they suggest that things have not been going well in the search for effective methods of personality appraisal. Dissatisfaction with the progress of personality study had been expressed in several recent articles, including Carlson (1971) and Mischel (1977a, 1977b).

Mischel emphasizes a consideration to which other people have given first priority: namely, the need to investigate the concepts and methods that observers themselves use in their assessments of others. This is to turn personality study inside out, as it were, and to examine the process of appraisal itself. Such a reaction is not at all unusual in science, since lack of progress in basic research and applications often leads scientists to re-examine their assumptions, concepts and procedures.

When we make an appraisal of another person we bring to that appraisal certain assumptions and rules of inference which are usually tacit rather than explicit. Research into implicit, construct and attributional processes in personality appraisal has been of interest particularly since the work of Asch (1946), Kelley (1955) and Heider (1958) – see, for example, Smith (1966), Warr and Knapper (1968), Bannister (1970), Hastorf, Schneider and Polefka (1970), Jones *et al.* (1972), Rosenberg and Jones (1972), Schneider (1973) and Shaver (1975).

When making statements about personality, the level of abstraction and generality of the rule is of the utmost importance. For example, if we describe a person as 'neat' or 'honest', without reservation or further specification, we commit ourselves to a highly abstract and general rule covering many aspects of that person's behaviour. Such statements can be easily disproved. But if we describe a person as 'neat in appearance' or 'honest in scientific matters', we commit ourselves to a much less abstract and less general rule and greatly restrict the range of actions covered by the rule. Such statements are correspondingly more resistant to falsification.

Livesley and Bromley (1973), Bromley (1977) and Bilsbury (1977) have made a particular study of the natural language of personality description. Ordinary language enables us to move without difficulty up and down the ladder of abstraction, it enables us to relate general rules to particular instances, and to make connections between overt behaviour and covert psychological processes. In their attempts to construct objective methods for personality appraisal and to develop definitive terms for personality description, psychologists have been scornful of commonsense concepts and have not made full use of the infrastructure of ordinary language. It is as if we had tried to build a house without sufficient regard for the natural qualities of our raw materials or for the foundations on which we were building. It is not surprising that the walls keep falling down and we still have no roof over our heads!

The problem of personality appraisal is to explain or predict individual behaviour. This means being able to specify: first, the particular dispositions, abilities and other characteristics of the person; second, the circumstances relevant to his adjustment; and third, the subjective meaning that the circumstances have for that person.

Personality appraisal is difficult because human responses are subject to many influences and can become associated with all sorts of stimuli in highly specific ways – for example, they can be influenced by another person's actions, opinions or facial expressions. Consider also a trait like aggressiveness: it may function in association with other general or specific traits, such as an inability to take criticism or emotional instability; its expression may be modified by inhibitions against direct aggression or by opportunities for displaced aggression, as in bullying, aggression may be triggered by the presence of aggression-stimulating objects such as guns, knives or custard pies; it may increase if there is no risk of retaliation, or if the person's level of arousal is high; alcohol, stress and social influences may increase or decrease aggression. These and other factors enter into the complex conditions governing personal adjustment, partly by modifying the meaning of the situation from the actor's point of view. They help to explain variations in the behaviour of a person in apparently similar situations.

Normally, behaviour is regulated by stabilizing dispositions *within* the person and by stabilizing conditions *outside* the person; but, in addition, the person's *subjective view* of himself and his situation is a major factor determining his behaviour. Thus we should think less about 'personality' and more about 'persons in situations'.

PERFORMANCE APPRAISAL

The slow and uncertain development of personality study has been partly attributable to the narrow focus of clinical psychology on psychopathology, working with what has been called a 'medical model' of abnormal behaviour. This focus has changed drastically over the past decade or so, and clinical psychology is now much less concerned with psychometric assessment and disease entities and much freer than it was to identify relevant problems and to deal with them in terms of recently developed concepts and methods. Many of these procedures are effective in dealing with individual cases and provide conceptual routines for the analysis of cases falling within a general class, e.g. marital disharmony, school phobia, sexual dysfunction. Both educational and clinical psychology have moved closer to the study of behaviour in its natural settings. In many areas of social work, in its widest sense, knowledge of modern psychological concepts and methods is of the utmost importance in understanding problematical behaviour in everyday life, although the ability to provide practical help often requires additional knowledge and skills, e.g. in administration and law.

The shift towards a more naturalistic approach to personality is reflected in some recent contributions to psychoanalytic research: LeVine (1973) emphasizes the sociocultural environment; Schafer (1976) translates psychoanalytic terminology into more direct, natural forms of language; Cheshire (1975) examines the logic and functions of psychodynamic interpretation.

Modern behaviourism adopts a functional approach to the problem of personal adjustment by examining the *organization* of behaviour as a whole, i.e. of the individual person in his total environment. In this approach, any particular piece of behaviour is looked at in its wider context. Although one may talk sensibly about a pattern of behaviour being under stimulus control, it makes even more sense to relate those controlling stimuli to whatever central processes are responsible for the organization of behaviour. The relevance of internal, dispositional and mentalistic processes is obvious in relation to the problem of self-control (see Thoresen and Mahoney 1974). Our understanding and control of 'self' and 'other' are closely related psychologically and developmentally, see Bromley (1977) and Bromley (in press). Even so, it may be possible to modify behaviour in a piecemeal fashion without fully understanding the central organizing processes which underlie it.

The history of personality study reveals continual shifts of emphasis between these two approaches: one emphasizes personal or psychological factors, the other emphasizes environmental or situational factors. But we must avoid thinking of them as alternatives or as being in some way opposed to one another. They are, rather, complementary views. They give us a new kind of perspective on the person when used in combination that we could never get from either view separately. There have been sustained efforts recently to describe and analyze the *interaction* between psychological and situational factors in the production of individual behaviour, and the interactionist approach to the study of personality is now widely accepted, not only in principle but also in practice – see, especially, Magnusson and Endler (1977).

There has been a growing resistance to personality testing. This resistance is based on two main considerations. The first and most important of these is the extent to which the tests seem to be unreliable, invalid, useless and even misleading, in a word – unscientific. The second consideration is that personality testing may be unethical: it may probe into private aspects of a person's life that have little or no direct bearing on the purpose for which the person is being assessed and it may be used to discriminate against minority groups – see Miller (1975).

By contrast, there is a growing interest in performance appraisal in natural settings. The advantages are: (i) the aim of the exercise is limited in scope and clearly stated at the outset; (ii) the admissible evidence is relevant, objective and direct; (iii) subjective views can be given a rightful place in relation to the interpretation of the evidence; (iv) the conclusions do not go far beyond the information given, in the sense that any appraisals that are made are at a relatively low, functional, level of abstraction and generality, i.e. they tend to state how the individual, with his particular characteristics, has reacted or is likely to react, in specified circumstances.

The quasi-judicial nature of the performance appraisal exercise will be clear to those who have some acquaintance with evidence and procedures in jurisprudence (legal science). Bromley (1977) has recently tried to show that quasi-judicial methods are the key to personality appraisal. They are more laborious and time-consuming than psychometric tests and we have a long way to go in developing the psychological case-law that will bring some kind of order into this chaotic area of psychology. Nevertheless, the failure of the personality testing movement to establish a firm body of knowledge justifies the exploration of other research methods. The case-study method could be used much more extensively, with a view to generating the sort of psychological case-law that is appropriate to a given area – whether that area is industry, education, social work or clinical psychology.

There are obvious similarities between performance appraisal procedures in industry and behaviour modification procedures in clinical psychology, education and social case-work. They all attempt to establish base-line measures of performance; they investigate the circumstances which govern that performance; they seek ways of improving the individual's behaviour through counselling, reinforcement and environmental change; they try to identify problems and obstacles which hinder improvement; they try to set realistic standards and behavioural objectives against which changes in performance can be assessed.

The current emphasis in applied psychology, therefore, is on performance appraisal rather than personality appraisal; this ties in with Mischel's views.

Nevertheless, we delude ourselves if we think we need never go beyond behavioural or performance data. This would be to limit ourselves to the simplest sorts of description, hardly venturing to classify or to correlate or to seek causal connections. Science is concerned with conceptual advances, and psychology is no exception. Therefore we need theories to explain the *organization* of individual behaviour. We need to analyze the reasons and causes for personal conduct. Hence we must find ways of relating the covert mentalistic and dispositional processes (referred to earlier as the central organizing processes of personality) to overt behaviour and the circumstances in which that behaviour occurs.

This leads on to a consideration of theories of personality which is too large a topic to deal with here. Maddi (1976), however, provides an unparalleled conspectus of personality theories and also identifies their common features and provides a way of analyzing and assessing their relative merits and demerits.

DEVELOPMENTAL ASPECTS

The infant's and young child's experiences are dominated by the contact he has with human beings. So much so that he understands the world first of all animistically, i.e. as if everything in it had human characteristics. The child has to learn *not* to think animistically and this takes him a long time. Similarly he has to learn *not* to rely on his own subjective, egocentric, view of other people, but to think *objectively,* i.e. in ways that he can share with other people. This too, takes him a long time and vestiges of animism and egocentricism are to be found in most of us, even as adults. The developmental psychology of social cognition (self-understanding and understanding others) is a rapidly developing area of research, see Livesley and Bromley (1973) and Shantz (1975).

Some of the research work on self-understanding and understanding others has been centred on two simple questions. First, what sorts of information are contained in personality descriptions in ordinary language? Second, how is this information organized? A diversity of approaches to these problems can be seen by reference to Peevers and Secord (1973), Jones and Rosenberg (1974), Gordon (1976) and others.

The answer to the first question is that there are as many sorts of information (or as few) as one cares to distinguish depending upon how fine or how coarse one wishes to make the analysis. About thirty categories of information are sufficient for most purposes. These categories refer to facets of personality such as traits, motives, expressive behaviour, morality, social relationships, appearance and so on. In actual personality descriptions, however, one may find that only a few of the conceptual categories are used. Unfortunately and somewhat surprisingly, the conceptual boundaries between some of these categories are fuzzy and none of the schemes that have been developed is unambiguous, much less are they definitive – see Bromley (1977).

The answer to the second question is that the words and phrases that make up the diverse contents of personality descriptions are formed into complex syntactical structures and semantic patterns in ways which so far defy complete analysis. It is certainly possible to identify some of the more obvious semantic distinctions and logical forms, but we have a long way to go in this direction.

Livesley and Bromley (1973) discovered that normal children between the ages of seven and fifteen years gradually acquire certain kinds of words and phrases pertaining to behaviour and psychological processes. They learn to put these words and phrases together in increasingly complex syntactical forms, so as to structure their experience into patterns of meaning which they share with other people in the society in which they grow up. Our conceptions of human nature generally and of individual persons develop throughout life as *social constructions,* made possible by mapping natural forms of language onto natural forms of experience. We grow up in a semantic environment and learn to think with socially derived meanings. Further research carried out by Bilsbury (1977) using more advanced methods of investigation into children's psycholinguistic abilities revealed that self-understanding and understanding others was severely impoverished in moderately retarded ESN children.

PERSONAL VIEWPOINT

Bromley (1977) has surveyed the whole area of personality description at the level of commonsense and natural language. He describes and illustrates the extraordinary power that language has in shaping our understanding and experience of ourselves and other people, and in regulating our behaviour. The words and concepts we use to describe psychological and behavioural processes are closely interlocked. Personality appraisal and performance appraisal at a professional level in clinical psychology and social case-work rest upon this infrastructure of commonsense and natural language.

It can be argued that the personality testing movement and the study of individual differences are off-course, if not completely misdirected, and that the paradigm for scientific research in the study of personality and adjustment should be drawn from legal science not natural science. Personality study should shift its emphasis towards the study of individual cases and develop systematic case-law; it should not be confined to the investigation of so-called universal dimensions of individual differences or general laws of behaviour. The philosophy and logic of personality study should not be narrowly stated in terms of experimental and quantitative methods – important as they are in some areas of psychology; instead, they should be broadly stated so as to encourage *any* mode of inquiry or argument which is objective, rational and empirical.

REFERENCES

Asch, S. E. 1946. 'Forming impressions of personality,' *J. abnorm. soc. Psychol.* *41*, 258-90.

Bannister, D. (ed.) 1970. *Perspectives in personal construct theory*. London: Academic Press.

Bilsbury, C. 1977. *Person perception in educationally subnormal children*. Unpublished Ph.D. thesis. Liverpool: University of Liverpool.

Block, J. 1971. *Lives through time*. Berkeley, Calif.: Bancroft Books.

Block, J. 1977. 'Advancing the psychology of personality: paradigmatic shift or improving the quality of research.' In D. Magnusson and N. S. Endler (eds) *Personality at the crossroads: current issues in interactional psychology*. Hillsdale, N. J.: Lawrence Erlbaum.

Bromley, D. B. 1977. *Personality description in ordinary language*. London: Wiley.

Bromley, D. B. (in press). 'Natural language and the development of the self.' In C. B. Keasey (ed.) *Nebraska symposium on motivation 1977*. Lincoln, Nebraska: Univ. Nebraska Press.

Burnham, J. C. 1968. 'Historical background for the study of personality.' In E. F. Borgatta and W. W. Lambert (eds) *Handbook of personality theory and research*. Chicago: Rand McNally.

Butcher, J. N. (ed.) 1972. *Objective personality assessment: changing perspectives*. New York: Academic Press.

Carlson, R. 1971. 'Where is the person in personality research?' *Psychol. Bull.* *75*, 203-19.

Carlson, R. 1975. 'Personality.' *Ann. Rev. Psychol. 26*, 393-414.

Cattell, R. B. and Dreger, R. M. (eds) 1977. *Handbook of modern personality theory*. Washington: Hemisphere Publishing Corporation.

Cheshire, N. M. 1975. *The nature of psychodynamic interpretation*. London: Wiley.

Eysenck, H. J. and Eysenck, S. B. G. 1969. *Personality structure and measurement*. London: Routledge and Kegan Paul.

Fiske, D. W. 1971. *Measuring the concepts of personality*. Chicago: Aldine.

Goodstein, L. D. and Lanyon, R. I. 1971. *Readings in personality assessment*. New York: Wiley.

Gordon, C. 1976. 'Development of evaluated role identities.' In *Ann. Rev. of Sociology. 2*, 405-33.

Hastorf, A. H., Schneider, D. J. and Polefka, J. 1970. *Person perception*. Reading, Mass.: Addison-Wesley.

Heider, F. 1958. *The psychology of interpersonal relations*. New York: Wiley.

Holt, R. R. 1969. *Assessing personality*. New York: Harcourt Brace Jovanovich.

Jones, E. E., Kanouse, D. E., Kelley, H. H., Nisbett, R. E., Valins, S. and Weiner, B. 1972. *Attribution: perceiving the causes of behavior*. Morristown: General Learning Press.

Jones, R. A. and Rosenberg, S. 1974. 'Structural representations of naturalistic descriptions of personality.' *Multivariate Behav. Res. 9*, 217-30.

Kelley, G. A. 1955. *The psychology of personal constructs*. New York: W. W. Norton.

Kleinmuntz, B. 1967. *Personality measurement, an introduction*. Homewood, Ill.: Dorsey Press.

LeVine, R. A. 1973. *Culture, behaviour and personality*. London: Hutchinson.

Livesley, W. J. and Bromley, D. B. 1973. *Person perception in childhood and adolescence*. London: Wiley.

McReynolds, P. 1975. 'Historical antecedents of personality assessment.' In P. McReynolds (ed.) *Advances in psychological assessment 3*. Palo Alto, Calif.: Science and Behavior Books.

Maddi, S. R. 1976. *Personality theories: a comparative analysis*, 3rd edn. Homewood, Illinois: Dorsey Press.

Magnusson, D. and Endler, N. S. (eds) 1977. *Personality at the crossroads: current issues in interactional psychology*. Hillsdale, N. J.: Lawrence Erlbaum.

Meehl, P. E. 1954. *Clinical versus statistical prediction*. Minneapolis: University of Minnesota Press.

Miller, K. M. (ed.) 1975. *Psychological testing in personnel assessment*. Epping: Gower Press.

Mischel, W. 1968. *Personality and assessment*. New York: Wiley.

Mischel, W. 1976. *Introduction to personality* 2nd edn. New York: Holt, Rinehart and Winston.

Mischel, W. 1977a. 'The interaction of person and situation.' In D. Magnusson and N. S. Endler (eds) *Personality at the crossroads: current issues in interactional psychology*. Hillsdale, N. J.: Lawrence Erlbaum.

Mischel, W. 1977b. 'On the future of personality measurement.' *Amer. Psychologist 32*, 246-64.

Peevers, B. H. and Secord, P. F. 1973. 'Developmental changes in attribution of descriptive concepts to persons.' *J. Pers. soc. Psychol. 27*, 120-8.

Rosenberg, S. and Jones, R. 1972. 'A method for investigating and representing a person's implicit theory of personality: Theodore Dreiser's view of people.' *J. Person. soc. Psychol. 22*, 372-86.

Ryle, G. 1954. *Dilemmas*. Cambridge: Cambridge University Press.

Sarason, I. G. and Smith, R. E. 1971. 'Personality.' *Ann. Rev. Psychol. 22*, 393-446.

Sawyer, J. 1966. 'Measurement *and* prediction, clinical *and* statistical.' *Psychol. Bull. 66*, 178-200.

Schafer, R. 1976. *A new language for psychoanalysis*. New Haven: Yale University Press.

Schneider, D. J. 1973. 'Implicit personality theory: a review.' *Psychol. Bull. 79*, 294-309.

Shantz, C. U. 1975. 'The development of social cognition.' In E. M. Hetherington (ed.) *Review of child development research 5*. Chicago: Univ. Chicago Press.

Shaver, K. G. 1975. *An introduction to attribution processes*. Cambridge, Mass.: Winthrop Publishers.
Smith, H. C. 1966. *Sensitivity to people*. New York: McGraw-Hill.
Thoresen, C. E. and Mahoney, M. J. 1974. *Behavioral self-control*. New York: Holt, Rinehart and Winston.
Warr, P. B. and Knapper, C. 1968. *The perception of people and events*. London: Wiley.

Chapter 2

Attitudes

J. RICHARD EISER

THE THREE-COMPONENT DEFINITION
OF ATTITUDES

To appreciate current trends in attitude research, it is first necessary
to remind ourselves of the point which this field of social psychology
had reached by the early 1960s. At that time there was a surprising
amount of agreement among researchers concerning how attitudes
should be conceptualized. One of the most influential theoretical
approaches of the time was the three-component definition of attitudes,
according to which attitudes were conceived of as consisting of
affective, cognitive and behavioural components, as portrayed in the
following diagram (Figure 2.1) taken from Rosenberg and Hovland
(1960, p. 3).

Neither this diagram (nor the theoretical discussion which surrounds
it) makes it clear to what extent the three components are expected
to covary with each other, whether they are assumed to be influenced
by common or distinct antecedent stimuli, and most important of all,
whether they are assumed to have any influence on one another.
The placement of the box labelled 'attitudes' under the category of
'intervening variables' also assumes a kind of 'black-box' notion
according to which attitudes are unobservable entities inferred from
observable events, inferred, that is, to fill a missing link in a *causal*
chain. The applicability of the notion of causal inference in this
context, however, remains highly questionable.

Many of the theoretical issues with which more recent research has
been concerned may therefore be traced to the ambiguities implicit in
the Rosenberg and Hovland model and contemporary preconceptions.
Without necessarily accepting the validity of any hard-and-fast

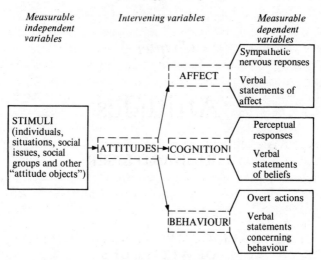

Figure 2.1 Schematic conception of attitudes. Reproduced with permission of the Yale University Press, from M. J. Rosenberg *et al.* 1960. *Attitude organization and change: an analysis of consistency among attitude components.* New Haven: Yale University Press.

distinctions between affective, cognitive and behavioural processes, it may therefore be useful to consider recent research in terms of their inter-relationships, under the respective headings of affect and behaviour, cognition and behaviour, and affect and cognition.

Affect and Behaviour

Perhaps the most embarrassing criticism ever made of social psychology is that verbal measures of attitude are of little or no value in predicting actual social behaviour. This criticism strikes at the very foundations of social psychological theory and method, questioning its practical utility and its claim to any kind of scientific status.

At first sight, there seem good grounds for this criticism. As early as 1934 La Piere reported little correspondence between the actual hospitality of a sample of American restaurateurs and hoteliers towards a Chinese couple and their verbally expressed unwillingness to accommodate 'members of the Chinese race'. Although this study is open to numerous criticisms, it is not an isolated example. More recently, Wicker (1969) reviewed a large number of studies in which attempts had been made to predict overt behaviour from verbal measures of attitude, and concluded that such verbal measures generally had little predictive value.

One of the reasons for the resilience of the three-component view of attitudes was its invulnerability to the findings of such studies, whichever way they turned out. If measures of affect predicted behaviour, this showed that attitudes indeed were cohesive combinations of different components. If no correlations were found, this merely demonstrated the importance of distinguishing between the different components. One study, however, makes this escape seem less viable. Ostrom (1969) presented subjects with a scale which contained verbal measures of affect, belief and behaviour towards the church, and then obtained measures of their actual church attendance and other indices of church attendance. Even though the three kinds of verbal measures intercorrelated highly, none was particularly successful in predicting overt behaviour. Thus, the so-called 'attitude-behaviour discrepancy' cannot necessarily be attributed to a lack of correlation between different attitude components.

Over the last few years, however, Ajzen and Fishbein have developed a theoretical position which goes a very long way towards clearing up this muddle (Ajzen and Fishbein 1973, 1977; Fishbein and Ajzen 1975). Their main argument is that many so-called attitude-behaviour studies involve a fairly general measure of affect towards an attitude object on the one hand and a very specific index of behaviour on the other, and that such differences in levels of specificity lead to low correlations between the two kinds of measures. As they point out in their most recent paper (Ajzen and Fishbein 1977, p. 889).

Attempts to predict behavior from attitudes are largely based on a general notion of consistency. It is usually considered to be logical or consistent for a person who holds a favorable attitude toward some object to perform favorable behaviors, and not to perform unfavorable behaviors, with respect to the object . . . The apparent simplicity of this notion is deceptive, since there is usually no theoretical basis for the assumption that a behavior has favorable implications for the object under consideration. In the absence of an explicit and unambiguous definition of attitude-behavior consistency, therefore, many tests of the attitude behavior relation reduce to little more than tests of the investigator's intuition.

In attempting to provide a suitable definition of consistency, Ajzen and Fishbein emphasize four 'elements' that need to be specified for both attitudinal (affective) and behavioural indices. These are 'the *action*, the *target* at which the action is directed, the *context* in which the action is performed and the *time* at which it is performed.' They argue the strength of any attitude-behaviour relation depends on the correspondence between these four 'elements'.

Examples of studies where they argue that such correspondence is completely absent include ones which have attempted to use attitudes towards an ethnic group in general as a predictor of conformity to an opinion expressed by a particular member of that group (Berg 1966; Boyanowski and Allen 1973; Schneider 1970) or success of verbal conditioning by a black or white experimenter (Smith and Dixon 1968). Other studies have come nearer to using attitude measures that specify the action in question more precisely, but still fail to specify the target precisely. For instance in the study by La Piere (1934) the general reference to 'members of the Chinese race' did not adequately specify the particular middle-class Chinese couple towards whom the hospitality was shown.

Other studies have shown correspondence between attitudinal and behavioural targets, but have used attitude measurements which leave the action element unspecified. The results here are very varied. Sampson and Insko (1964) were able to predict conforming responses as a function of liking for another, but a variety of studies using attitudes towards a partner as a predictor of co-operation or competition in the Prisoner's Dilemma game have yielded inconsistent findings (Gardin, Kaplan, Firestone and Cowan 1973; Oskamp and Perlman 1966; Tornatsky and Geiwitz, 1968).

Higher correlations are found when a specific action is in the attitude measure, as in Kothandapani's (1971) study of birth control attitudes and practices, and where the behavioural index is based on a variety of possible behaviours, rather than a single act, as in the Bandura, Blanchard and Ritter (1969) study of snake phobia. Voting behaviour also seems quite predictable from attitudes towards political candidates (e.g. Fishbein and Coombs 1974).

The clearest evidence for the Ajzen and Fishbein position, however, comes from studies which have included a number of attitude measures varying in their degree of specificity. For instance Weinstein (1972) showed that a measure of attitudes towards an issue predicted petition-signing less well than a measure of attitudes towards 'signing a petition' on the issue in question.

It might be argued that the Ajzen and Fishbein approach is good at explaining low attitude-behaviour correlations, where these occur, but cannot as yet always account for why some specific behaviours seem relatively predictable from rather more general attitude measures, and others do not. It is not altogether clear, for instance, why voting behaviour should be so much more predictable from political attitudes than co-operative behaviour in an experimental game should be from interpersonal attitudes. But notwithstanding such difficulties, the contribution of Ajzen and Fishbein enables social psychologists to be more confident now than ten years ago that verbal attitude measures, adequately specified, can validly be used to predict behaviour.

Cognition and Behaviour

Turning back again to the early 1960s, the most influential theory of attitudes at the time was undoubtedly Festinger's (1957) theory of cognitive dissonance. The mid-1960s, however, saw the theory coming under attack from so many sides (Bem 1965, 1967; Chapanis and Chapanis 1964; Rosenberg 1965) that its survival must have seemed very uncertain. Yet the theory has survived, albeit with some qualification and refinements, and the questions which it raises remain among the most vital in social psychology.

The best-developed alternative to cognitive dissonance theory has been Bem's (1965, 1967) self-perception theory, and although this particular debate has fortunately quietened down over the last few years, a brief account of it is necessary to explain current trends in dissonance research. The distinction between the two theories is best seen in relation to the so-called 'forced compliance' paradigm. This paradigm involves the subject being induced to comply with a request to perform an act which is presumed to be inconsistent with his beliefs, e.g. to tell a waiting confederate of the experimenter that a boring task was in fact interesting (Festinger and Carlsmith 1959). According to Festinger, the knowledge that one has acted in this way creates a state of mental tension or cognitive dissonance, which the individual will seek to reduce by any of a number of means. He could, for instance, look for any extrinsic benefits that might accrue from his act (e.g. a large monetary reward) or he could change his cognition about the attitude object (his belief that the task was boring) to bring it more into line with his behaviour. It is predicted that cognitive changes of the latter kind will be less likely to occur as the result of counter-attitudinal behaviour in the presence of large as opposed to small extrinsic rewards – an apparent contradiction of the principle of reinforcement.

Bem's (1965, 1967) position is that individuals called upon to make an attitude response following such a manipulation offer an interpretation of their own behaviour as it would appear to an outside observer. Behaviour performed for a small reward, on this account, would be seen as relatively unlikely to be counter-attitudinal ('Why should I lie, if I don't get anything for it?') whereas behaviour performed for a large reward could be adequately explained by the presence of that reward, without the need to assume anything about the individual's attitude. Bem maintains that attitude responses are the outcome of self-observations which take the situation into account essentially in the manner proposed by attribution theorists (c.f. Jones *et al.*, 1971).

A number of experimenters have attempted to pit the two theories against each other in 'crucial' tests, principally by varying the salience to the subject of attitude responses made prior to any 'dissonance' manipulation, (Bem and McConnell 1970; Green 1974; Ross and Shulman 1973; Snyder and Ebbesen 1972). Greenwald (1975) has argued that such tests are inconclusive, pointing out that reminding subjects of their prior attitudes could reduce attitude change either, according to self-perception theory, by providing subjects with a broader informational base from which to infer current attitudes, or, according to dissonance theory, by increasing subjects' commitment to their prior attitudes and thus making it more likely that they would seek an alternative means of dissonance reduction. There is also the question in these studies of how well subjects remember their pre-manipulation attitudes. Dissonance theory implies that subjects could reduce dissonance by selectively forgetting cognitions concerning their prior attitudes where these were inconsistent with later behaviour – a prediction supported by Shaffer (1975).

Other aspects of Bem's approach, particularly his method of 'interpersonal simulations' (Bem 1965, 1967) have been severely criticized by Wicklund and Brehm (1976). However, in confronting issues of this kind, dissonance theory has itself changed into a far more cognitively orientated theory, increasingly dealing with concepts within the sphere of interest of attribution theory (Jones *et al.* 1971). This is particularly so with respect to the notions of perceived responsibility and freedom of choice.

A number of studies have manipulated the extent to which subjects feel responsible for persuading others to adopt a position contrary to their own point of view. In a modified replication of the Festinger and Carlsmith (1959) study, Cooper and Worchel (1970) induced subjects to try and convince a waiting stooge that a boring task would in fact be interesting. Only when the stooge acted as though he was convinced by the subject were the Festinger and Carlsmith findings replicated. In a later study, Cooper and Goethals (1974) found that it was more important that subjects *expected* that a speech they recorded, which was contrary to their own attitude, would be used in a way that might lead others to be persuaded than that their speech was *actually* used in such a way. Collins and Hoyt (1972) also found that writing a counter-attitudinal essay produced no 'dissonance' effect if subjects signed a disclaimer stating, 'I am in no way responsible for its contents'.

These studies suggest that negative effects of one's own behaviour arouse dissonance to the extent that they appear pre-meditated. This conclusion is supported by a number of studies which have manipulated subjects' perceived freedom of choice to perform the counter-attitudinal behaviour. Linder, Cooper and Jones (1967) found that subjects who were given no choice, in contrast to those who were led to feel they were choosing freely, showed no attitude change following counter-attitudinal behaviour, the assumption being that they experienced no dissonance. Reiss and Schlenker (1977) manipulated subjects' perceived choice in a similar way through experimental instructions, but also gave subjects supposed details of raters' impressions of their delivery of the counter-attitudinal speech. When told that they appeared to the raters to have had no choice but to deliver the speech, subjects showed no attitude change, even in the condition when they had initially been led to believe they were choosing freely.

A study by Zanna and Cooper (1974) is interesting in that it employs a classic paradigm of attribution research (Schachter and Singer 1962) to test a central assumption of dissonance theory. Subjects wrote a counter-attitudinal essay under conditions of high or low perceived choice, after being given a placebo pill that they were told would either make them feel tense, or relaxed, or about which they were given no information. The Linder *et al*, (1967) effect (i.e. change towards the counter-attitudinal position under high but not low perceived choice) was replicated in the 'no information' condition, enhanced in the 'relaxed' condition, but eliminated in the 'tense' condition. The implication is that dissonant behaviour under free choice conditions produces tension, which the subjects attributed either to the pill, or to the fact that their behaviour was counter-attitudinal, depending on their expectations of the pill's effects.

Recently, an important challenge to dissonance theory has been proposed by Nuttin (1975). According to his 'response-contagion' theory of persuasion, the results of forced-compliance studies do not arise from any strictly *cognitive* dissonance, but are due to the general arousal effects of novel or unusual situations. The first assumption of dissonance theory which is put under scrutiny is that small incentives produce more attitude change than large incentives because they are *just sufficient* to elicit the counter-attitudinal behaviour but not large enough to provide a justification for such compliance.

Nuttin points out that this assumption has never been properly tested by seeing what would happen if no incentive was provided. In a series of experiments, Nuttin found that Belgian students were prepared to deliver speeches against their own viewpoints on the issue of the examination system to a female experimenter posing as a reporter from the national broadcasting company, even when no monetary incentive was offered. When subjects received a small monetary reward, they shifted their attitudes towards the position for which they had argued, as predicted by dissonance theory. However, subjects in the zero reward condition, like those who received a large reward, showed no shift. On the other hand, subjects in a 'relative deprivation' condition, who were told that others had been paid but that they could not be as the funds were now used up, showed even more marked shifts than those in the low reward condition. These results suggest that it is not so much that a large reward reduces dissonance (created by the knowledge that one has acted counter-attitudinally), but that the inequitable witholding of a reward, or the provision of an inequitably low reward, gives rise to dissonance. If, however, the question of payment for the task never arises, the absence of a reward need not create dissonance.

Nuttin goes on to report further experiments where attitude shifts occur towards an advocated position as a result of other kinds of 'inappropriateness' in the situation where compliance was elicited – e.g. when the same experimenter in her true role of teaching assistant and then lecturer offered to fiddle examination marks to benefit her male student subjects, or else conducted the session dressed in 'hotpants' and a low-necked T-shirt! Nuttin's interpretation of these findings is that attitudinal responses elicited under arousing conditions of whatever kind generalize to later attitude-testing situations. Moreover, the changes observed are specific to the actual words used in the counter-attitudinal advocacy and the subsequent attitude measure – a result which leads Nuttin to argue that attitude change, in the sense of a change in some all-embracing cognitive structure rather than a specific verbal response, is an 'illusion'.

Affect and Cognition

One of the enduring issues of social psychology is whether it is possible to predict a person's overall evaluation of an attitude object from the specific beliefs held, or information received, about that object. A large body of literature has been devoted to defining the mathematical functions required for such predictions, and the 1960s saw a debate between advocates of summative (Fishbein 1963) and averaging models (Anderson 1965). Since then, Anderson's 'information integration theory', which assumed that specific beliefs or items of information are combined according to a weighted average model, has gained ground over most of its rivals and has been applied to an expanding range of theoretical areas from psychophysical judgement (Anderson 1970) to attribution processes (Anderson 1974) and equity theory (Anderson 1976). At the same time an influential approach to the study of interpersonal attraction has been concerned with predicting a person's liking for another as a linear function of the proportion of opinions which they hold in common (Byrne 1961; Byrne and Nelson 1965).

Such approaches treat attitudes, in the sense of overall evaluative responses, as very much the end-product of cognitive processes, i.e. attitudes have typically been the dependent rather than the independent variables in such experiments. However, important questions still remain as to how an individual's cognitive processes may be influenced by attitudinal factors, and another research tradition, dating back to the late 1940s and early 1950s, is continuing to examine these. This latter tradition has received rather less attention than the former, even though they are clearly complementary to each other.

One important question is how attitudinal information is remembered. A useful framework for examining this issue has recently been proposed by Lingle and Ostrom (in press). In a discussion which relies heavily on research in psycholinguistics and general cognitive psychology, they suggest that items of information are typically encoded according to a particular 'thematic framework', one result of which is that information encoded within one framework is less easily retrieved in terms of another framework (Tulving and Thomson 1973). For instance, we learn the names of months in temporal sequence, so it is difficult to recall them in alphabetic order. The presence of such a 'thematic framework' will also be important in determining the perceived implications of specific items of information. Lingle and Ostrom argue that attitudes function as thematic frameworks, influencing how information is encoded and recalled. Sulin and Dooling (1974) for instance, found that recognition errors for sentences were influenced by whether they concerned a fictitious or a famous character (Adolf Hitler). Other studies have examined whether the influence of attitudes on recognition primarily reflects differences in sensitivity or in response bias (Dorfman, Keeve and Saslow 1971; Eiser and Monk 1978; Upmeyer and Layer 1974).

Attitudes (i.e. overall evaluative responses) as the end-products of implicational processes, appear to be stored in memory separately from the individual items of information from which they were derived. Anderson and Hubert (1963) read subjects a list of personality trait descriptions and asked them to give an overall evaluation of the person so described. Later subjects were given a surprise recall test and showed better recall of the later traits in the list, even though their overall impressions, as remembered, were more closely related to the earlier traits. Greenwald (1968) also found that the number of persuasive arguments a subject could remember in a message was a poor predictor of the amount of attitude change the message produced. A better predictor was the subject's own set of inferences and abstractions from the information in the message.

Such studies suggest that attitudes may have an important organizing and labelling function over and above the specific evaluative beliefs on which they were originally based. Research on attitudinal judgement supports this conclusion particularly strongly. Hovland and Sherif (1952) first drew attention to the fact that judgements of the degree of favourability of attitude statements towards an issue are influenced by the judges' own attitudes. Since then, a frequently replicated finding has been that judges with different attitudes will differ in the polarization or extremity of their ratings (Eiser and Stroebe 1972). For instance when the attitude issue has been 'the social position of the Negro', American studies have consistently found that the judgements given by black subjects and white subjects who hold strong integrationist views tend to be more polarized (i.e. show greater use of the categories at both extremes of the rating scale) than those given by segregationist white subjects (Hovland and Sherif 1952; Selltiz, Edrich and Cook 1965; Upshaw 1965; Zavalloni and Cook 1965). Comparable effects in judgements of statements concerned with drug-use have been found by Eiser (1971) and Reich (1974).

Such studies, based upon Thurstone's method of equal-appearing intervals for the construction of attitude scales, have involved subjects rating the statements presented to them on a single scale. In a series of studies, we have departed from this standard procedure and required subjects to give ratings on a number of scales defined by adjectives chosen so as to imply a definitive evaluative bias. On some of the scales, therefore, the 'pro' end is marked by an evaluatively positive label and the 'anti' end by a negative label, and on other scales these implicit value connotations are reversed. Thus, in a study on the drug issue (Eiser 1973), the scales permissive – restrictive, liberal – authoritarian and broadminded – narrow-minded were chosen as ones where the 'pro-drug' term (the first in each pair) would tend to carry more positive value connotations, and the scales immoral – moral and decadent – upright were chosen so that the 'anti-drug' term would be the more positive. In two studies on the issue of teenagers' attitudes towards adult authority (Eiser and Mower White 1974a, 1975) scales such as adventurous – unadventurous were chosen to label the 'anti-authority' extreme more positively, and scales such as disobedient – obedient to label the 'pro-authority' extreme more positively. This manipulation of response scale labels is similar to the device suggested by Peabody (1967) for unconfounding the evaluative and descriptive aspects of personality trait inferences.

These studies show very clearly that judges' attitudes and the value connotations of the response language have an interactive effect on polarization of judgement. Judges whose own attitudes on an issue are 'pro' will tend to give more polarized judgements on scales where the 'pro' end is labelled positively and 'anti' subjects will tend to give more polarized ratings on scales where the 'anti' end is labelled positively. It has often been argued that polarization of judgement may be an index of the salience or personal significance of a particular dimension to an individual. (e.g. Tajfel and Wilkes 1964). Following this reasoning, it is suggested that individuals may prefer to think of attitudinal issues in terms of language which allows them to apply evaluatively positive labels to positions they accept and evaluatively negative labels to positions they reject. Differences in attitude thus directly predict differences in how individuals label attitude-relevant material.

IMPLICATIONS FOR ATTITUDE CHANGE

Although the question of how attitudes may be changed remains a pre-eminent concern, it is largely contingent on antecedent questions concerning the definition of attitudes and the predictive validity of attitude measures. This chapter has concentrated on such antecedent questions, rather than on so-called 'techniques of persuasion'. The research that has been reviewed here, however, carries a number of important implications for attitude change.

The research on the attitude-behaviour relation (Ajzen and Fishbein 1977) alerts one to the issue of specificity. There is little point in producing a change in attitude at a verbal level if this fails to have an impact on one's criterion behaviour. Changes in a given specific behaviour, however, are by no means a necessary consequence of changes in some general social attitude. Communication therefore, should aim, in terms of the Fishbein and Ajzen (1975) approach, to change evaluative beliefs and/or subjective norms concerning the *specific* behaviour in question. Convincing a smoker that smoking damages health, for instance, does not necessarily persuade him to make a determined attempt to stop.

The research on cognitive dissonance theory and its alternatives also implies that achieving a general change in a person's general social attitude may not be the easiest goal for the would-be persuader nor necessarily the most effective means of inducing a change in behaviour. Indeed, this whole body of literature testifies to the possibility that behaviour change can be as much the precursor as the result of changes in verbally expressed attitudes. The definition of the situational factors that produce so-called dissonance effects remains an important and challenging area. In this context, the individual's perceived freedom of choice is a variable of crucial significance. Again to use the example of smoking, a smoker who admits the health hazards of smoking may not necessarily be in a state of cognitive dissonance if he regards himself as an addict, unable to choose not to smoke (Eiser 1978). Nuttin's (1975) contribution to this field is particularly notable, raising as it does the whole question of what attitude change is and emphasizing the importance of attending to the particular language employed both by the subject in his counter-attitudinal advocacy and by the experimenter in his choice of a verbal response measure.

The interrelationship between attitudes and language is also critical for an understanding of social judgement processes. The classic question of how attitudes affect basic processes of perception and memory is deservedly receiving renewed attention. The notion of attitudes as thematic frameworks (Lingle and Ostrom in press) relies partly but explicitly on studies concerned with the cognitive processing of linguistic material. Our own research suggests a strong link between a person's attitude and his preferred use of particular kinds of verbal labels. One implication of this research which has received preliminary support is that it should be possible to influence people's attitudes by inducing them, either through questionnaire instructions (Eiser and Mower White 1974b), or through essay-writing procedures (Eiser and Ross 1977; Eiser and Pancer 1979), to construe attitudinal issues in terms of language which implies a particular evaluative bias. For instance, Eiser and Ross (1977) found that Canadian students shifted their attitudes towards capital punishment in a more abolitionist direction after writing an essay on the topic which had to include a number of words with an anti-capital punishment bias (e.g. callous, barbaric), as compared to others who had to incorporate anti-abolition words (e.g. over-sentimental, irresponsible) in their essays. In general terms, it seems that persuasion need not be contingent on the provision of new information, but may often, as probably in the case of much commercial and political propaganda, depend upon the communication of a specific thematic framework or set of verbal labels and concepts in terms of which both new and existing information may be interpreted.

Like many other topics in social psychology, the study of attitudes has suffered in the past from approaches that appeared to be searching for causal mechanisms 'inside the heads' of isolated individuals. Recent research is moving encouragingly towards a more interactionist position. To understand linguistic behaviour, we need to assume that statements have meaning. To understand communication and social behaviour, we need to assume that people have attitudes. The relationship in each case is logical, not causal. The continuing task of attitude research is thus to understand the shared and personal meanings in terms of which people account for their actions and interpret their experience.

REFERENCES

Ajzen, I. and Fishbein, M. 1973. 'Attitudinal and normative variables as predictors of specific behaviors.' *J. Pers. soc. Psychol. 27*, 41-57.

Ajzen, I. and Fishbein, M. 1977. 'Attitude-behaviour relations: a theoretical analysis and a review of empirical research.' *Psychol. Bull. 84*, 888-918.

Anderson, N. H. 1965. 'Averaging versus adding as a stimulus-combination rule in impression formation.' *J. exp. Psychol. 70*, 394-400.

Anderson, N. H. 1970. 'Functional measurement and psychophysical judgment.' *Psychol. Rev. 77*, 153-70.

Anderson, N. H. 1974. 'Cognitive algebra: integration theory applied to social attribution.' In L. Berkowitz (ed.) *Advances in experimental social psychology 7*. New York: Academic Press.

Anderson, N. H. 1976. 'Equity judgments as information integration.' *J. Pers. soc. Psychol. 33*, 291-9.

Anderson, N. H. and Hubert, S. 1963. 'Effects of concomitant verbal recall on order effects in personality impression formation.' *J. verb. Learn. verb. Behav. 2*, 379-91.

Bandura, A., Blanchard, E. B. and Ritter, B. 1969. 'Relative efficacy of desensitization and modelling approaches for inducing behavioral, affective and attitudinal changes.' *J. Pers. soc. Psychol. 13*, 173-99.

Bem, D. J. 1965. 'An experimental analysis of self-persuasion.' *J. exp. soc. Psychol. 1*, 199-218.

Bem, D. J. 1967. 'Self-perception: an alternative interpretation of cognitive dissonance phenomena.' *Psychol. Rev. 74*, 183-200.

Bem, D. J. and McConnell, H. K. 1970. 'Testing the self-perception explanation of dissonance phenomena.' *J. Pers. soc. Psychol. 14*, 23-31.

Berg, K. E. 1966. 'Ethnic attitudes and agreement with a Negro person.' *J. Pers. soc. Psychol. 4*, 215-20.

Boyanowski, E. O. and Allen, V. L. 1973. 'Ingroup norms and self-identity as determinants of discriminatory behavior.' *J. Pers. soc. Psychol. 25*, 408-18.

Byrne, D. 1961. 'Interpersonal attraction and attitude similarity.' *J. abnorm. soc. Psychol. 62.* 713-15.

Byrne, D. and Nelson, D. 1965. 'Attraction as a linear function of proportion of positive reinforcements.' *J. Pers. soc. Psychol. 1*, 659-63.

Chapanis, N. J. and Chapanis, A. C. 1964. 'Cognitive dissonance; five years later.' *Psychol. Bull. 61*, 1-22.

Collins, B. E. and Hoyt, M. F. 1972. 'Personal responsibility-for-consequences: an integration and extension of the "forced compliance" literature.' *J. exp. soc. Psychol. 8*, 558-93.

Cooper, J. and Goethals, G. R. 1974. 'Unforeseen events and the elimination of cognitive dissonance.' *J. Pers. soc. Psychol. 29*, 441-5.

Cooper, J. and Worchel, S. 1970. 'The role of undesired consequences in arousing cognitive dissonance.' *J. Pers. soc. Psychol. 16*, 199-206.

Dorfman, D. D., Keeve, S. and Saslow, C. 1971. 'Ethnic identification: a signal detection analysis.' *J. Pers. soc. Psychol. 18*, 373-9.

Eiser, J. R. 1971. 'Enhancement of contrast in the absolute judgment of attitude statements.' *J. Pers. soc. Psychol. 17*, 1-10.

Eiser, J. R. 1973. 'Judgement of attitude statements as a function of judges' attitudes and the judgemental dimension.' *Brit. J. soc. clin. Psychol. 12*, 231-40.

Eiser, J. R. 1978. 'Discrepancy, dissonance and the "dissonant" smoker.' *Int. J. Addictions 13*, in press.

Eiser, J. R. and Monk, A. F. 1978. 'Is the recognition of attitude statements affected by one's own opinion?' *Eur. J. soc. Psychol. 8*, 529-33.

Eiser, J. R. and Mower White, C. J. 1974a. 'Evaluative consistency and social judgment.' *J. Pers. soc. Psychol. 30*, 349–59.

Eiser, J. R. and Mower White, C. J. 1974b. 'The persuasiveness of labels: attitude change produced through definition of the attitude continuum.' *Eur. J. soc. Psychol. 4*, 89-92.

Eiser, J. R. and Mower White, C. J. 1975. 'Categorization and congruity in attitudinal judgment.' *J. Pers. soc. Psychol. 31*, 769-75.

Eiser, J. R. and Pancer, S. M. 1979. 'Attitudinal effects of the use of evaluatively biased language.' *Eur. J. soc. Psychol. 9*, in press.

Eiser, J. R. and Ross, M. 1977. 'Partisan language, immediacy and attitude change.' *Eur. J. soc. Psychol. 7*, 477-89.

Eiser, J. R. and Stroebe, W. 1972. *Categorization and social judgement.* London: Academic Press.

Festinger, L. 1957. *A theory of cognitive dissonance.* Evanston, Illinois: Row, Peterson.

Festinger, L. and Carlsmith, J. M. 1959. 'Cognitive consequences of forced compliance.' *J. abnorm. soc. Psychol. 58*, 203-10.

Fishbein, M. 1963. 'An investigation of the relationships between beliefs about an object and the attitude toward that object.' *Human Relations 16*, 233-40.

Fishbein, M. and Ajzen, I. 1975. *Belief, attitude, intention and behavior: an introduction to theory and research.* Reading, Mass.: Addison-Wesley.

Fishbein, M. and Coombs, F. S. 1974. 'Basis for decision: an attitudinal analysis of voting behavior.' *J. appl. soc. Psychol. 4*, 95-124.

Gardin, H., Kaplan, K. J., Firestone, I. J. and Cowan, G. A. 1973. 'Proxemic effects on cooperation, attitude and approach-avoidance in a Prisoner's Dilemma game.' *J. Pers. soc. Psychol. 27*, 13-18.

Green, D. 1974. 'Dissonance and self-perception analyses of "forced compliance": when two theories make competing predictions.' *J. Pers. soc. Psychol. 29*, 819-28.

Greenwald, A. G. 1968. 'Cognitive learning, cognitive response to persuasion and attitude change.' In A. G. Greenwald, T. C. Brock and T. M. Ostrom (eds) *Psychological foundations of attitudes*. New York: Academic Press.

Greenwald, A. G. 1975. 'On the inconclusiveness of "crucial" cognitive tests of dissonance versus self-perception theories.' *J. exp. soc. Psychol. 11*, 490-9.

Hovland, C. I. and Sherif, M. 1952. 'Judgmental phenomena and scales of attitude measurement: item displacement in Thurstone scales.' *J. abnorm. soc. Psychol. 47*, 822-32.

Jones, E. E., Kanouse, D. E., Kelley, H. H., Nisbett, R. E., Valines, S. and Weiner, B. 1971. *Attribution: perceiving the causes of behavior*. Morristorn, N. J.: General Learning Press.

Kothandapani, V. 1971. 'Validation of feeling, belief and intention to act as three components of attitude and their contribution to prediction of contraceptive behavior.' *J. Pers. soc. Psychol. 19*, 321-33.

La Piere, R. T. 1934. 'Attitudes versus actions.' *Social Forces 13*, 230-7.

Linder, D. E., Cooper, J. and Jones, E. E. 1967. 'Decision freedom as a determinant of the role of incentive magnitude in attitude change.' *J. Pers. soc. Psychol. 6*, 245-54.

Lingle, J. H. and Ostrom, T. M. in press. 'Principles of memory and cognition in attitude formation.' In R. E. Petty, T. M. Ostrom and T. C. Brock (eds) *Cognitive responses in persuasive communications: a text in attitude change*. New York: McGraw-Hill.

Nuttin, J. M. Jr. 1975. *The illusion of attitude change: towards a response contagion theory of persuasion*. London: Academic Press.

Oskamp, S. and Perlman, D. 1966. 'Effects of friendship and disliking on cooperation in a mixed-motive game.' *Journal of Conflict Resolution 10*, 221-6.

Ostrom, T. M. 1969. 'The relationship between the affective, behavioral and cognitive components of attitude.' *J. exp. soc. Psychol. 5*, 12-30.

Peabody, D. 1967. 'Trait inferences: evaluative and descriptive aspects.' *J. Pers. soc. Psychol. Monog. 7*, (2, Pt. 2, Whole No. 642).

Reich, J. W. 1974. 'Involvement and response language effects in attitude scaling.' *J. exp. soc. Psychol. 10*, 572-84.

Reiss, M. and Schlenker, B. R. 1977. 'Attitude change and responsibility avoidance as modes of dilemma resolution in forced-compliance situations.' *J. Pers. soc. Psychol. 35*, 21-30.

Rosenberg, M. J. 1965. 'When dissonance fails: on eliminating evaluation apprehension from attitude measurement.' *J. Pers. soc. Psychol. 1*, 28-42.

Rosenberg, M. J. and Hovland, C. I. 1960. 'Cognitive, affective and behavioral components of attitudes.' In M. J. Rosenberg, C. I. Hovland, W. J. McGuire, R. P. Abelson and J. W. Brehm *Attitude organization and change: an analysis of consistency among attitude components*. New Haven, Conn.: Yale University Press.

Ross, M. and Shulman, R. F. 1973. 'Increasing the salience of initial attitudes: dissonance versus self-perception theory.' *J. Pers. soc. Psychol. 28*, 138-44.

Sampson, E. E. and Insko, C. A. 1964. 'Cognitive consistency and performance in the autokinetic situation.' *J. abnorm. soc. Psychol. 68*, 184-92.

Schachter, S. and Singer, J. E. 1962. 'Cognitive, social and physiological determinants of emotional state.' *Psychol. Rev. 69*, 379-99.

Schneider, F. E. 1970. 'Conforming behaviors of black and white children.' *J. Pers. soc. Psychol. 16*, 466-71.

Selltiz, C., Edrich, H. and Cook, S. W. 1965. 'Ratings of favorableness about a social group as an indication of attitude toward the group.' *J. Pers. soc. Psychol. 2*, 408-15.

Shaffer, D. R. 1975. 'Some effects of consonant and dissonant attitudinal advocacy on initial attitude salience and attitude change.' *J. Pers. soc. Psychol. 32*, 160-8.

Smith, E. W. L. and Dixon, T. R. 1968. 'Verbal conditioning as a function of race of the experimenter and prejudice of the subject.' *J. exp. soc. Psychol. 4*, 285-301.

Snyder, M. and Ebbesen, E. 1972. 'Dissonance awareness: a test of dissonance theory versus self-perception theory.' *J. exp. soc. Psychol. 8*, 502-17.

Sulin, R. A. and Dooling, D. J. 1974. 'Intrusion of thematic ideas in retention of prose.' *J. exp. Psychol. 103*, 255-62.

Tajfel, H. and Wilkes, A. L. 1964. 'Salience of attributes and commitment to extreme judgements in the perception of people.' *Brit. J. soc. clin. Psychol. 3*, 40–9.

Tornatsky, L. and Geiwitz, P. J. 1968. 'The effects of threat and attraction on interpersonal bargaining.' *Psychon. Sci. 13*, 125-6.

Tulving, E. and Thomson, D. M. 1973. 'Encoding specificity and retrieval processes in episodic memory.' *Psychol. Rev. 5*, 352-73.

Upmeyer, A. and Layer, H. 1974. 'Accentuation and attitude in social judgement.' *Eur. J. soc. Psychol. 4*, 469-88.

Upshaw, H. S. 1965. 'The effect of variable perspectives on judgements of opinion statements for Thurstone scales: equal-appearing intervals.' *J. Pers. soc. Psychol. 2*, 60-9.

Weinstein, A. G. 1972. 'Predicting behavior from attitudes.' *Public Opinion Quarterly 36*, 355-60.

Wicker, A. W. 1969. 'Attitudes versus actions: the relationship of overt and behavioral responses to attitude objects.' *J. soc. Issues. 25*, 41-78.

Wicklund, R. A. and Brehm, J. W. 1976. *'Perspectives on cognitive dissonance.'* Hillsdale N.J.: Erlbaum.

Zanna, M. P. and Cooper, J. 1974. 'Dissonance and the pill: an attribution approach to studying the arousal properties of dissonance.' *J. Pers. soc. Psychol. 29*, 703-9.

Zavalloni, M. and Cook, S. W. 1965. 'Influence of judges' attitudes on ratings of favorableness of statements about a social group.' *J. Pers. soc. Psychol. 1*, 43-54.

Chapter 3

Psychology of Art

G. W. GRANGER

As the psychology of art receives scarcely any attention in university courses, I see my task as providing the reader with some initial orientation in an unfamiliar but fascinating field, of central importance to the study of man (Young 1971, p. 519). This being so, my chapter will assume a more historical form than those dealing with recognized core topics in psychology. My strategy will be to use one particular author, carefully chosen for the depth and breadth of his knowledge, readability and arousal potential. Using his ideas as a starting-point, I will then introduce you to some of the main alternatives.

ART AND THE AESTHETIC

Objets d'Art, Objets Trouvés, Objets?

For the present purpose, art is to be understood in its narrower, but widely-accepted, meaning as denoting the visual arts of painting, sculpture, etc. (cf. Gombrich 1972a; Read 1974). But already, this usage covers a bewildering variety of objects: e.g. the Venus of Milo and the 'Venus' of Willendorf (c. 16,000 years B.C.), Michelangelo's 'David', Andre's Tate Gallery 'brickwork', the Lascaux cave-paintings (c. 15,000 years B.C.), Leonardo's 'Mona Lisa', Picasso's 'Les Demoiselles d'Avignon', Warhol's 'Four Campbell Soup Cans' and a Pollock 'action painting'. (See Walker (1975) on the contemporary erosion of traditional boundaries between painting, sculpture and pure and applied art.)

Some Problems of Definition

Little wonder, therefore, that no one has yet come up with a crisp answer to the question, 'What is a work of art?', in terms of necessary and sufficient defining conditions. Many philosophers have given up the attempt and suggested that 'work of art' might better be regarded as a Wittgenstein family-resemblance concept. However, Dickie (1974) has recently offered a definition in terms of the conventional matrix (artworld) in which artworks are embedded. But see Goodman (1977) for an interesting suggestion that, instead of asking, '*What* objects are (permanently) works of art?' a better question might be, '*When* is an object a work of art?'

As for the term aesthetic (introduced as a neologism in the 18th century for the science of perceptible beauty and eagerly taken up as a generic term to cover both the enjoyment of artefacts and nature) no philosopher has yet succeeded in defining it or the scope of aesthetics to the satisfaction of most other philosophers in the field. Goodman (1968, pp. 252-5) suggests we look for 'aspects or symptoms', a symptom being '. . . neither a necessary nor sufficient condition for, but merely tends in conjunction with other such symptoms to be present in, aesthetic experience . . .,' an approach which seems likely to prove more fruitful.

Speculative versus Empirical Aesthetics

Confused and frustrated by all this wrangling, many psychologists have decided to draw a sharp line separating *empirical* from *speculative* aesthetics and remain aloof from the latter. Speculative aesthetics includes the hermeneutic[1] disciplines of *philosophical aesthetics* and *art theory* (the nearest English equivalent for the French *sciences de l'art* and German *Kunstwissenschaft*), which derives from *art history* and *art criticism*. Empirical aesthetics covers psychology and other disciplines that make use of the methods of science in the 'English' sense, as distinct from the French *science* and German *Wissenschaft*, which carry the meaning of scholarship (Berlyne 1974, pp. 2-4).

Speculative and Empirical Aesthetics: Conjectures and Refutations

While agreeing with Berlyne (1971) on three basic issues, I disagree with him in several other respects. I agree: that, as psychologists, we must take a cool look at art *in relation to other human activities*; that because art is such a widespread feature of human cultures, it must

[1]Which '. . . rely heavily on interpretative examination of particular specimens . . . of art' (Berlyne 1974, p. 2).

be presumed to be rooted in fundamental characteristics of the nervous system; and that we must, therefore, search for rudimentary forms of artistic/aesthetic activities among our collateral relatives in the animal kingdom. However, I think Berlyne and others like him, misguided in their attempt to remain aloof from speculative aesthetics, because so-called speculative aestheticians not only serve as valuable critics of the assumptions underlying empirical aesthetics, but have generated interesting and potentially-testable ideas about art which psychologists would be foolish to ignore.

Moreover, Berlyne has misrepresented the methods used by contemporary art historians, which *are* in part scientific (English sense) – not that psychologists could afford to remain aloof from art history, even if it were nothing more than scholarship. Also he holds an outmoded view that psychology and philosophy are totally independent disciplines (cf. Wollheim 1977, p. 173). Further he ignores 'artists on art' (Leonardo, Klee, Picasso[1] *et al.*) which provides another valuable source of ideas and criticism.

A Suggested Approach from 'Art Theory'

Though there are many possible approaches, my own preference is in favour of starting from within the framework provided by the *Kunstwissenschaft* tradition, while, at the same time, attempting to remain receptive to the words, as well as the works, of the artists themselves (the image men, as well as the professional word men – the scholars). I propose taking up a few psychological issues which have arisen within the theory of art, viz. representation, expression and communication, before considering the contribution of psychological aesthetics, as this is usually understood. I shall start by outlining the theme of a highly stimulating and readable book by the eminent art historian, Ernst Gombrich, *Art and illusion*.

THE PSYCHOLOGY OF REPRESENTATION IN PICTORIAL ART

Why Does Representational Art Have a History?

This is the basic question Gombrich (1977) sets out to answer. Like many of us, he is struck by the enormous variety of ways in which

---

[1] Who is a marvellously deft hand at throwing a spanner into the works of aestheticians!

artists have represented the world. Gombrich anticipates inevitable criticism that art is *essentially* self-expression by declaring that, whether we like it or not, the representation of nature *has* been (and *continues to be*) one aim of artists, which is both legitimate and cogent.

**Figure 3.1   Dürer: Self-portrait, c. 1491. Pen and ink: 204 × 208 mm. Erlangen, Graphische Sammlung der Universität, B 155ᵛ. Reproduced by permission.

The Myth of the Innocent Eye

To cut a long and absorbing story regrettably short, what Gombrich does is to examine the various theories that have been proposed to solve the riddle of style (cf. Figures 3·1 and 3·4), in particular, the very influential theory of *seeing and knowing*, the doctrine of the *innocent eye*, still held by some contemporary artists (e.g. Heron 1975, p. 158) in a quite different, non-figurative, context. According to this theory, artists concerned with the faithful portrayal of nature have had to strive to rid themselves of the burden of *knowledge*.

Gombrich argues that the innocent eye is a myth, because seeing cannot be separated from knowing. Moreover, he rejects the idea, shared by all earlier theorists, that the artist can transcribe directly what he sees, independent of conventional elements: he can only translate, in terms of the limitations imposed by his medium[1] and the role of projection which occurs in all image reading, the beholder's share.

The Theory of 'Making and Matching': Art and Illusion

The upshot is that Gombrich proposes an alternative theory of making and matching (and making comes before matching). The real problem for the naturalistic artist is not that of discarding his knowledge of the world but rather of inventing comparisons which work. Gombrich's theory is essentially Popperian in conception, emphasizing the part played by anticipations and tests. Artists cannot copy what they see, but only manipulate ambiguous clues until the made image becomes indistinguishable from reality. A painting is realistic to the extent that it succeeds as an *illusion*, leading the viewer to believe that it has the characteristics of what it represents.

Alternative Theories of Pictorial Representation

Gombrich's account has its difficulties (e.g. the artist tends to become entrapped in his own schemata (cf. Neisser 1976; Wollheim 1970) and several alternatives have been proposed, though no author, other than Gombrich, has attempted such a wide-ranging art-historical (ecologically-valid, cf. Neisser 1976) test of his ideas. Theories range from the optically-based point-projection (central perspective) theory (Pirenne 1970; Gibson 1971, pp. 27-9); through Gibson's attempt to take a new look at the problem in terms of his theory of *information pickup* (Gibson 1971); to Goodman's (1968) *semiotic* theory. Like Gombrich, Goodman emphasizes the relativity of vision and representation, but regards perspective as a convention, which Gombrich insists has a natural basis in optics.

Some empirical support for Gibson's approach comes from Kennedy's (1974) review of work on outline drawings which, elsewhere, he suggests were discovered not invented; though, more recently, he has expressed doubts about Gibson's theory of pictorial perception (e.g. Kennedy and Ostry 1976). For detailed accounts of the various

---

[1] E.g. pigment range; colour interactions on canvas (cf. Ruskin, in Gombrich 1977, p. 261; Matisse, in Chipp 1968, p. 134 and Albers 1971).

theories, see Gibson (1971), Kennedy (1974), Gombrich (1975) and Wollheim (1977) who makes an important point about *representational seeing*, which requires of the observer that, besides seeing something or other *in* the configuration, he should also be aware of the configuration itself (cf. Gibson 1968, 1971, on the pictorial attitude).

The Perspective Issue in Art: Central or Perverted?

On the specific issue of perspective, Carter (1970, pp. 840-61) provides a thorough review of the various types, scientific and otherwise. Gibson (1971) argues against Goodman's (1968) view of perspective as a convention, to which Goodman (1971) replies, claiming (*contra* Gibson) that reverse perspective *can* be consistently applied. But see, especially, Arnheim (1972) who raises the issue of inverse perspective to launch a general attack on what he calls the illusionistic doctrine of art which rests on a Renaissance conception of the nature of pictorial form. (See also Léger (1973, esp. pp. 3, 15), and many other twentieth century artists on art, Chipp 1968.) Though widely adopted as a norm, 'A collector of antiques can discover many fine specimens in the writings of psychologists, art historians, aestheticians and even artists.' It fails abysmally not only to account for twentieth century Western art, as exemplified by Picasso, but 'all styles of world art . . .' (Arnheim 1972, p. 125). I shall have more to say about Arnheim's own viewpoint later, in relation to expression.

Works of Art as Systems of Symbols

Though several of the other alternatives merit serious consideration, I single out for special mention Goodman's semiotic theory (Goodman 1968), because it exemplifies an increasingly *cognitive* approach to art[1] in recent years. Goodman regards works of art as systems of symbols (cf. Picasso, in Ashton 1972, p. 68) and makes interesting comparisons between pictorial representation and verbal description. Whereas most popular discussion tends to emphasize the sharp contrast between the verbal and the visual – language being serial and conventional, vision immediate, natural and wholistic – Goodman has pointed to some important similarities as well as differences.

---

[1]Including child art, a field rich in artworks, but in a very uncultivated state, scientifically. Goodnow (1977) and Freeman (1977) provide good introductions to the vast literature on the subject, and Freeman presents cogent arguments in favour of a *cognitive*, experimental, approach. And, of course, don't fail to look at and ponder upon Nadia's drawings (Selfe 1977). (See Figure 3·2).

That 'reading' pictures and reading texts *do* have something in common is evident, at least at an elementary level, in the sense that reading text involves visual discrimination and scanning. Moreover, there is evidence that although people agree to some extent in what they look at (e.g. in viewing Hokusai's picture, 'The Great Wave') there is wide

Figure 3.2   Nadia: Cockerel. Pen drawing: approximately 27 × 15 cm. Drawn when the artist was about six years of age. (Reproduced from Selfe, L. 1977. *Nadia: a case of extraordinary drawing ability in an autistic child.* London: Academic Press, by permission of the publishers.)

variation in the sequence of their looks (Buswell 1935); they 'read' pictures in different ways, just as they do text. In both cases, they appear to work from a stored data-base in order to interpret the features of a 'complex stimulus sequence sampled over time' (Kolers 1977).

Can Artists Invent New 'Languages of Vision'?

But, although the analogy between linguistic and pictorial symbol systems seems a very fruitful one to explore, Hochberg has argued that the 'symbols of art are not in general arbitrary; they are not learned in the same sense that we learn to read' (Hochberg 1972, p. 66). See Kennedy (1974) for relevant evidence. The 'artist is not free to design just any old language of *vision* that strikes his fancy' (Hochberg 1972, p. 69).

Gibson (1971) makes a similar point against the 'languages of vision'. idea, prevalent in writings on art. Although he rejects the point-projection theory, as (literally) providing too restrictive a viewpoint, he nevertheless considers the structure of a picture has a closer affinity with *natural optics* (of the Gibsonian, ecological, kind) than with the structure of language. Pictures do have a 'sort of grammar' but this arises from the 'informative structure of ambient light' (Gibson 1971, p. 34). While accepting that artists can educate our attention, he rejects the idea that they can invent a new mode of visual perception.

ART AS EXPRESSION AND COMMUNICATION

From Representation to Expression

In Chapter 11 Gombrich (1977) turns from representation to expression, taking up this issue again in *Meditations on a hobby horse* (Gombrich 1971). As he puts it, '. . . a growing awareness that art offers a key to the mind as well as the outer world has led to a radical change of interest on the part of artists.' While accepting this as a perfectly 'legitimate' shift, he thinks it a pity if these 'fresh explorations' (surely not in world art as a whole?) 'failed to profit from the lessons of tradition'. He notes a '. . . curious reversal of emphasis in recent critical writings . . .' naturalism being now widely accepted as a form of convention; the 'language of forms and colours, on the other hand, that explores the inner recesses of the mind . . . as right by nature. Our nature'. (Gombrich 1977, p. 305).

The Natural Resonance Hypothesis of Expressionist Art

What Gombrich argues against is the *natural resonance* hypothesis, held by Kandinsky (see Read 1974, pp. 165-75, p. 372) and certain other, non-figurative,[1] artists of this century. On this view, the artist's emotion naturally spills on to the canvas in the sense that the blue pigment (which to Kandinsky himself emerged dolorously from the paint tube) charges the canvas with the artist's blues, which are then transmitted direct to the beholder. Whereas the communication of information depends on *codes* that rest on conventions, the expression of emotion is supposed to work through symptoms that are *natural* and unlearned.

Expressionism, Gestalt 'Brain Fields' and Information Pickup

Whether he was directly influenced by Gestalt theory, as has been suggested, Kandinsky (and other, similar expressionists) would certainly have had the support of Gestalt psychology. Arnheim (1974), for instance, their chief living spokesman on art insists that expression which, in his view, is what art is essentially about, resides in the visual patterns themselves and is the direct outcome of perceptual forces or visual dynamics. When he speaks of forces, he does not mean 'merely figures of speech' but the direct psychological counter-part of 'field processes' in the brain (Arnheim 1974, pp. 16-17). Unfortunately, Arnheim's case rests on a concept which, as an explanatory principle in perceptual theory, is widely-regarded as 'totally defunct'[2] (Hochberg 1972, p. 52). And, though the idea of *natural resonance* might also be attractive to Gibson, it is difficult at the present time to understand how, in other than a metaphorical sense, his perceptual systems could be said to resonate (Gibson 1968, p. 5) to the expressive information available in the light, structured by artifice or art (*op. cit.*, p. 224); but see Pratt (1961, pp. 77-8) for a more sanguine view.

Gombrich's Arguments Against the Natural Resonance Hypothesis

Maybe metaphor has got more to do with expression in art than either Arnheim or Gibson would have us believe. Gombrich (1971,

---

[1]cf. 'Nor is there any "figurative" and "non-figurative" art' (Picasso, in Ashton 1972, p. 9).

[2]In saying this, I do not wish for a moment to detract from the value of Arnheim's (1974) book as a whole: he has a great many interesting and important things to say about perceptual phenomena (shape, colour, etc.) in relation to art.

p. 14) thinks it has, as does Goodman (1968, p. 85) who regards expression as *metaphorical exemplification*, speaking as a philosopher!

Gombrich thinks the natural resonators are badly mistaken when they suppose that the artist's emotion can, as it were, overflow into his painting and infect others with it (Tolstoy's way of putting it). Instead, he must make a particular choice (of colour, line or shape) that corresponds to the emotion he wants to convey, within a set of alternatives provided by his palette, repertoire, style or social context within which he works. Contrary to the natural resonance hypothesis, he cannot *transpose* his emotion into an 'unstructured medium' (Gombrich 1971, pp. 56-69).

Importance of the Choice Situation in Judgements of Expression

And, from the beholder's viewpoint, it is only when *he* is aware of the alternatives open to the artist that he can get the (emotional) message. He must be aware of the choice situation. As with his 'reading' of the images of representational art, so with his response to expression, 'expectations of possibilities and probabilities must come into play' (Gombrich 1977, p. 316). The more we know about the artist's palette, repertoire and style, the more likely we are to grasp the intended meaning; we need all the contextual aids we can lay our hands on.

In support of his case, Gombrich mentions three specific examples which I invite you to consider: Mondrian's 'Broadway Boogie-Woogie' (Gombrich 1977, pp. 311-3); Kandinsky's 'At Rest' (Gombrich 1971, pp. 67-8); and Van Gogh's 'Bedroom at Arles' (Gombrich 1972b, p. 96). Note that Gombrich does *not* say you need collateral information about repertoire, style and social context before you can *enjoy* these three paintings: only that it seems unlikely that you will hit on the expressive meaning *intended* by the artist (there's the rub!), unless you have additional contextual clues.

A Possible Natural Basis for Expression

Although Gombrich considers that expression depends heavily on convention, he admits that it rests on a natural basis: 'some inborn disposition . . . to equate certain sensations with certain feeling tones' (Gombrich 1971, p. 58). Though the range of alternatives confronting an artist *is* a matter of convention, it is not a matter of convention *which* alternative, in *contrast to some other*, conveys a particular emotion. Though red as such has no fixed expressive meaning, where there is a choice between red and blue, 'the move towards the blue is more likely to be felt as a move towards the sad end of the spectrum' (Gombrich 1971, p. 61).

Thus, he implies a *natural* correspondence between a gamut of colours or forms, on the one hand, and emotional states or meanings on the other. His basic assumption seems to be that the two ends of the spectrum (now in a wider sense than the visible) from which the artist's palette or repertoire is selected, are correlated naturally with particular emotional states and that the ordinal relations (redder-than, bluer-than, warmer-than, cooler-than, etc.) within this spectrum also have a natural basis. 'There may be a layer deep down in our mind . . . for which these sensory categories are only different aspects of the same experience.' But, Gombrich remains sceptical and goes on to say that, 'perhaps it is precisely because they all converge in one particular point that even the directions seem extraordinarily unstable' (Gombrich 1971, pp. 61-2). Note also, the possible effect of contextual variables in the stimulus pattern itself (e.g. simultaneous contrast in shifting a given colour from warm to cool (cf. Ruskin, quoted earlier in Gombrich 1977, p. 261).

Evidence for Cross-cultural Universals of Expressive Meaning

Osgood's semantic differential has an obvious empirical bearing on Gombrich's theory. I will give but a single reference, to the massive collection of data assembled from cross-cultural studies using the semantic differential in its graphic, as well as its ordinary form. Osgood, May and Miron (1975) claim that there are cross-cultural universals of affective (including expressive) meaning. Moreover, they suggest, that the synaesthetic metaphors with which they deal do indeed originate in a 'layer deep down in our mind' or, rather, brain, *viz.* '. . . the non-specific projection system as it mediates reactions from hypothalamus, reticular or limbic systems to the frontal lobes . . .' (Osgood *et al.* 1975, p. 395). Though based on factor-analysis which suffers from severe limitations as a hypothesis-testing technique (*op. cit.* p. 44), their extensive data, lists of references and speculations merit attention by the psychologist of art though one must bear in mind that meaning in semantic differential terms is imposed, as distinct from spontaneously expressed. For a good summary of earlier research on expression relevant to art, see Pratt (1961). I shall have something more to say about Gombrich's ideas on the subject later.

ART AS PLEASURE AND AROUSAL

Up to this point, I have approached the psychology of art from within the framework of art theory. In this section I propose introducing the reader to the more traditional approach adopted by psychologists *via* the concept of the aesthetic, as developed first by Fechner and, more recently, by Berlyne (1971). I shall not distinguish between the old Fechnerian (c. 1876-1960) and the new empirical aesthetics (c. 1960-), as Berlyne does, because they are based on the same underlying hedonistic concept of the aesthetic and related assumptions that stem from eighteenth century philosophy. For an introduction to the Fechnerian phase see Berlyne (1971) who provides an adequate supply of references. I shall concentrate upon the second phase as developed by Berlyne (1971, 1974).

The Hedonic as a Paradigm of the Aesthetic

What Berlyne has done, in effect, is to develop the old Fechnerian aesthetics, which rested on a mentalistic form of hedonism (in terms of judgements of affect) and an atomistic theory of perception, along more behaviouristic and biological lines. On the stimulus side, he has extended it to include a new class of informational as distinct from energy variables; on the response side, to include non-verbal measures besides affective judgements; and has re-interpreted the ancient *unity in variety* principle in terms of a psychophysiological analysis of the Wundt curve (Berlyne 1971, p. 86) based on the concept of arousal.

The Wundt Curve and Arousal Potential

Besides Fechnerian *psychophysical* variables, the stimulus properties that constitute *arousal potential* include ecological variables (e.g. sign stimuli) and 'collative' variables (e.g. complexity, novelty, ambiguity) – collative because they involve collation of information from two or more sources. Berlyne's thesis is that his collative variables 'seem to be identifiable with the irreducibly essential ingredients of art and of whatever is aesthetically appealing . . .' (Berlyne 1971, p. vii): they can be identified with the factors that constitute 'form' and 'structure' or 'composition' in art (*op. cit.*, p. 70).

The horizontal axis of the inverted U-shaped Wundt curve now represents, not simply a single characteristic of stimulus energy, but also ecological and, more importantly for aesthetics, collative (informational) variables, while the vertical axis represents behavioural indices of hedonic value (e.g. attractiveness, reward value) as well as verbal reports of pleasingness and the like. Berlyne regards this curve as the algebraic summation of two antagonistic curves that represent the supposed degrees of activation of two antagonistic brain systems (see Berlyne (1971, pp. 88-89) and Figure 3·3).

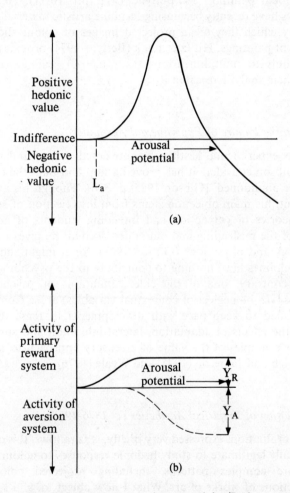

Figure 3.3 a The Wundt curve, as reinterpreted by Berlyne, representing relations between hedonic value and arousal potential. b Hypothetical curves representing activity of a primary reward system and an aversion system in the brain, whose resultant produces the Wundt curve. (Based on material contained in Figures 2 and 3, from Berlyne, 1974, pp. 10-11, courtesy, Hemisphere Publishing Corporation.)

From the Synthetic to the Analytic

Berlyne and his colleagues have recently moved from their synthetic phase, using relatively simple stimulus patterns (exemplified by Fechner's original work on the golden rectangle), to the analytic, characterized by Fechner's study of preferences between two versions of a Holbein painting (see Berlyne 1971, pp. 10-11). He and his colleagues have recently been using 'genuine artistic material' (*op. cit.*, p. 11), by which they mean projected images of colour slide reproductions of paintings. His later book (Berlyne 1974) provides a useful introduction to multidimensional (non-metric) scaling techniques, used in their analytic research.

Gibson on the Failure of Experimental Aesthetics

What has experimental aesthetics contributed to our understanding of art? Gibson considers it has proved a flop and that 'the enterprise should be abandoned' (Gibson 1975, p. 320). Though his arguments are cogent, his main objection stems from his rejection of sensation-based theories of perception and intending students of art should beware of the misleading and outmoded account he gives of sensory psychology and physiology (Gibson 1968), for it might suggest that these disciplines have nothing to contribute to the psychology of art. On the contrary, one of the chief limitations of psychophysical aesthetics (*viz.* its neglect of contextual variables) arose from the fact that it failed to keep pace with developments in these disciplines (e.g. on the effects of adaptation, lateral inhibition and summation, etc.). For examples of the value of a sensory approach to paintings, see Hurvich and Jameson (1975) and Weale (1976).

An Evaluation of Empirical Aesthetics (c. 1876-1978)

My own evaluation, expressed very briefly, is as follows. It is obviously scientifically legitimate to study hedonic responses to colours, shapes and more complex patterns, including projected colour slide reproductions of works of art. What I now object to, and I speak as a former experimental aesthetician of the 'old' school (cf. Granger 1956, 1973), is the uncritical and very slippery way in which the term aesthetic has been, and continues to be, used: pleasure becomes aesthetic pleasure, hedonic value becomes aesthetic value, etc. Moreover, I consider the hedonic and evaluative aspect has been overemphasized, oversimplified and overvalued, at the expense of the cognitive (cf. Goodman, 1972, pp. 120-121, on 'Merit as Means').

Berlyne's work is about the motivational effect of collative stimulus variables: a kind of perceptual hedonics, as contrasted with Fechner's sensory hedonics (but see Gibson 1968). What he has *not* demonstrated is that his collative variables constitute the 'irreducibly essential ingredients of art and of whatever else is aesthetically appealing', even though arousal potential may well have something to do with the initial orienting responses to works of art and natural objects.

His key concepts are not only difficult to pin down experimentally, but they are connected by loose chains of reasoning (e.g. Berlyne 1971, p. 81). Even at the synthetic level, he has not produced any compelling evidence for reproducible U-shaped curves in individuals; only for bits of what might be Wundt curves, from data averaged over groups, drawn from a limited population, under conditions which lack ecological validity (cf. Neisser 1976). Though, to be fair to Berlyne on the issue of generality, in the period before his recent untimely death he was in the process of extending his work cross-culturally (Berlyne 1978).

Despite the extravagant claims he makes at times about the significance of the new experimental aesthetics for our understanding of art, he concludes his second book with a very modest and frank admission that, 'the new experimental aesthetics has not yet gone very far beyond its first twitchings and gasps for breath' (Berlyne 1974, p. 327).

The Psychobiological Roots of Art

As I mentioned at the outset, one of the features of Berlyne's approach which appeals strongly to me is the psychobiological aspect and I recommend Berlyne (1971) as a valuable introduction to research on 'intrinsically-rewarding' activities, as shown, for instance, by the scribbling, drawing and painting of apes (Morris 1962), a line of research that ought to be pursued in relation to work on the representational skills of young children and the evolution and ontogeny of hand function in primates (Connolly and Elliott 1972). See also Young (1971, pp. 499-540), Brothwell (1976) and, especially, Whiten's (1976) review of work on primate aesthetics, but note that Humphrey and Keeble (1977) now doubt their earlier claim that rhesus monkeys find blue light more pleasant than red. The going is hard in experimental primate 'aesthetics'.

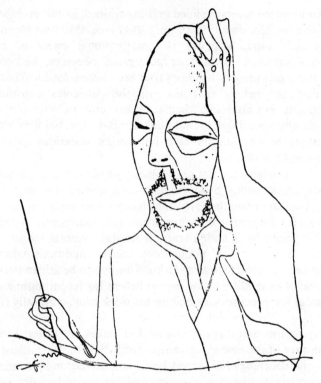

Figure 3.4   Klee: Artist's picture (self-portrait), 1919. Pen drawing: 23 × 14 cm. Present owner unknown. (Reproduced from Paul Klee Notebooks: Vol. 1: *The thinking eye*. London: Lund Humphries, 1961, by permission of the publishers.) ['The meaning of art?']

THE MEANING OF ART?

The Need for Collateral Information: Code, Caption and Context

Having suggested Gombrich as your initial guide and mentor, I will now offer a few more statements from the same source in the hope that they will provoke you to further thought and research. They bear directly on the themes touched on in the earlier sections.

Following Karl Bühler's division of the functions of language in terms of arousal, expression and description (signal, symptom and symbol), Gombrich (1972b) suggests: (i) that the visual image is 'supreme in its capacity for arousal'; (ii) 'that its use for expressive purposes is problematic'; and (iii) 'that unaided it altogether lacks the possibility of matching the statement function of language' (Gombrich 1972b, p. 86). To add to this list, from *Meditations on a hobby horse*, reflect also on the following: '. . . art is not the "universal language" that could link classes and civilizations . . .' (Gombrich 1971, p. 28); '. . . we must not confuse response with understanding, expression with communication . . .' (*op. cit.*, p. 49); 'I am by no means sure that art can be wholly described as "communication" . . . in . . . any sense' (*op. cit.* p. 54).

Gibson on the Information Available

Compare these statements with a selection from Gibson (1971). 'It is surely true that picturing is a means of communication and a way of storing, accumulating and transmitting knowledge to successive generations of men.' 'Both pictures and language *have* structure, to be sure . . . But the informative structure of ambient light is richer and more inexhaustible than the informative structure of language.' 'As every artist knows, there are thoughts that can be visualized without being verbalized' (*op. cit.* p. 34). ['Take the proverbial apples by Cézanne' (the watercolour, 'Apples, bottle and chair' in the Courtauld Galleries, London) . . . 'They say infinitely more than can be summed up in words . . .' (Gombrich 1971, p. 99). But, to be fair to Gombrich, he does place 'say' in inverted commas.]

Picasso on Intentions and Captions

On the issue of the artist's real intentions, a recurring theme in Gombrich's writings, I can only appeal to Picasso for help. 'To know what you want to draw, you have to begin drawing it. If it turns out to be a man, I draw a man – if it's a woman, I draw a woman. There's an old Spanish proverb: "If it has a beard, it's a man; if it doesn't have a beard, it's a woman"' (Ashton 1972, p. 107). As for the significance of captions, which entered the world of art relatively late in its history, the same artist, noting the 'mania of art dealers, collectors . . . for christening pictures', is reported to have said, 'When they ask me for a title, I say the first thing that comes into my head' (*op. cit.* p. 97).

Allowing the Beholder His Fair Share

What meaning a painting or other work of art conveys poses a very difficult problem for the psychologist, especially when the experimenter still has to rely so heavily on verbal reports about meanings that perhaps cannot, from their very nature, be adequately 'summed up in words' (cf. Gombrich 1971 above). We do, of course, have a number of non-verbal measures at our disposal, as Berlyne has pointed out, but these remain in a relatively undeveloped state. We might, of course, consider asking the subject to paint his response, but that method also is not without its problems.

But, even though our existing techniques have their limitations, we ought at least to allow our subject a little more *time* than we normally do in order to discover just how much meaning he could extract from, say, an original work of art, unassisted by any of the contextual aids on which Gombrich places so much emphasis. Perhaps a period of perceptual learning, of the Gibsonian discrimination type, would help the beholder to get rather more from the stimulus configuration than he is able to pick up, either in a tachistoscopic experiment using colour slides or from a quick trot round an art gallery, paying a casual glance here and there, as part of an initial orienting reaction of the Berlynian kind.

A Final Word: The Potency of Great Works of Art

But even supposing that, at the end of the day, we (now as beholders) still fail to get the message, we can surely agree with Gombrich that 'a great work of art is so rich in structure that it remains potent even when misunderstood' (Gombrich 1971, p. 67). And when he talks here of potency, I think we can safely assume that he means more than mere arousal potential.

REFERENCES

Albers, J. 1971. *Interaction of color*. New Haven and London: Yale University Press.

Arnheim, R. 1972. 'Inverted perspective in art: display and expression.' *Leonardo 5*, 125-36.

Arnheim, R. 1974. *Art and visual perception; the new version*. Berkeley and Los Angeles: University of California Press.

Ashton, D. 1972. *Picasso on art: a selection of views*. London: Thames and Hudson.

Berlyne, D. E. 1971. *Aesthetics and psychobiology*. New York: Appleton-Century-Crofts.

Berlyne, D. E. (ed.) 1974. *Studies in the new experimental aesthetics; steps toward an objective psychology of aesthetic appreciation*. Washington, D.C.: Hemisphere Publishing Corporation.

Berlyne, D. E. 1978. 'Psychological aesthetics.' In H. C. Triandis *et al.* (eds), *Handbook of cross-cultural psychology 2*. Boston: Allyn and Bacon.

Brothwell, D. 1976. 'Visual art, evolution and environment.' In D. Brothwell (ed.) *Beyond aesthetics*. London: Thames and Hudson.

Buswell, G. T. 1935. *How people look at pictures*. Chicago: University of Chicago Press.

Carter, B. A. R. 1970. 'Perspective.' In H. Osborne (ed.) *The Oxford companion to art*. Oxford: Clarendon Press.

Chipp, H. B. 1968. *Theories of modern art: a source book by artists and critics*. Berkeley, Los Angeles and London: University of California Press.

Connolly, K. and Elliott, J. 1972. 'The evolution and ontogeny of hand function.' In N. Blurton Jones (ed.) *Ethological studies of child behaviour*. London: Cambridge University Press.

Dickie, G. 1974. *Art and the aesthetic: an institutional analysis*. Ithaca and London: Cornell University Press.

Freeman, N. 1977. 'How young children try to plan drawings.' In G. Butterworth (ed.) *The child's representation of the world*. New York and London: Plenum Press.

Gibson, J. J. 1968. *The senses considered as perceptual systems*. London: George Allen and Unwin.

Gibson, J. J. 1971. 'The information available in pictures.' *Leonardo 4*, 27-35.

Gibson, J. J. 1975. 'Pickford and the failure of experimental aesthetics.' *Leonardo 8*, 319-21.

Gombrich, E. H. 1971. *Meditations on a hobby horse*. London: Phaidon Press.

Gombrich, E. H. 1972a. *The story of art*. London: Phaidon Press.

Gombrich, E. H. 1972b. 'The visual image'. *Scientific American 223*, 82-96.

Gombrich, E. H. 1975. 'Mirror and map: theories of pictorial representation.' *Phil. Trans. Roy. Soc. Lond. B.*, *270*, 119-49.

Gombrich, E. H. 1977. *Art and illusion*. London: Phaidon Press.

Goodman, N. 1968. *Languages of art*. Indianapolis and New York: Bobbs-Merrill.

Goodman, N. 1971. 'On J. J. Gibson's new perspective.' *Leonardo 4*, 359-60.

Goodman, N. 1972. *Problems and projects*. Indianapolis and New York: Bobbs-Merrill.

Goodman, N. 1977. 'When is art?' In D. Perkins and B. Leondar (eds) *The arts and cognition*. Baltimore and London: The Johns Hopkins University Press.

Goodnow, J. 1977. *Children's drawing*. London: Fontana/Open Books.

Granger, G. W. 1956. 'Expériences récentes d'Esthétique Visuelle.' *Rev. d'Esthétique 9*, 10-49.

Granger, G. W. 1973. ' "Colour harmony" in science and art.' In *Colour 73*. London: Hilger.

Heron, P. 1975. 'The shape of colour.' In B. Smith (ed.) *Concerning contemporary art*. Oxford: Clarendon Press.

Hochberg, J. E. 1972. 'The representation of things and people.' In E. H. Gombrich, J. Hochberg and M. Black *Art, perception and reality*. Baltimore and London: The Johns Hopkins University Press.

Humphrey, N. K. and Keeble, G. R. 1977. 'Do monkeys' subjective clocks run faster in red light than in blue?' *Perception 6*, 7-14.

Hurvich, D. and Jameson, L. M. 1975. 'From contrast to assimilation: in art and in the eye.' *Leonardo 8*, 125-31.

Kennedy, J. M. 1974. *A psychology of picture perception.* San Francisco and London: Jossey-Bass.

Kennedy, J. M. and Ostry, D. J. 1976. 'Approaches to picture perception: perceptual experience and ecological optics.' *Can. J. Psychol. 30*, 90-8.

Kolers, P. 1977. 'Reading pictures and reading text.' In D. Perkins and B. Leondar (eds) *The arts and cognition.* Baltimore and London: The Johns Hopkins University Press.

Léger, F. 1973. *The functions of painting.* London: Thames and Hudson.

Morris, D. 1962. *The biology of art.* London: Methuen.

Neisser, U. 1976. *Cognition and reality.* San Francisco: W. H. Freeman.

Osgood, C. E., May, W. H. and Miron, M. S. 1975. *Cross-cultural universals of affective meaning.* Urbana: University of Illinois Press.

Pirenne, M. H. 1970. *Optics, painting and photography.* Cambridge: Cambridge University Press.

Pratt, C. C. 1961. 'Aesthetics.' *Ann. Rev. Psychol. 12*, 71-92.

Read, H. 1974. *A concise history of modern painting.* London: Thames and Hudson.

Selfe, L. 1977. *Nadia: a case of extraordinary drawing ability in an autistic child.* London: Academic Press.

Walker, J. A. 1975. *Art since pop.* London: Thames and Hudson.

Weale, R. A. 1976. 'Trompe l'œil to rompe l'œil: vision and art.' In D. Brothwell (ed.) *Beyond aesthetics.* London: Thames and Hudson.

Whiten, A. 1976. 'Primate perception and aesthetics.' In D. Brothwell (ed.) *Beyond aesthetics.* London: Thames and Hudson.

Wollheim, R. 1970. *Art and its objects.* Harmondsworth: Pelican Books.

Wollheim, R. 1977. 'Representation: the philosophical contribution to psychology.' In G. Butterworth (ed.) *The child's representation of the world.* New York and London: Plenum Press.

Young, J. Z. 1971. *An introduction to the study of man.* London: Oxford University Press.

FURTHER READING

Relevant articles are widely scattered among the psychological journals, but I would single out *Perception* for special mention. On the philosophical side, *The Journal of Aesthetics and Art Criticism* and *British Journal of Aesthetics* carry articles and book reviews of interest to the psychologist of art. *Scientific Aesthetics* (the new version of *Sciences de l'Art*) and *Leonardo* have the advantage of being multidisciplinary in approach. Within the art world, I offer the following selection for anyone wishing to keep in touch with contemporary happenings: *Artforum, Artscribe, Art Monthly, Art International* and, for the really avant-garde, *Flash Art!*

Chapter 4

Perception and Cognition in Infancy

PAUL HARRIS

In debating the validity of some of our basic conceptual categories, philosophers of the 17th and 18th centuries frequently made proposals about the origin of those categories. For example the empiricists argued that our knowledge of space depends upon prior sensory experience. Berkeley in particular, claimed that we do not perceive depth directly at birth, but must learn to interpret visual cues – such as the clarity of the retinal image or the angle of convergence of our eyes. An interpretation of these cues can be made when they have been associated with other experiences such as touching and reaching out for visible objects at various distances. The rationalists claimed on the other hand that certain interpretations of our perceptual experience are based on innate ideas rather than experience. Thus Kant argued that the categories of space and time, among others, are imposed upon and not derived from perceptual experience. The empiricists might insist on the didactic role of certain experiences, such as tactual experience, for the interpretation of visual cues, but innate ideas must supply an initial interpretation of our tactual experience.

Such questions about the origins of knowledge can be answered, at least in part, by experiments on infants. This is not to say that psychologists always carry a philosophy text with them into the infant laboratory, but it will be clear from the remainder of this chapter that those philosophical speculations have not been completely forgotten by psychologists.

I shall discuss four basic issues: the origin of shape perception; the perception of space; the relationship between the senses and the problem of object permanence. This is by no means an exhaustive review of current research on human infancy. In particular, I shall not discuss the infant's capacity for interaction with other people nor his capacity for speech perception (Haith and Campos 1977).

SHAPE PERCEPTION

Detection of Visual Configuration

Consider a newborn infant looking at his mother's face for the first time in his life. Can the baby perceive the shape of the face despite its total unfamiliarity? Most current texts and reviews of infant perception (Bronson 1974; Haith and Campos 1977; Salapatek 1975; Rosinski 1977) suggest that during the first weeks of his life, the baby does not respond to a stimulus like a face as an organized visual configuration. The baby can detect edges because he spends more time looking at a striped black and white card than a plain grey one (Karmel and Maisel 1975) but if the edges are organized into a shape he does not appear to notice. For example given the choice of looking at a picture of a face or a picture where the parts of the face have been jumbled, the infant below about ten weeks spends the same amount of time looking at each (Haaf and Brown 1976). Indeed even if the neonate is given a real face to look at, he only appears to examine it in a fragmentary fashion – typically he fixates a limited portion of the perimeter of the face (Maurer and Salapatek 1976).

This picture changes at around two months in several ways. The infant begins to fixate the inner features of a shape (Maurer and Salapatek 1976) and he begins to prefer a familiar organized configuration such as a face to a jumble of fragments (Haaf and Brown 1976).

From these findings, it is tempting to infer a lack of competence from a lack of performance: to claim that since the infant does not respond to a configuration, he cannot. Thus the newborn seeing his mother's face sees edge-transitions from light to dark – but no organized configuration. In order to imagine what this would be like, take a look at Figure 4·1.

You will immediately see the various transitions from light to dark, but it may be difficult for you to see a face in the picture. Tempting though it may be to think of the newborn as deficient in this way, some recent research indicates that the neonate can indeed perceive visual configuration.

First Meltzoff and Moore (1977) have recently confirmed earlier

Figure 4.1 The hidden man (after Porter, 1954). If you cannot see the figure immediately, it may be helpful to know that only his head and shoulders are visible; the line of his nose is indicated by the edge in the top centre of the figure which is almost vertical.

suggestions in the literature (Zazzo 1957) that the newborn can imitate. Meltzoff and Moore (1977) report that infants of two or three weeks can copy an adult modelling tongue or lip protrusion, mouth opening or sequential finger movements. Because the neonate's imitation is highly discriminative – for example he can see a difference between protrusion of the tongue and protrusion of the lips – he must be capable of perceiving the shape of a stimulus, even when this shape is a component feature of some larger stimulus.

Second, Goren, Sarty and Wu (1975) report that babies only a few minutes old will track a moving face-like stimulus. When the features of the face are jumbled this following response is much reduced. Third, during the first month of life the baby can distinguish between his mother's face and the face of a stranger (Carpenter 1974; Maurer and Salapatek 1976). This type of selectivity also suggests that the baby can perceive visual configuration, since the stimuli are approximately equal in amount of contour, brightness and mobility.

One can reasonably ask why so many investigators have concluded that the newborn is insensitive to visual configuration. I think there are two related factors. In discussing the early work of Ebbinghaus on memory for nonsense syllables, Bartlett (1932) argued that the results were misleading because subjects were almost totally deprived of the variable which typically determines the memorability of material: meaningfulness. Thus, in his efforts to simplify the stimulus situation, Ebbinghaus presented subjects with a task which was straining their

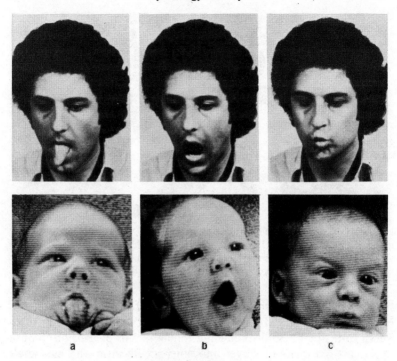

a   b   c

Figure 4.2   Imitation of facial gestures by 2- to 3-week-old infants.

normal competence and therefore, from the subjects' point of view
(rather than the experimenter's) was more, not less, complex than
memory for meaningful material. Similarly, investigators into the
origins of visual perception, in their efforts to 'simplify' the stimulus
situation may have presented their subjects with the visual equivalent
of nonsense syllables. For example, most investigators present subjects
with static stimuli. It is possible that the motion present in the studies
mentioned above (Meltzoff and Moore 1977; Goren *et al.* 1975;
Carpenter 1974) helped the infants to perceive the visual configuration.

    A second and related factor has been the elemental approach
favoured by many investigators. It has been assumed along the lines
of Hebb (1949) that infants construct configurations from a successive
fixation of elements. Thus by studying the infant's successive fixations
(Salapatek and Kessen 1966; Salapatek and Kessen 1973) one might
have been able to study the infant engaged in shape construction.
Recent evidence, however, suggests that it is most unlikely that the
neonate's scanning activities will provide any clues as to how visual
configurations are perceived: Harris and Bassett (1977) found that

neonates could discriminate between configurations which were presented repeatedly but for only 300 msec on any given occasion – far too short for systematic scanning to occur.

Discrimination and Categorization

To what extent can the infant recognize similarities between stimuli that he can discriminate? Both McGurk (1972) and Fagan (1974) have examined this issue. Fagan's studies will be used as an illustration. He gave 4-5 month infants a face to look at. Afterwards, the infants were shown two faces – the one they had seen before plus a second, novel face. The infants spent more time looking at the novel face[1], showing that they recognized the familiar face and preferred to look at the unfamiliar one. In a later set of experiments, Fagan (1976) has begun to probe this capacity for recognition. Suppose that the infant has been presented with a picture of a man and is then shown this same picture paired with one of a woman (see Figure 4.3). Any preference for the woman might be due to the infant's capacity to recognize the man as a specific individual face or as a face having a particular orientation.

Since the man and the woman in Figure 4·3 differ in individual identity

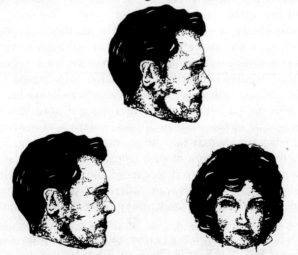

Figure 4.3   After exposure to the upper face, infants prefer the relative novelty of the lower right-hand face.

[1]The selective reduction of attention to a previously exposed stimulus as compared to a relatively unfamiliar stimulus is known as habituation. Habituation occurs from the earliest months of infancy to stimuli in various modalities. Models of the process have recently been proposed (Fagan 1977).

and in orientation, we cannot tell how the infant distinguishes them. Fagan has shown however that even if the novel and the familiar faces differ only in orientation with identity held constant (Figure 4·4a) or in identity with orientation held constant (Figure 4·4b), infants of five months are still able to distinguish between them.

In subsequent experiments subjects were familiarized with one face and then asked to distinguish between a face similar in either orientation or identity to the familiar one and a completely unfamiliar face. Figure 4·5a and 4·5b illustrate these experiments.

In Figure 4·5a, one of the two test faces is similar to the familiarized stimulus in identity although its orientation is different. In Figure 4·5b on the other hand, one of the two test stimuli is similar in orientation to the familiarized stimulus but different in identity. In both experiments, the infants recognized the similarity and spent more time looking at the completely novel stimulus instead.[1]

These results are very intriguing because they show that the infant can see similarities between two faces that he can distinguish; remember that Fagan had already shown that infants could distinguish faces differing only in orientation (Figure 4·4a) or identity (Figure 4·4b). Thus in answer to the question posed earlier, we can assert that the infant can detect subtle changes in identity and orientation but he can also recognize similarities despite those differences. Such an abstractive ability is vital if the infant is to form categories. For example Fagan was also able to show that although infants of five months can distinguish between different male faces, they can also detect their relative similarity as compared to a female face. The formation of such categories is an obvious foundation for language which relies on the infant's ability to apply the word 'man' or 'cat' not to a unique instance but to a whole category of instances. Over the next few years we may hope to see more research concerned with the prelinguistic formation of such categories. In particular we need to know how the ability to detect more and more subtle differences between instances (e.g. between different types of face) develops alongside the ability to see similarities among all those instances.[2]

[1] N.B. We can only conclude that the infant is able to perceive similarities in stimuli which differ in orientation. We cannot assume that the infant recognizes that the same faces pictured in different orientations are different views of an otherwise identical object. For further discussion of this point, see Harris and Allen (1974).

[2] When presented with two visual stimuli side-by-side, young infants frequently shift their gaze back and forth between the two stimuli (Harris 1973a; Ruff 1977). Such shifting would presumably facilitate the detection of both similarities and differences between adjacent stimuli. Future studies of habituation (Note 1) should examine the effect of presenting two similar stimuli for familiarization rather than a single stimulus or two identical stimuli.

Figure 4.4a After exposure to the upper face, infants prefer the relative novelty of the lower right-hand face.

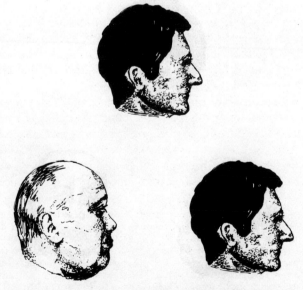

Figure 4.4b After exposure to the upper face, infants prefer the relative novelty of the lower left-hand face.

Figure 4.5a   After exposure to the upper face, infants prefer the relative novelty
of the lower left-hand face.

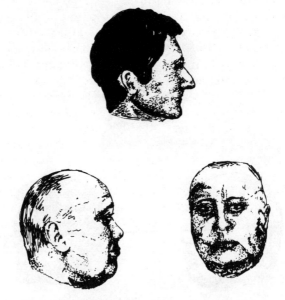

Figure 4.5b   After exposure to the upper face, infants prefer the relative novelty
of the lower right-hand face.

SPACE PERCEPTION

The Left-right and Up-down Dimensions

Several recent experiments (Harris and Macfarlane 1974; Aslin and Salapatek 1975; Macfarlane, Harris and Barnes 1976) have shown that so far as the left-right and up-down dimensions are concerned, the newborn's perception is probably much the same as an adult's. When presented with a stimulus above, below or to one side of his fixation point, the neonate initiates an eye-movement in the appropriate direction. The eye-movements are rarely large enough to reach their target in one saccade (Aslin and Salapatek 1975) but they do move directly toward the target. Since infants in some of these experiments were only two or three days old, it is tempting to conclude that there is an innate organization linking various peripheral positions to eye-movements in a given direction, contrary to the empiricist hypothesis first put forward by Helmholtz that such eye-movements could only develop on the basis of an initial period of trial and error. However Helmholtz could in fact defend his position quite effectively despite the above evidence. Eye-movements have highly consistent consequences in that a shift in any given direction brings stimuli in the direction of that shift onto the fovea – the central and most sensitive region of the retina. Thus a newborn could learn within a couple of days that a particular cue (i.e. a stimulus in a specific peripheral direction) will be followed by a particular consequence (i.e. foveal vision) if an eye-movement is made in a given direction. Although this sounds like a complicated piece of learning, analogous problems have been solved by newborns. For example, Siqueland and Lipsitt (1966) found that newborns could learn that a particular tone was followed by a taste of a sweet drink if a head movement was made in a given direction. Accordingly, we shall only fully understand the origin of directional eye-movements by studying infants immediately after birth. However, as we shall see later, there is some evidence that babies only a few minutes old can make directionally appropriate eye movements to sound (Wertheimer 1961) and they can follow a moving stimulus (Goren *et al.* 1975). Thus the evidence clearly points to a nativist interpretation.

The Third Dimension

Turning to the near-far dimension, the situation is complicated from a developmental point of view by the wide variety of cues which might

specify it. There are important monocular cues such as linear
perspective, density gradients and optical expansion (see, for example,
Bower 1974 and 1977). I shall concentrate on binocular cues for
depth which have received extensive experimental analysis recently.

It is now clear that although binocular convergence increases in
probability and latency during the first six months of life (Aslin 1977)
a limited ability to adjust the angle of convergence in accordance
with the distance of the object is available from birth. (Slater and
Findlay 1975a and b).

It is not possible to state from these results whether the infant can
adjust convergence with sufficient precision to achieve stereopsis:
fusion of the images available from each eye. Haith and Campos
(1977) point out that even a minute amount of deconvergence – an
amount too small to be detected by current measurement techniques –
will prevent stereopsis. Nonetheless there is some evidence that shows,
at a minimum, that two-month-old infants can detect a shift from
non-disparity to disparity (Appel and Campos 1977; Atkinson and
Braddick 1976), a detection which has been thought to presuppose
the ability to achieve stereopsis at least some of the time.

These various experiments show only that the infant may have
cues for depth available to him, namely convergence and disparity.
They do not show that he can interpret them correctly. This distinction
was, made in fact by Berkeley himself. His argument was not that
the baby could not detect convergence or disparity but that he must
learn the meaning of such cues. In order to show that the infant can
interpret cues for depth as specifying depth, we must show that the
infant exhibits behaviour appropriate to objects at different distances.
For example, can the infant adjust his reaching to the distance of an
object? We know that the infant of five months is less likely to reach
for an object if it is beyond his reach (Field 1976). Are binocular
cues sufficient to lead to this adjustment? To investigate such a
possibility, the infant must be presented with an object whose depth
is specified by binocular cues only. This can be achieved if the infant
is fitted with a pair of prisms or lenses which alter the apparent
distance of an actual object or, with the aid of a stereoscopic shadow
caster, produce a 'virtual' image – an object which looks tangible but
is in fact an optical illusion. In both of these experimental arrangements
the infant adjusts his reach to the distance of the object (van Hofsten
1977; Gordon and Yonas 1976). Accordingly we can conclude that by
about five months the infant can not only detect binocular cues for
depth, but he can interpret them so as to guide his behaviour
appropriately. Nonetheless, it must be admitted that it is not yet clear

how this adjustment emerges. The five month infant has had some experience of reaching for objects, experience which could in principle teach him how to interpret binocular cues, if their interpretation is not given directly by visual inspection.

Indeed, experimenters face a dilemma: because the motor abilities of the neonate are limited, it is often necessary to assess his perceptual abilities by indirect measures such as habituation. However in order to know that the infant can interpret the cues he is able to detect we usually need to observe his motor responses to those cues. Yet the latter approach leaves open the possibility that motor experience has already influenced the infant's interpretation of his visual experience.

So far as visual experience *per se* is concerned the evidence is now quite convincing that it plays a role in the attainment of mature depth perception. We know from work with cats and monkeys that deprivation of binocular experience – for example, by covering one eye during infancy – prevents the accurate perception of depth in infancy (Blakemore 1973). Evidence of the contribution of early experience has also been found for human subjects. A squint will reduce or eliminate binocular experience and leads to deficits in mature binocular functioning. Surprisingly, a squint in the first four to six months seems to have no permanent damaging effect (Banks, Aslin and Letson 1975; Hohmann and Creutzfeld 1975). Why is it that the first six months of binocular experience are not critical for later functioning? It will be remembered that the convergence movements of the neonate are rather slow and inflexible. Accordingly at least some of his perceptual experience may be effectively monocular. Nature appears to have forestalled any deleterious effects of this monocular experience, by postponing the influence of experience in the long term until such time as the baby can guarantee obtaining consistently binocular experience (Aslin 1977).

CROSS-MODAL INTEGRATION

In a famous question to Locke, Molyneux asked whether a blind man who had his sight restored would instantly recognize a cube as distinct from a sphere. This query contains the kernel of the cross-modal issue: discriminations available in one modality (e.g. touch in the case of the blind man) might immediately transfer to another modality. Alternatively we might have to experience the tactual feel and the visual appearance of a sphere simultaneously in order to recognize their equivalence. The empiricist tradition sees the developmental problem as one of co-ordinating initially separate modalities by means of association. The rationalist position implies, on the other hand, that there are innate co-ordinations between the modalities from birth.

Before examining the experimental evidence, it will be helpful to distinguish various levels at which cross-modal integration might occur. At a basic level, we might expect information in one modality to provide directional information for the receptors in another modality. Such an expectation is reasonable on purely physical grounds. An object which provides auditory or tactual information from a particular direction will usually provide visual information from the same source. Sometimes, for example at the cinema, the sources of visual and auditory information are artificially separated, but nature typically offers us information from the same source. Thus nature might have built into the infant a system for capitalizing on this coincidence such that auditory information guides the eyes or visual information the hand.

At a second level, information in one modality could lead to the expectation of feedback in a second modality, following an appropriate adjustment of the receptors in that second modality. For example, an object visible straight ahead could lead to the expectation of tactual feedback after reaching. Finally, one modality could yield predictions about a specific type of feedback in the other modality. Visual information might lead one to expect to feel a solid, round object.

Vision and Touch

Experiments on vision and touch illustrate the three levels of integration. First, it seems likely that there is a basic level of translation from visual direction into appropriate reaching movements: Bower, Broughton and Moore (1970a) placed objects at various positions around two week old infants. The infants typically reached in the correct direction – to the left, to the right or straight ahead, even though their movements did not always lead to tactual contact with object. Indeed early reaching is in most cases ballistic: the direction of the reach is not corrected en route toward the object (Bresson, Maury, Pieraut-Bonniec and de Schönen 1976). Yet the visible position of the object is translated into a reach which is aimed in the approximate radial direction.

Turning to the second level, the expectation of tactual feedback, the evidence is contradictory. Bower, Broughton and Moore (1970b) presented a virtual object that looked solid and tangible but which was in fact an optical illusion providing no tactual feedback whatsoever. The authors claimed that infants from two weeks to six months showed surprise when they reached out to touch the object and found nothing there. Two recent experiments, however (Gordon and Yonas 1976; Field 1977) have failed to replicate these findings for five month infants: although subjects reached out for the virtual object they exhibited no visible surprise when their hands passed through the intangible image.

At the third level of more precise expectations, the evidence is also inconclusive. On the one hand Bower, Broughton and Moore (1970b) claimed that infants exhibit hand-shaping prior to actually touching the object – and hence had specific tactual expectations based upon visual appraisal of the object. However, Gordon and Yonas (1976) do not report any such hand-shaping. Instead they state that: 'the infant often closed his hand in front or to the side of the object, undershot or overshot the object or hit the object with the back of the hand.' The precision reported by Bower, Broughton and Moore (1970b) and the inaccuracy reported by Gordon and Yonas (1976) clearly do not fit together.

The picture is more consistent if we examine experiments concerned with the translation from touch to vision rather than from vision to touch. Bryant, Jones, Claxton and Perkins (1972) and Gottfried, Rose and Bridger (1977) report evidence that infants of eight months upwards selected on the basis of visual appearance an object they had previously felt but not seen. Thus we appear to have a story with a fairly clear ending and beginning but an unresolved middle section. The evidence indicates that at a basic level the eye can guide the hand from an early age. Much later, at around nine months evidence of a rather precise cross-modal dictionary is available at least for translations from touch to vision rather than vision to touch. The intervening development is far from clear. The capacity for visual guidance of the hand by the eye might provide a basis for the kind of associative experience which the empiricists argued was necessary for cross-modal translations concerning solidity and shape. Certainly the infant of six months and upwards spends a good deal of time exploring objects by means of simultaneous visual and tactual inspection (Harris 1972). Conversely, the kind of cross-modal ability established by Bryant *et al.* (1972) and Gottfried *et al.* (1977) might be based on some type of automatic inbuilt rules of translation, limited only in their capacity by the discriminative capacity of each sensory modality considered separately (Bryant 1968).

Vision and Hearing

Sound-making objects provide an infant with the possibility of both visual and auditory information located in the same direction. Since the newborn can, as we have seen, shift his gaze toward a peripheral visual stimulus, it would not be surprising if he could also shift his gaze toward a peripheral auditory stimulus. This would correspond to the basic level of cross-modal integration described earlier. Wertheimer (1961) reported that a newborn only two minutes old could make such directed eye-movements toward sound. These observations obviously cast doubt on the empiricist account as proposed by Helmholtz for peripheral visual stimuli. This finding has been replicated recently – albeit with infants two or three days old rather than two minutes old (Mendelson and Haith 1976).

Granted that the neonate looks toward a sound source, does he expect to see anything there? This would correspond to the second level of cross-modal integration described earlier: expectation of co-located inputs. Aronson and Rosenbloom (1971) examined this question with the help of the disruption technique used by Bower, Broughton and Moore (1970b) for vision and touch. By means of a loudspeaker, Aronson and Rosenbloom presented young infants with a sight – their mother – separated from a sound – her voice. They claimed that infants were distressed by this separation but later studies (McGurk and Lewis 1974; Condry, Haltom and Neisser 1977) have not been able to replicate this finding.

If we turn to the higher levels of integration described for touch and vision, it is clear that the physical world does not always offer an obvious correlation between visual and auditory input. There is a necessary relation between visual and tactual information because one cannot alter the touchable surface of an object without simultaneously altering its visual appearance. However no such necessary correlations exist between for example a person's voice and his external shape. Indeed some sounds have no visible accompaniment whatsoever. Accordingly, some investigators (e.g. Lyons-Ruth 1977) have looked at the young infant's ability to learn and expect an essentially arbitrary relationship between a sight and a sound. Nonetheless, subtle correlations do exist between sights and sounds over time. For example there is a temporal correlation between the movements of the lips and tongue in speech and the sounds produced. All of us have noticed our sensitivity to this temporal correlation in watching badly-dubbed films. Spelke (1976) has reported that infants are sensitive to this correlation at four months because they prefer to look at a film which corresponds to a sound-track. Future research may uncover the extent to which the infant expects not simply a general temporal link between sound and movement but a more precise link between particular types of sounds and particular types of movement or the fusion of visual and auditory cues into a single auditory percept as recently reported for older subjects (McGurk and MacDonald 1976).

There also exist systematic correlations between the visible appearance of an object and the way in which it reflects sound. The invention of sonar took advantage of such correlations by using reflected sound as a substitute for vision. Similarly a blind infant might use reflected sound as a visual surrogate. Bower (1976) has reported that a blind infant fitted with a sonar device could indeed use reflected sound instead of vision to orientate his motor activity and to identify objects. From the evidence so far available it is not clear however whether infants can spontaneously use reflected sound in the same way as visual information or alternatively whether they must learn how to use sound as a surrogate.

In summary, whether we examine the relation between vision and touch or between vision and hearing, there is reasonable evidence of an early ability to orientate toward bi-modal input in the same place or direction. In the middle of the first year, the infant can translate in a fairly precise fashion between two modalities, but the origins of this translation are still not understood.

OBJECT PERMANENCE

In the previous section, we discussed the extent to which information in one modality could be used to predict the information available in another modality. The notion of object permanence concerns a related type of prediction. We can use prior perceptual information (for example the disappearance of an object under a cloth) to predict future perceptual information (for example the fact that the object will be visible if we lift the cloth). Piaget (1954) argued that young infants cannot make such predictions because, unlike adults, they do not believe that objects continue to exist in the interval between disappearance and reappearance. This is obviously a bold hypothesis: it implies that the phenomenal world of the infant is quite different from that of the adult. For the infant, objects are continually being annihilated as they disappear and then arbitrarily recreated when they reappear. For the adult, on the other hand the disappearance of an object rarely implies annihilation and appearance rarely implies creation.

Piaget supported his hypothesis with a variety of observations. For example the infant of six months does not search for an object if it disappears under a cloth. Although he has the manual ability to lift a cloth, he does not do so, thereby supporting Piaget's claim that he ceases to believe in its existence once it has disappeared. Somewhat later, at about nine months, the infant will search under a cloth but even then he makes mistakes. Suppose that there are two cloths, A and B; the infant will search accurately at A if the object is hidden there a couple of times but if it is then hidden at B, the infant is liable to return to A, ignoring B. Piaget's interpretation of this error is that the infant's search is not prompted by a belief in the permanence of the invisible object during its disappearance, but by his own apparent success in 'recreating the object'; accordingly he repeats his previously successful act of creation and ignores B in favour of A.

Recent research shows that Piaget's claims concerning the slow development of accurate search during infancy are substantially correct (Miller, Cohen and Hill 1970). Moreover, it is clear that the errors and difficulties exhibited by the infant are difficult to explain solely in terms of perceptual, motor or mnemonic deficiencies (Harris 1975). Currently, therefore most investigators agree with Piaget in viewing the development of search as an index of the infant's cognitive development (Bower 1974; Gratch 1975; Harris 1975). There is nonetheless a continuing debate about whether Piaget has diagnosed the nature of the infant's cognitive difficulties accurately. Whereas Piaget focused on the issue of permanence there are various indications that the difficulty might be more general and more fundamental. The infant appears to have difficulty in knowing where an object is and not whether it continues to exist. An analogy might help to explain this difference more clearly: when a magician makes his assistant mysteriously disappear, we as adults do not doubt her continued existence. Rather we are puzzled as to her whereabouts. Similarly the infant might not consider whether or not a hidden object continues to exist but he may well be puzzled as to where it has gone. If the infant's difficulty is with position rather than permanence, we may make two sets of predictions counter to Piagetian theory.[1] First the infant may sometimes be confused about an object's location even if no difficulties about its continued existence could arise (e.g. it remains

---

[1]One might defend Piaget (1954) by arguing that he acknowledges the infant's spatial naivete. While this is certainly true, he consistently explains the infant's errors in search as a problem of permanence rather than position.

fully visible.) Second, the infant may search accurately for an invisible object provided its position is understood. There are now several experiments showing that position errors occur despite the visibility of the object. For example, Harris (1974) and Butterworth (1977) have found that infants will try to retrieve an object from a previous location even though it is visible at a new location. In support of the second prediction, Bower and Wishart (1972) have found that the infant will reach out for an invisible object if it is made to disappear by turning out the lights rather than by covering it with a cloth.

Piaget's theory is rich and complicated, and as a result not easily falsified. The experiments just cited are open to alternative interpretations *à la* Piaget. For example, Harris (1974) pointed out that turning back to a previous location away from the object's new visible location could be interpreted as strong support for Piaget's claim that the infant believes the object to be at the disposal of his own actions. Perhaps the infant believes he can recreate the object at its old position irrespective of its current visible position. To dispose of this interpretation we require a situation in which the infant turns back to an old location even though he has never retrieved the object from that location. In this case it becomes impossible to argue that the infant is repeating a previously successful action and expecting magical recreation. Lucas and Uzgiris (1977) have recently reported such a situation. They found that if an object was placed in front of a landmark and then covered and moved away from the landmark, infants of seven or eight months frequently approached the landmark as if they expected the object to be there even though they had not previously retrieved the object from that location. Thus the infant's return to a prior position of the object appears to be due to his confusion about its whereabouts not to an egocentric faith in the efficacy of his own previous actions in restoring the object.

Turning to the observations made by Bower and Wishart (1972) one could claim that the infants were already reaching before the lights were out. In this case the typically ballistic reach of the young infant would continue in the darkness until the target was reached. This interpretation would mean that the infant's search for an invisible object was really the extension of retrieval of a visible object. To answer this objection we need more information about how quickly the infant recruits a reaching response following the introduction of a visible object.

If the hypothesis of spatial difficulty is accepted we need to specify it more precisely to render it testable. The infant would appear to have two possible ways of encoding the position of an object. On the one hand he can encode its position relative to himself e.g. to the right, left, straight ahead and so forth. Such a coding is vital, as we have seen, if the infant is going to make eye or hand movements in the correct direction toward an object. Such a code could, in principle, be effective for invisible objects. If I remember that an object was straight ahead before the lights went out and plunged it into darkness, I can still reach out to that remembered position to retrieve it. Such a code could therefore explain the success of the infants observed in darkness by Bower and Wishart (1972). An alternative type of spatial code involves locating an object relative to some landmark. The object can be on, in front of, under etc. such a landmark. The infant appears to have difficulties in developing this second externally related type of spatial code (Harris 1977). In particular, as we have seen, the infant is liable to return to an old landmark such as cloth A, rather than search at a new hiding place B. One possible interpretation of this error is that delay forces the infant to resort to the use of an out-dated landmark coding. If the object disappears from view, the infant can remember where it was before it disappeared and reach out toward that spot if he acts quickly. In particular, if he reaches before changing his posture, the object will be in the same place relative to his own body. If he waits, however, and moves relative to the object's position, his reach for the object would require redirecting. Instead, therefore he can guide his reach, not in terms of the object's remembered position relative to his own body but in terms of its proximity to some visible landmark. The object has last appeared at A (N.B. the infant has seen the object disappear under cloth B, but not reappear) hence the infant mistakenly directs his search toward A. This account explains the infant's perseverative search at a landmark whether he has searched at that landmark before (Harris 1974) or not (Lucas and Uzgiris 1977). Moreover it predicts that search will be accurate at B, if the infant searches immediately (Harris 1973b, Gratch *et al.* 1974), but not if he is forced to wait before searching.

In the future, we may expect a broadening of research on cognitive development. Hitherto, investigators have concentrated on the development of search because of the clarity with which Piaget describes the sequence of stages. However, if we are to get a representative view of the origins of intelligence and indeed the cognitive foundations of language we shall have to study the infant's grasp of a wider range of causal and spatial concepts. Piaget, himself, was well aware of the need for breadth (Piaget 1952; 1954).

SUMMARY AND CONCLUSIONS

The following general conclusions have emerged from this review. First, contrary to the traditional empiricist position, the neonate can detect visual configuration. Moreover, it is extremely unlikely that this is achieved by successively scanning and integrating a series of visual elements. Second, the young infant can perceive visual categories in so far as he can recognize similarities among discriminable stimuli. The extent and origin of this capacity, which is fundamental to language, remain as yet unexplored. Third, by the middle of the first year of life, the infant is able to recognize stimuli across modalities, touch and vision or vision and hearing. These various abilities of the young infant all indicate that he rapidly comes to live in a world of objects which have a recognizable identity.

To what extent are these identifiable objects located in a three-dimensional space? First, even the newborn infant can make appropriate eye-movements depending on the position of an object in the near-far, up-down or left-right dimension. Second, these visually-specified positions can be translated within the first six months into appropriately directed hand movements. Thus, the evidence indicates that by about six months the infant can perceive identifiable objects in a three-dimensional space. Nonetheless, difficulties remain for the infant. These difficulties do not appear to be attributable to a lack of object permanence in the young infant. Rather, he has difficulties in grasping or up-dating the relationship between an object and some other landmark such as a screen or cover. Thus, the infant can readily locate objects relative to himself but has difficulty with the spatial relations which can temporarily exist between two objects. In this sense, at least, the infant lives in a different spatial world from the adult.

Finally, it is important to bear in mind that we have a fairly narrow view of the infant's perceptual and cognitive world. Most research has concentrated on identity and space – as did the philosophers. We need to remember that the world even for the infant is not simply a space plus some objects, a stage and some recognizable props; it is a place where there is a continuous live performance.

I thank S. Hampson, H. McGurk, B. Netelembos and A. Slater for their helpful comments on the manuscript.

REFERENCES

Appel, M. and Campos, J. 1977. 'Binocular disparity as a discriminable stimulus parameter in early infancy.' *J. exp. Child Psychol. 23*, 47-56.

Aronson, E. and Rosenbloom, S. 1971. 'Space perception in early infancy: perception within a common auditory visual space.' *Science 172*, 1161-3.

Aslin, R. N. 1977. 'Development of binocular fixation in human infants.' *J. exp. Child Psychol. 23*, 133-50

Aslin, R. N. and Salapatek, P. 1975. 'Saccadic localization of peripheral targets by the very young human infant.' *Percep. and Psychophys. 17*, 293-302.

Atkinson, J. and Braddick, O. 1976. 'Stereoscopic discrimination in infants.' *Perception 5*, 29-38.

Bartlett, F. C. 1932. *Remembering*. Cambridge: Cambridge University Press.

Banks, M. S., Aslin, R. N. and Letson, R. D. 1975. 'Critical period for the development of human binocular vision.' *Science 190*, 675-7.

Blakemore, C. 1973. 'Environmental constraints on development in the visual system.' In R. A. Hinde and J. Stevenson Hinde (eds) *Constraints on learning*. London: Academic Press.

Bower, T. G. R. 1974. *Development in infancy*. San Francisco: Freeman.

Bower, T. G. R. 1976. 'Auditory surrogates for vision.' Paper presented at XXIst International Congress of Psychology, Paris.

Bower, T. G. R. 1977. *A primer of infant development*. San Francisco: Freeman.

Bower, T. G. R., Broughton, J. and Moore, M. K. 1970a. 'Demonstration of intention in the reaching behaviour of neonate humans.' *Nature 228*, 5172.

Bower, T. G. R., Broughton, J. and Moore, M. K., 1970b. 'The coordination of visual and tactual input in infancy.' *Percep. and Psychophys. 8*, 51-3.

Bower, T. G. R. and Wishart, J. 1972. 'The effects of motor skill on object permanence.' *Cognition 1*, 165-71.

Bresson, F., Maury, L., Pieraut-Bonniec, G. and de Schönen, S. 1976. 'Organisation and lateralization of reaching in infants: an instance of asymmetric function in hand collaboration.' *Neuropsychologica 15*, 311-20.

Bronson, G. 1974. 'The post-natal growth of visual capacity.' *Child Develop. 45*, 873-90.

Bryant, P. E. 1968. 'Comments on the design of cross-modal matching and cross-modal transfer experiments.' *Cortex 4*, 127-37.

Bryant, P. E., Jones, P., Claxton, V. and Perkins, J. 1972. 'Recognition of shapes across modalities by infants.' *Nature 240*, 303-4.

Butterworth, G. 1977. 'Object disappearance and error in Piaget's stage IV task.' *J. exp. Child Psychol. 23*, 391-401.

Carpenter, G. C. 1974. 'Visual regard of moving and stationary faces in early infancy.' *Merrill-Palmer Quart. 20*, 181-94.

Condry, S. M., Haltom, M. Jr. and Neisser, U. 1977. 'Infant sensitivity to audio-visual discrepancy.' *Bull. Psychonomic Soc. 9*, 431-2.

Fagan, J. F. III 1974. 'Infant recognition memory: the effects of length of familiarization and type of discrimination task.' *Child Develop. 45*, 351-6.

Fagan, J. F. III 1976. 'Infants' recognition of invariant features of faces.' *Child Develop. 47*, 627-38.

Fagan, J. F. III 1977. 'An attention model of infant recognition.' *Child Develop. 48*, 345-59.

Field, J. 1976. 'The adjustment of reaching behaviour to object distance in early infancy.' *Child Develop. 47*, 304-8.

Field, J. 1977. 'Coordination of vision and prehension in young infants.' *Child Develop. 48*, 97-103.

Gordon, F. R. and Yonas, A. 1976. 'Sensitivity to binocular depth information.' *J. exp. Child Psychol. 22*, 413-22.

Goren, C. C., Sarty, M. and Wu, P. Y. K. 1975. 'Visual following and pattern discrimination of face-like stimuli by newborn infants.' *Pediatrics 56*, 544-9.

Gottfried, A. W., Rose, S. A. and Bridger, W. H. 1977. 'Cross modal transfer in human infants.' *Child Develop. 48*, 118-23.

Gratch, G., Appel, K. J., Evans, W. F., Le Compte, G. K. and Wright, N. A. 1974. 'Piaget's stage IV object concept error: evidence of forgetting or object conception?' *Child Develop. 45*, 71-7.

Gratch, G. 1975. 'Recent studies based on Piaget's view of object concept development.' In L. B. Cohen and P. Salapatek (eds) *Infant perception from sensation to cognition II*. London: Academic Press.

Haaf, R. A. and Brown, C. J. 1976. 'Infants' response to facelike patterns: developmental changes between 10 and 15 weeks.' *J. exp. Child Psychol. 22*, 155-60.

Haith, M. M. and Campos, J. J. 1977. 'Human infancy'. In *Ann. Rev. Psychol. 28*, 251-93.

Harris, L. J. and Allen, T. W. 1974. 'Role of object constancy in the perception of object orientation.' *Hum. Develop. 17*, 187-200.

Harris, P. L. 1972. 'Infants' visual and tactual inspection of objects.' *Perception 1*, 141-6.

Harris, P. L. 1973a. 'Eye movements between adjacent stimuli; an age-change in infancy.' *Brit. J. Psychol. 64*, 215-8.

Harris, P. L. 1973b. 'Perseverative errors in search by young infants.' *Child Develop. 44*, 28-33.

Harris, P. L. 1974. 'Perseverative search at a visibly empty place by young infants.' *J. exp. Child Psychol. 18*, 535-42.

Harris, P. L. 1975. 'Development of search and object permanence during infancy.' *Psychol. Bull. 82*, 332-44.

Harris, P. L. 1977. 'The child's representation of space.' In G. Butterworth (ed.) *The child's representation of the world*. New York: Plenum.

Harris, P. L. and Macfarlane, A. 1974. 'The growth of the effective visual field from birth to seven weeks.' *J. exp. Child Psychol. 18*, 340-8.

Harris, P. L. and Bassett, E. 1977. 'Discrimination by young infants of stimuli presented discontinuously.' *Perception 6*, 685-90.

Hebb, D. O. 1949. *The organization of behaviour*. New York: Wiley.

Hohmann, A. and Creutzfeld, O. D. 1975. 'Squint and the development of binocularity in humans.' *Nature 254*, 613-14.

Karmel, B. Z. and Maisel, E. B. 1975. 'A neuronal model for infant visual attention.' In L. B. Cohen and P. Salapatek (eds) *Infant perception: from sensation to cognition I*. London: Academic Press.

Lucas, T. C. and Uzgiris, I. C. 1977. 'Spatial factors in the development of the object concept.' *Develop. Psychol. 13*, 492-500.

Lyons-Ruth, K. 1977. 'Bimodal perception in infancy: response to auditory visual incongruity.' *Child Develop. 48*, 820-7.

McGurk, H. 1972. 'Infant discrimination of orientation.' *J. exp. Child Psychol. 14*, 151-64.

McGurk, H. and Lewis, M. 1974. 'Space perception in early infancy: perception within a common auditory-visual space?' *Science 186*, 649-50.

McGurk, H. and MacDonald, J. 1976. 'Hearing lips and seeing voices.' *Nature* *264*, 5588.

Macfarlane, A., Harris, P. and Barnes, I. 1976. 'Central and peripheral vision in early infancy.' *J. exp. child Psychol. 21*, 532-8.

Maurer, D. and Salapatek, P. 1976. 'Developmental changes in the scanning of faces by young infants.' *Child Develop. 47*, 523-7.

Meltzoff, A. and Moore, M. K. 1977. 'Imitation of facial and manual gestures by human neonates.' *Science 198*, 75-8.

Mendelson, M. and Haith, M. M. 1976. 'The relation between audition and vision in the human newborn.' *Monogr. soc. res. Child Develop.* Serial No. 167.

Miller, D., Cohen, L. and Hill, K. 1970. 'A methodological investigation of Piaget's theory of object concept development in the sensory motor period.' *J. exp. Child Psychol. 9*, 59-85.

Piaget, J. 1952. *The origins of intelligence in children.* New York: International Universities Press.

Piaget, J. 1954. *The construction of reality.* London: Routledge and Kegan Paul.

Rosinski, R. R. 1977. *The development of visual perception.* Santa Monica: Goodyear.

Ruff, H. 1977. 'The function of shifting fixations in the visual perception of infants.' *Child Develop. 46*, 857-65.

Salapatek, P. 1975. 'Pattern perception in early infancy.' In L. Cohen and P. Salapatek (eds) *Infant perception from sensation to cognition I.* London: Academic Press.

Salapatek, P. and Kessen, W. 1966. 'Visual scanning of triangles by the human newborn.' *J. exp. Child Psychol. 3*, 155-67.

Salapatek, P. and Kessen, W. 1973. 'Prolonged investigation of a plane geometric triangle by the human newborn.' *J. exp. Child Psychol. 15*, 22-9.

Siqueland, E. R. and Lipsitt, L. P. 1966. 'Conditioned head-turning in human newborns.' *J. exp. Child Psychol. 3*, 356-76.

Slater, A. M. and Findlay, J. M. 1975a. 'The corneal reflection technique and the visual preference method: sources of error.' *J. exp. Child Psychol. 20*, 240-7.

Slater, A. and Findlay, J. M. 1975b. 'Binocular fixation in the newborn baby.' *J. exp. Child Psychol. 20*, 248-73.

Spelke, E. 1976. 'Infants intermodal perception of events.' *Cog. Psychol. 8*, 553-60.

van Hofsten, C. 1977. 'Binocular convergence as a determinant of reaching behaviour in infancy.' *Perception 6*, 139-44.

Wertheimer, M. 1961. 'Psycho-motor coordination of auditory-visual space at birth.' *Science 2*, 135-42.

Zazzo, P. 1957. 'La probleme de l'imitation chez le nouveau-ne.' *Enfance 2*, 135-42.

Chapter 5

Language and Human Mentality

P. N. JOHNSON-LAIRD

> Credit requires that the walls
> of coffers be opaque, and the
> interchange of human things
> between men requires that
> brains be impenetrable.
>
> – Paul Valéry

What happens when a speaker communicates an idea to a listener in a language common to both of them? One answer is easily stated: the speaker formulates the meaning of the intended message, finds the appropriate words in a mental lexicon, arranges them in suitable grammatical relations and finally articulates the required speech sounds. The listener works in the opposite direction, from the speech sounds to the meaning of the message. This simplified account of communication provides us with some convenient labels and levels of analysis: speech sounds, words, grammar, meaning. It also provides us with one idea: the psychological processes at each level are independent and do not interact with each other. The aim of this essay is to explore this influential notion of linguistic *autonomy*,[1] to reject it and to draw some general conclusions about human mentality.

SPEECH SOUNDS

One of the correlates of a knowledge of a written language based on an alphabet is that it is natural to think of speech sounds as strung

---

[1] The notion is that such processes as the identification of words, syntactic analysis and semantic analysis, occur independently of one another. They may overlap in time, but the outcome of one such process has no facilitatory effect upon the others.

together like beads on a string: to think, for example, that the sound of 'cat' is equivalent to 'c'+'a'+'t'. But, an alphabet is a very abstract model and the real nature of speech sounds as acoustic events or articulatory movements eludes our conscious inspection (Liberman, Mattingly and Turvey 1972). In fact, speech is not a single series of sounds one after another, but a staggered sequence of parallel events that overlap one another. Take a slice through continuous speech at one moment in time, and you will often find in it information about adjacent sounds laid out like geological strata. Indeed, many consonants do not have an acoustic pattern common to all their occurrences. The 'd' sound of 'dee', for instance, is very different to the 'd' sound of 'do'. If you watch your lips in a mirror as you pronounce these two words, you will immediately see why: your mouth moves into a position to articulate both the consonant and its subsequent vowel at virtually the same time. You cannot produce the 'd' sound unsullied by the following vowel; the actions involved in speaking are carried out in parallel.

Why is speech produced in such a complicated way? The basic reason is probably because it allows sounds to be uttered at a faster rate than a simple serial process (Liberman, Cooper, Shankweiler and Studdert-Kennedy 1967). Although various 'sound alphabets' have been invented – with a separate sound for each letter in the alphabet – the rate at which highly practised subjects can understand these serial stimuli is only a tenth that of actual speech. The way to speed up performance is to do things in parallel and thereby overcome the inertia of nerve cells and muscle fibres. A speaker is able to produce sounds at a faster rate than that at which any single part of the vocal apparatus can change its state. The fact that the resulting acoustic cues overlap one another allows a listener sufficient time to identify them, but plainly their perceptual effect will depend heavily on the context in which they occur.

If the central nervous system has to operate in parallel, it is important that separate speech events are properly interrelated. They must constitute a pattern in time rather than a random arrangement. There must be predictable temporal landmarks and an obvious way to establish them is to demarcate regular intervals of time. This underlying metrical pulse can be used as a sort of carrier wave that allows separate parallel processes to be synchronized where necessary. There is indeed considerable evidence for the rhythmic nature of speech (Lenneberg 1967; Martin 1972). Languages are sometimes categorized either as having stresses at equal intervals of time, e.g. English, or as having syllables at equal intervals of time, e.g. French.

In fact, it turns out that stresses do not occur at exactly equal intervals in English, but their perception is more regular than their objective distribution warrants (C. Darwin and A. Donovan, personal communication). Quite why this regularity is perceptually imposed remains a mystery, but there is no doubt about the importance of rhythm in the control and perception of language.

WORDS

There are no very good cues to the beginnings and ends of words in fluent speech, because one word may succeed another without a pause. A sentence spoken in an ordinary conversational intonation is very different from the same string of words spoken in isolation from one another. 'Cats chase mice' is not equivalent to 'cats'+'chase'+ 'mice'. The articulation of ordinary speech is often imprecise, yet if carefully articulated words are spoken in isolation and then joined together, the result is not very intelligible (Huggins 1972). In continuous speech, the fundamental pitch of a speaker's voice does not remain constant (unless he is trying to imitate a science-fiction robot): it varies relatively smoothly, rising and falling, according to certain underlying principles that demarcate clauses, draw attention to important information and express the speaker's attitudes and feelings. One is aware of the effects of intonation, not how they are obtained. Few people realize that in order to express incredulity, as in uttering, say 'Cats chase DOGS???', they do not so much increase the intensity of their voice as its pitch – sometimes by as much as two octaves.

A listener must somehow segment phonemes (the speech sounds of the language) into word-like units and find the corresponding words in the mental lexicon. What is puzzling is how the listener can establish the right segments unless he already knows what the words are. Perhaps it is a matter of trial and error, with the listener checking, as each new phoneme is identified, whether the current string corresponds to a word in the lexicon. But, if there were no more to the process of recognizing words, recognition would be impossible whenever a noise obliterated a phoneme. In fact, listeners often fail to notice that a sound has been masked or mispronounced and perceive whatever word fits the context (Warren 1970; Cole 1973). Sometimes, when a mispronunciation occurs, a listener can be aware of both what the speaker said and what he intended to say.

There can be little doubt that context plays an important role in recognition, if only because the identification of the end of one word is a good cue to the start of the next word. However, theorists committed to the autonomy of word recognition argue that syntactic and semantic cues have their effect only after a word has been accessed in the lexicon (Forster 1976). Perhaps the best evidence against this view comes from studies in which subjects repeat aloud a tape-recorded passage in which there are deliberate mispronunciations (but see also Lieberman 1963). Subjects in such shadowing tasks regularly correct these 'mistakes' without even noticing them, provided that the restored word is syntactically and semantically congruent with the preceding context. They can do so after they have heard so small a fragment of a word that its recognition on the basis of sound alone is most unlikely (Marslen-Wilson 1976). When a mis-pronunciation is gross, fluent corrections are more likely to occur if it is located in the last syllable of a word, e.g. 'tomorrane' instead of 'tomorrow', and if the word is highly predictable in context. This effect of manipulating the position of the mispronunciation and the predictability of the word itself is much greater than a simple addition of the independent effects of the two variables, contrary to the principle of autonomy (Marslen-Wilson and Welsh, 1978).

Most theories that incorporate effects of context do so by postulating that the recognition of one word may make it easier to recognize other semantically related words (e.g. Morton 1970; Marslen-Wilson and Welsh 1978). This assumption is plausible, but it fails to go far enough. If someone says to you, 'Because the meal was exquisite, I left a large . . .' and is then nearly drowned out by a pneumatic drill, you may nevertheless pick up enough cues to recognize the word, 'tip'. There is no single word here that suggests it. What you are using is not just an association between one word and another, but a knowledge of the frequent and stereotyped event of dining out in a restaurant. A number of workers in artificial intelligence have argued that this knowledge takes the form of 'scripts', which are necessary in order to bridge gaps in discourse, to disambiguate words and to assign referents to pronouns and other referring expressions (see Minsky 1975; Schank and Abelson 1975). I believe that scripts also mediate the recognition of words, though there is as yet no direct evidence for this proposition.

If a speaker says, 'The pilot put the plane into a spin just before landing on the field,' you are unlikely to have any difficulty in under-standing what he means. Yet, every word in this sentence (apart perhaps from the articles) is ambiguous. Since the most frequently used words in the language tend also to be the most ambiguous (see Miller 1951, p. 112), it is a reasonable inference that the processes of comprehension can rapidly establish the intended sense of a word from the context in which it occurs. Nevertheless, there is some evidence that even when preceded by a disambiguating context such ambiguities take time to deal with: they slow down a subject's ability to detect the presence of a particular target phoneme in a sentence (e.g. Foss and Jenkins 1973) and they make it harder to repeat back a sentence displayed one word after another in a Rapid Serial Visual Presentation, the so-called 'RSVP' procedure (Holmes, Arwas and Garrett 1977). There is also some evidence that the effects of ambiguity disappear when context disambiguates words (Swinney and Hakes 1976). The issue is important because if the retrieval of lexical meanings is an autonomous process, ambiguity should always retard comprehension. The evidence does not yet permit us to draw a definite conclusion, particularly because the predictability of the word bearing the target phoneme determines the speed with which it is detected (Morton and Long 1976) and this factor has often been uncontrolled. However, if semantic context can affect the recognition of words, certain aspects of their meaning may well be recovered in the process of identifying them.

A fluent speaker is seldom aware of having to choose words, and can even construct a running commentary without effort. Yet, to find an appropriate name plainly requires that the relevant object is recognized, and this process must rely on a variety of different sorts of knowledge. Miller and Johnson-Laird (1976) have set out a general theory of the meanings of words, which is designed both to relate their fundamental semantics to perceptual, motor and cognitive processes, and to establish how meanings are mentally organized so as to allow rapid lexical choice. Sometimes, of course, a speaker makes a mistake in his choice of words. He may say, to take an example from my own repertoire, 'mirror box' when he means 'bathroom cabinet'. This error is clearly close in meaning to the intended item. On another occasion, I remarked, 'The doctors may be picketing the hospital with their stereoscopes to make a cordon,' where the error is close to the sound rather than the sense of the intended word, 'stethoscopes'. Fay and Cutler (1977), who have collected a considerable corpus of such 'malapropisms', argue that the lexicon must be arranged so that similarly sounding words are adjacent to one another. In fact, there are good grounds for supposing it to be also organized in terms of the similarity of words in their written form, frequency of usage, age at which they were acquired, meaning, and role in 'scripts'. No-one has yet managed to discover the actual framework that accommodates all these constraints.

GRAMMAR

All natural languages are governed by grammatical constraints. In English, for example, there are numerous restrictions on the ordering of the constituents of sentences and on syntactic agreements that must hold between them. Violations of such constraints are immediately apparent – as an *au pair* remarked, 'My works is many and my salary are few' – yet it is not easy to discern the underlying principles that govern language. The study of syntax is one of the oldest of human intellectual activities, but to this day there is no complete grammar of any natural language. Traditional linguists often relied on intuition in exercising their postulated rules; modern linguists have been much influenced by Chomsky's (1957) precept that a theory of syntax should be wholly explicit and place no reliance on intuition in its operation. Only since this principle won general approval has it become apparent how little is known about grammar. One cannot, unfortunately, recover either the form or the content of the rules of syntax by conscious introspection. The process has to be indirect: a linguist like any other scientist seeks an underlying explanation of the observed phenomena – in this case, judgements about the grammaticality of sentences, relations between them and so on. A grammar is accordingly neither a list of 'do's and don'ts', nor a psychological model of mental processes, but a theory of the structural principles underlying language.

One reason that natural language is so hard to elucidate can be brought out by comparing it with an artificial language such as that of mathematics. An expression such as $(x+2)$ has a standard interpretation, carry out the operation signified by '$+$' on x and 2, regardless of the formula into which it is embedded. However, an expression such as 'two feet in the air', behaves in one way in the sentence, 'The ball bounced two feet in the air', and in a very different way in the sentence, 'The dog put its front two feet in the air'. The syntax of many an expression depends on the linguistic context in which it occurs. This is just one of the phenomena that led Chomsky (1965) to distinguish two levels of syntactic analysis for any sentence: a surface structure that segments the sentence into its superficial grammatical constituents – noun phrases, verb phrases, etc. and a deep structure that (re-) arranges these constituents in a way that unequivocally identifies the subject and object of the sentence and other such underlying grammatical relations. Deep structures are mapped onto surface structures by transformational rules that permute, delete or add constituents.

Although transformational grammar is not intended as a model of psychological mechanisms, many psycholinguists assume that in order to understand a sentence it is necessary to build up a mental representation of linguistic structure (e.g. Fodor, Bever and Garrett 1974). They argue that deep structure is recovered by perceptual processes that are guided by cues in surface structure. To take a familiar example, if the verb following an initial noun phrase is of the form, '. . . was eaten,' it constitutes a definitive cue to the sentence being in the passive voice and so the initial noun phrase is the underlying object of the sentence. Once the underlying grammatical relations of a sentence have been established, they can be used as a blueprint for obtaining its meaning.

This theory of comprehension suggests that syntactic processes are autonomous: grammatical structure is established without regard to any aspect of meaning. This is an important but controversial claim. The evidence in favour of it comes from experiments in which syntactic and semantic variables have been found to have purely additive effects on performance. Forster and Olbrei (1973) obtained such results in a task where subjects had to decide whether or not a given string of words made up a sensible well-formed sentence. Other studies have obtained additive effects when subjects had to repeat back a sentence using the RSVP procedure (Forster 1978). Yet, there are a number of difficulties with the autonomy proposal.

One direct problem is that there is evidence that runs counter to it. These findings arose in the following way. For a number of years, I have argued that there is no unequivocal evidence that either speakers or listeners set up a mental representation of deep structure and I have recently proposed a theory based on this assumption (Johnson-Laird 1977a). Mark Steedman has implemented one version of the theory in a computer program in which comprehension consists in translating a sentence directly into its semantic representation, speaking consists in translating a semantic representation directly into a sentence, and an explicit representation of deep structure plays no role in either process (Steedman and Johnson-Laird 1978). The program builds up a semantic representation, roughly constituent by constituent, as it progresses through a sentence, and it takes into account both semantic and syntactic information in a way that flagrantly contradicts the principle of autonomy. In fact, Gerry Quinn and I have observed the sort of interactions predicted by the theory in a series of unpublished experiments. Sentences of the form, 'The chairman sold the manager the player,' are reliably harder to understand, as reflected in the time spent perusing them before answering a question, than sentences in which there is an explicit syntactic cue to the indirect object, e.g. 'The chairman sold the player to the manager'. However, the difference disappears if the sentence contains a good *semantic* cue to the indirect object, e.g. 'The chairman sold the manager the desk.'

An indirect difficulty for the autonomy hypothesis arises from the study of language acquisition. A transformational grammar is very nearly unlearnable in principle (Anderson 1975), yet children pick up their native tongue virtually uninstructed and with little of the theoretically necessary information about the set of ungrammatical strings of words (see Brown 1973). One resolution of the paradox is, as Chomsky (1965) proposes, that there are innate constraints that guide children in their choice of grammatical hypotheses. An alternative proposal is that children use semantics to predict syntax. A common perceptual strategy that young children adopt is to treat the initial noun phrase of a sentence as its underlying subject (Bever 1970). They accordingly misinterpret a sentence such as, 'The boy is easy to help,' and assume that it is the boy who is doing the helping (Chomsky 1969; Cromer 1975). A sentence can always be paraphrased, of course, and it can sometimes be construed from the context in which it occurs. Hence, a child may come to understand the correct meaning of a sentence, know the meanings of the words it contains, and remain ignorant only of the syntactic principles that relate the two. This puzzle is obviously soluble, and its solution establishes that the child's erstwhile strategy does not invariably work. There are at least two sorts of adjective: those like 'easy' require the initial noun phrase of such sentences as 'The boy is easy to help' to be treated as the object of 'help', and only those like 'kind' require the initial noun phrase to be treated as the subject of 'help'. Autonomy implies that the child has to learn the syntactic status of each adjective separately. The interactive hypothesis implies that in many cases the syntactic status of an adjective can be predicted from a knowledge of its meaning (Johnson-Laird 1975). How do you interpret, 'The child is esurient to help'? The answer is obvious once you know that 'esurient' means hungry. Because the grammatical behaviour of a word is not invariably correlated with its meaning, linguists tend to work on restricting the power of grammars in order to render them learnable (see Hamburger and Wexler 1975). Other cognitive scientists, however, have exploited the correlation between syntax and sense in developing computer programs that learn grammatical rules (Anderson 1975; Longuet-Higgins and Power 1978).

MEANING

There is a variety of psychologically oriented theories of meaning, but they tend to cluster into a number of distinct categories. First, some theorists assume that the meaning of a word is specified in the mental lexicon by a set of *semantic features* and that the meaning of a sentence is likewise composed of a combination of them according to its deep structure relations (e.g. Smith, Shoben and Rips 1974). Table 5.1 presents some simplified examples of such semantic

Table 5.1 *An example of the representation of meaning in terms of semantic features*

Words in the lexicon
  man: (noun) HUMAN, ADULT, MALE
  child: (noun) HUMAN, NOT(ADULT)
  lift: (verb) CAUSE(ACTIVITY X, UPWARDS(MOVE)Y),
          where X is the underlying subject
          and Y is the underlying object.
The representation of a sentence: 'A man lifts a child'.
  CAUSE(ACTIVITY(HUMAN, ADULT, MALE)),
    UPWARDS(MOVE)(HUMAN, NOT(ADULT))).

---

representations, though the details vary considerably from one specific theory to another. Second, another group of theorists argues that the mental lexicon takes the form of a *semantic network* that links words according to the relations between them (e.g. Lindsay and Norman 1977). Table 5.2 presents a simplified version of this sort of theory. The initial representation of the meaning of a sentence consists of a network centred around a representation of its main verb and with links from the words that it contains to their generic representations in the lexicon. The logical implications of the sentence can be established subsequently by following up the links in the lexicon. A third and analogous sort of theory has been couched in terms of *meaning postulates*, which are rules that specify the semantic relations between words (Kintsch 1974; Fodor, Fodor and Garrett 1975). This theory, which is illustrated in Table 5.3, proposes that comprehension consists in a fairly superficial translation into a mental

Table 5.2 *An example of the representation of meaning in terms of a semantic network*

Words in the lexicon

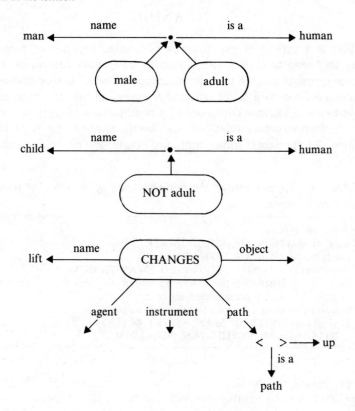

The initial representation of a sentence: 'A man lifts a child'.

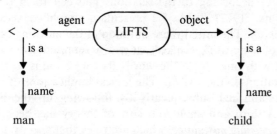

Note: Nodes represented by black dots correspond to generic nodes; nodes represented by ovals correspond to propositions that apply to other nodes; nodes represented by angle brackets represent specific instances of generic concepts.

Table 5.3 *An example of the representation of meaning in terms of meaning postulates*

Words in the lexicon
   man: MAN
   child: CHILD
   lift: LIFT

Meaning postulates
   FOR ANY X, IF X IS A MAN THEN X IS HUMAN
     AND X IS ADULT AND X IS MALE.

   FOR ANY X, IF X IS A CHILD THEN X IS HUMAN AND
     NOT (X IS AN ADULT).

   FOR ANY X AND Y, IF X LIFTS Y THEN X CAUSES Y TO MOVE
     UPWARDS

The initial representation of a sentence: 'A man lifts a child'.

   $((A\ MAN)_{NP}(LIFTS(A\ CHILD)_{NP})_{VP})_S$

where NP = noun phrase, VP = verb phrase, S = sentence.

---

language; the logical implications of a sentence are established subsequently by using meaning postulates.

There has been some argument about whether these three sorts of theory differ except on paper (e.g. Hollan 1975). The matter need not detain us, however, since in my view none of them is rich enough to be psychologically plausible. The trouble lies in their implicit assumption of the autonomy of semantic processing, i.e. that the mechanisms responsible for establishing the meaning of an expression operate independently of the mechanisms for establishing properties of its reference. In order to establish this point, consider the following simple valid inference:

> The man is at the office.
> The office is at the university.
> ---
> ∴ The man is at the university.

The three sorts of theory have the common aim of accounting for such logical implications of sentences. The transitivity of 'at' could here be captured by using a meaning postulate: for any x, y and z, if x is at y, and y is at z, then x is at z; and, presumably, it could also be handled by the other sorts of theory. But, now consider the following inference:

The man is at the desk.
The desk is at the window.

∴ The man is at the window.

If the premises are true, is the conclusion necessarily true? The
answer depends on the size of the desk and the window and how
they are arranged, etc. If you are to evaluate this inference, you need
to know, not just the meanings of the words, but also their referents
in the real world. This phenomenon is by no means unique to
spatial inferences, but it violates any psychological theory based on the
assumption that a semantic representation is set up autonomously
and without regard to the reference of expressions.

What sort of psychological theory of meaning is needed? The view
that I wish to take derives from what is sometimes known as
'procedural semantics' (e.g. Davies and Isard 1972; Miller and
Johnson-Laird 1976; Johnson-Laird 1977b). Utterances provide us
with clues for building models of the world in our minds. What is
important about these models is not their phenomenal content –
whether they take the form of visual images or whatever – but their
structure and the fact that we possess procedures for constructing,
manipulating and interrogating them. Many of these procedures can
be taken for granted by a speaker: his message is really a set of additional
instructions that assume a common background of information,
including knowledge of the linguistic context, the 'scripts' that govern
stereotyped activities, and the conventions governing discourse.
Obviously, a listener can to some extent vary the detail that he builds
into his mental model: he may allow the words simply to 'wash
over' him in a passive way or, alternatively, he may be alert to every
nuance in them and follow up their implications in much the same
way as a chess player explores the possibilities of a position in a
game.

A procedural semantics naturally suggests that the meaning of a
word should be treated as a procedure. But, this suggestion is an
oversimplification: a word can be used in many ways and it is more
appropriate to regard its meaning as something that can play a part
in many different procedures. The point can be illustrated by
considering briefly a simple computer program devised by the author.
Given statements such as 'A is on the right of B', 'C is in front of
B' and so on, the program builds up an internal two-dimensional
representation of the appropriate spatial arrangement of the entities
referred to and can draw conclusions about the relations between
them. Most of the program is concerned with building up spatial

arrays and manipulating and interrogating them. There is, for instance, a general procedure for verifying whether a specified relation holds between two items: it looks along a line whose origin is the second of the two objects in order to determine whether the first of them lies somewhere on that line. The direction of the line is defined in terms of two variables, Δx and Δy, which specify the increments that successively spell out the locations that are scanned. The semantic representations of the spatial prepositions are very simple and in marked contrast to the ways in which their meanings would have to be represented in other sorts of theory. The meaning of 'in front of' consists simply in the assignment of two specific values for Δx and Δy. Their effect is to convert a general procedure such as the one for verification into a more specific one based on a line representing a particular line of sight. The point to be emphasized is that transitivity is not explicitly asserted in the dictionary entry, yet it will always emerge when required. For many prepositions such as 'at' the actual shapes and sizes of objects affect the validity of inferences. The only way such factors could be taken into account would be by constructing an internal model of the sort described here. There is evidence that even when the properties of objects can be ignored, subjects nevertheless construct a mental model (Johnson-Laird and Steedman 1978).

HUMAN MENTALITY

The process of comprehension can be likened to a conveyor belt: the raw product, the speech wave form, comes in at one end and is submitted to a series of processes that ultimately yield the significance of the utterance. The notion of autonomy implies that the various stages of assembly are independent of one another, though they may overlap in time. However, the evidence suggests autonomy should be replaced by interaction. Speech perception is guided by a knowledge of words; word recognition is constrained by syntactic and semantic context; syntactic decisions are aided by semantic cues; and semantic interpretation takes a knowledge of referents into account. While the conveyor belt shifts the product in one direction, there is a flow in the opposite direction of specifications of what is needed, or predicted, by assembly processes higher up the line (Johnson-Laird 1977a).

Two points are worth recapitulating about the assembly processes. First, their categories and concepts are often not open to conscious inspection. You cannot in this way discover the nature of speech sounds, the meanings of common words, the rules of grammar or the form of semantic representations. Second, their operations invariably take context into account. The perception of a particular speech sound depends on acoustic cues and the context in which they are embedded; the syntax of an expression is sometimes a function of the structure in which it occurs; the meanings of words are often disambiguated by the other words with which they are collocated.

These two phenomena suggest that the human mind is organized to carry out many processes in parallel: it works at different levels of linguistic analysis simultaneously and at any level it can cope with an element and its context at one and the same time. Such a mechanism is extremely efficient, but it contains a potential danger. Two parallel processors may get into a state where each is waiting for the outcome of the other's computations. They might wait forever. One way to avoid such a 'deadly embrace' is to ensure that the programming language controlling the system does not permit it to occur. Computer programmers have devised such languages (e.g. Rumbaugh 1975) and nature may have devised them for organisms such as starfish that lack a central processor. Another way to avoid them is to have a high-level monitor that can detect such conflicts and override them. Consciousness may originally have emerged from the web of parallel processors in order to serve this purpose. Its evolution confers a definite biological advantage. Many ethologists have argued that deception is fundamental to animal communication; the best deception is a self-deception since it precludes involuntary tell-tale signs that might give the deceiver away (see Dawkins 1976). But, to deceive oneself necessarily presupposes that one part of the mind is inaccessible to another. It is evolutionarily advantageous that certain motives are unconscious and that advantage is made possible by the efficiency of ineffable mental processes. The interchange of ideas does indeed, as Valéry remarked, require that brains be impenetrable.

ACKNOWLEDGEMENTS

I am indebted to my colleagues, and particularly to Tony Ades, Anne Cutler, Chris Darwin, Kate Ehrlich, Steve Isard, Christopher Longuet-Higgins, Stuart Sutherland and Til Wykes, for taking the time to instruct me on the intricacies of language. I am also grateful to Stuart Sutherland for a critical reading of an early version of this paper. My research is supported by a grant for scientific assistance from the SSRC.

REFERENCES

Anderson, J. R. 1975. 'Computer simulation of a language acquisition system: a first report.' In R. L. Solso (ed.) *Information processing and cognition: the Loyola symposium.* Hillsdale, N.J.: Erlbaum.

Bever, T. G. 1970. 'The cognitive basis for linguistic structures.' In J. R. Hayes (ed.) *Cognition and the development of language.* New York: Wiley.

Brown, R. 1973. *A first language: the early stages.* London: Allen and Unwin.

Chomsky, C. 1969. *'The acquisition of syntax in children from 5 to 10.'* Cambridge, Mass.: M.I.T. Press.

Chomsky, N. 1957. *'Syntactic structures.'* The Hague: Mouton.

Chomsky, N. 1965. *'Aspects of the theory of syntax.'* Cambridge, Mass.: M.I.T.

Clark, H. H. and Clark, E. V. 1977. *Psychology and language: an introduction to psycholinguistics.* New York: Harcourt Brace Jovanovich.

Cole, R. A. 1973. 'Listening for mispronunciations: a measure of what we hear during speech.' *Percep. and Psychophys. 11*, 153-6.

Cromer, R. F. 1975. 'Are subnormals linguistic adults?' In N. O'Connor (ed.) *Language, cognitive deficits, and retardation.* London: Butterworth.

Darwin, C. J. 1976. 'The perception of speech.' In E. C. Carterette and M. P. Friedman (eds). *Handbook of perception VII: language and speech.* New York: Academic Press.

Davies, D. J. M. and Isard, S. D. 1972. 'Utterances as programs.' In D. Michie (ed.) *Machine intelligence 7.* Edinburgh: Edinburgh University Press.

Dawkins, R. 1976. *The selfish gene.* Oxford: Oxford University Press.

Denes, P. B. and Pinson, E. N. 1973. *The speech chain: the physics and biology of spoken language.* Garden City, New York: Anchor Books.

Fay, D. and Cutler, A. 1977. 'Malapropisms and the structure of the mental lexicon.' *Linguistic Inquiry 8*, 505-20.

Fodor, J. A., Bever, T. G. and Garrett, M. F. 1974. *The psychology of language.* New York: McGraw-Hill.

Fodor, J. D. 1977. *Semantics: theories of meaning in generative grammar.* Hassocks, Sussex: Harvester Press.

Fodor, J. D., Fodor, J. A. and Garrett, M. F. 1975. 'The psychological unreality of semantic representations.' *Linguistic Inquiry 4*, 515-31.

Forster, K. I. 1976. 'Accessing the mental lexicon.' In E. C. T. Walker and R. J. Wales (eds), *New approaches to language mechanisms.* Amsterdam: North-Holland.

Forster, K. I. 1978. 'Levels of processing and the structure of the language processor.' In W. E. Cooper and E. Walker (eds) *Sentence processing: psycholinguistic studies presented to Merrill Garrett.* (in press).

Forster, K. I. and Olbrei, I. 1973. 'Semantic heuristics and syntactic analysis.' *Cognition 2*, 319-47.

Foss, D. J. and Jenkins, C. 1973. 'Some effects of context on the comprehension of ambiguous sentences.' *J. verb. Learn. verb. Behav. 12*, 577-89.

Glucksberg, S. and Danks, J. H. 1975. *Experimental psycholinguistics: an introduction.* Hillsdale, N. J.: Erlbaum.

Hamburger, H. and Wexler, K. 1975. 'A mathematical theory of learning transformational grammar.' *J. Math. Psychol. 12*, 137-77.

Henderson, L. 1977. 'Word recognition.' In N. S. Sutherland (ed.) *Tutorial essays in psychology I.* Hillsdale, N. J.: Erlbaum.

Hollan, J. D. 1975. 'Features and semantic memory: set-theoretic or network model.' *Psych. Rev. 82*, 154-5.

Holmes, V. M., Arwas, R. and Garrett, M. F. 1977. 'Prior context and the perception of lexically ambiguous sentences.' *Memory and Cognition 5*, 103-10.

Huggins, A. W. F. 1972. 'On the perception of temporal phenomena in speech.' *J. Acoust. Soc. Amer. 51*, 1279-90.

Johnson-Laird, P. N. 1975. 'Commentary on R. F. Cromer 1975.' In N. O'Connor (ed.) *Language, cognitive deficits, and retardation*. London: Butterworth.

Johnson-Laird, P. N. 1977a. 'Psycholinguistics without linguistics.' In N. S. Sutherland (ed.) *Tutorial essays in psychology 1*. Hillsdale, N. J.: Erlbaum.

Johnson-Laird, P. N. 1977b. 'Procedural semantics.' *Cognition 5*, 189-214.

Johnson-Laird, P. N. and Steedman, M. J. 1978. 'The psychology of syllogisms.' *Cog. Psychol. 10*, 64-69.

Kintsch, W. 1974. *The representation of meaning in memory*. Hillsdale, N. J.: Erlbaum.

Lenneberg, E. H. 1967. *Biological foundations of language*. New York: Wiley.

Liberman, A. M., Cooper, F. S., Shankweiler, D. S. and Studdert-Kennedy, M. 1967. 'Perception of the speech code.' *Psych. Rev. 74*, 431-61.

Liberman, A. M., Mattingly, K. and Turvey, M. T. 1972. 'Language codes and memory codes.' In A. W. Melton and E. Martin (eds) *Coding processes in human memory*. Washington, D.C.: Winston.

Lieberman, P. 1963. 'Some effects of semantic and grammatical context on the production and perception of speech.' *Lang. and Speech 6*, 172-9.

Lindsay, P. H. and Norman, D. A. 1977. *Human information processing: an introduction to psychology*, Second Edition. New York: Academic Press.

Longuet-Higgins, H. C. and Power, R. 1978. 'Learning to count – a computational model of language acquisition.' *Proc. Roy. Soc. B. 200*, 391-417.

Lyons, J. 1970. *Chomsky*. London: Fontana.

Lyons, J. 1977. *Semantics 1 and 2*. Cambridge: Cambridge University Press.

MacNeilage, P. and Ladefoged, P. 1976. 'The production of speech and language.' In E. C. Carterette and M. P. Friedman (eds) *Handbook of perception VII: language and speech*. New York: Academic Press.

Marslen-Wilson, W. 1976. 'Linguistic descriptions and psychological assumptions in the study of sentence perception.' In E. C. T. Walker and R. Wales (eds) *New approaches to language mechanisms*. Amsterdam: North-Holland.

Marslen-Wilson, W. and Welsh, A. 1978. 'Processing interactions and lexical access during word recognition in continuous speech.' *Cogn. Psychol. 10*, 29-63.

Martin, J. G. 1972. 'Rhythmic (hierarchical) versus serial structure in speech and other behavior.' *Psych. Rev. 79*, 487-509.

Miller, G. A. 1951. *Language and communication*. New York: McGraw-Hill.

Miller, G. A. and Johnson-Laird, P. N. 1976. *Language and perception*. Cambridge: Cambridge University Press and Cambridge, Mass.: Harvard University Press.

Minsky, M. 1975. 'Frame-system theory.' In R. C. Schank and B. L. Nash-Webber (eds) *Theoretical issues in natural language processing*. Preprints of a conference at M.I.T., June, 1975. Reprinted in Johnson-Laird, P. N. and Wason P. C. (eds) *Thinking: readings in cognitive science*. Cambridge: Cambridge University Press, 1977.

Morton, J. 1970. 'A functional model for memory.' In D. A. Norman (ed.) *Models of human memory*. New York: Academic Press.

Morton, J. 1978. 'Word recognition.' In J. Morton and J. C. Marshall (eds) *Psycholinguistics II*. London: Paul Elek.

Morton, J. and Long, J. 1976. 'Effect of word transitional probability on phoneme identification.' *J. verb. Learn. verb. Behav. 15*, 43-51.

Rumbaugh, J. E. 1975. 'A parallel asynchronous computer architecture for data flow programs.' Unpublished Ph.D. dissertation, M.I.T., Project MAC.

Schank, R. C. and Abelson, R. P. 1975. 'Scripts, plans and knowledge.' *Proceedings of the Fourth International Joint Conference on Artificial Intelligence*, Tbilisi, 1975. Reprinted in Johnson-Laird, P. N. and Wason, P. C. (eds) *Thinking: readings in cognitive science*. Cambridge: Cambridge University Press, 1977.

Smith, E. E., Shoben, E. J. and Rips, L. J. 1974. 'Comparison processes in semantic memory.' *Psychol. Rev. 81*, 214-41.

Steedman, M. J. and Johnson-Laird, P. N. in press. 'A programmatic theory of linguistic performance.' In P. T. Smith and R. N. Campbell (eds) *Proceedings of the Stirling conference on the psychology of language*. London: Plenum.

Studdert-Kennedy, M. 1977. 'Speech perception.' In N. J. Lass (ed.) *Contemporary issues in experimental phonetics*. New York: Academic Press, 1977.

Swinney, D. A. and Hakes, D. T. 1976. 'Effects of prior context upon lexical access during sentence comprehension.' *J. verb. Learn. verb. Behav. 15*, 681-9.

Warren, R. M. 1970. 'Perceptual restoration of missing speech sounds.' *Science 167*, 392-3.

FURTHER READING

The three best recent text-books on psycholinguistics are Fodor, Bever and Garrett (1974), Glucksberg and Danks (1975), and Clark and Clark (1977). A good introduction to the production and perception of speech sounds is Denes and Pinson (1973) and recent work is excellently surveyed in Darwin (1976), MacNeilage and Ladefoged (1976) and Studdert-Kennedy (1977). The attentive reader will have observed that I have deliberately avoided the tricky question of how written words are recognized. Henderson (1977) and Morton (1978) are two stimulating guides to a massive literature. The earlier theories of Chomsky are elucidated without too many technical details in Lyons (1970). Lyons (1977) has also written a two-volume compendium on semantics from a linguistic standpoint; Fodor (1977) provides a more specialized treatment of theories of meaning developed within the framework of transformational grammar. Miller and Johnson-Laird (1976) survey much of what is known about meaning in the context of developing their account of procedural semantics.

Chapter 6

Motor Activity Mutants of *Drosophila*

WILLIAM D. KAPLAN

INTRODUCTION

Just as the sequential steps in a biochemical pathway have been dissected through the study of single gene mutations, it may be possible to unravel complex behaviour by altering the individual genes one by one by means of specific mutations. Genes code for proteins. By altering proteins we may influence neuronal and muscle membrane processes, synaptic transmission, sensory transduction, the properties of ion channels or the generation of action potentials. These are essentially molecular processes. Therefore, our understanding of behaviour at the molecular level is made possible. The development of the nervous system and integration of its many elements is opened to investigation by the use of appropriate mutants.

In the behavioural genetics of *Drosophila*, the primary interest has, until recently, been placed upon a multifactorial approach which has successfully exploited the use of selection experiments to demonstrate that such behaviours as phototaxis, geotaxis and spontaneous activity have a large heritability component (Manning 1961; Ewing 1963; Connolly 1966; Dobzhansky and Spassky 1969) and measurements have been made on the contributions of individual chromosomes (Hirsch 1967). Ultimately it becomes difficult to unravel the genetics of these high- and low-response lines and the difficulties under these conditions, of determining the molecular basis of a given behaviour, would seem to be almost insurmountable.

Mating behaviour has been extensively studied in *Drosophila*. The considerable literature has been reviewed by Manning (1965) and most recently by Burnet and Connolly (1974). Many studies that have utilized single gene changes and their effects upon mating have made use of spontaneous body or eye colour mutants or mutants of wing or bristle structure. It has been shown that in many cases the mating effects have resulted from a pleiotropism, following anatomical or activity changes, in a psychologically or physiologically unimportant sense (Wilcock 1969).

A better understanding of mating behaviour might stem from the study of mutants which dissect out the individual elements in the chain of events constituting the total sequence (Hotta and Benzer 1976; Hall 1977). Benzer (1967) proposed the induction of mutations followed by selection for specific types through appropriate screening techniques. In *Drosophila* there are almost automatic regimens for the induction and measurement of rates of mutation. The methods are readily adaptable for the isolation of behavioural mutants, the only limitations being the ingeniousness of the screening techniques and the need to screen large numbers of flies.

The mutant approach in *Drosophila* has been gaining wide acceptance as a powerful tool in neurobiology. It has been successful in studies on vision, mating behaviours, circadian rhythms, neurophysiology, sense perception and even for studies on learning (see review by Pak and Pinto 1976).

This chapter deals with a study of a group of mutants known as shakers. It will illustrate the several genetic techniques available in *Drosophila* that have been used to describe them, to determine the primary focus of the mutant defect and to gain some insight into the nature of the gene change.

DESCRIPTION OF MUTANTS

The shaker mutants are so named because of their reaction to diethyl ether. During the period of anaesthesia the legs of the flies shake rapidly in a regular, rhythmic fashion. The shaking is not simply a hyperactive state before or after anaesthesia nor is it a waking phenomenon. Flies kept in a closed system with a 3 per cent v/v concentration of ether reach a steady state and continue to shake for as long as 24 hours, or until they die of desiccation.

The four mutants discussed here were independent mutagenic events induced in the *Canton-S* wild-type strain by the mutagen ethylmethane-sulfonate (Kaplan and Trout 1969). All are sex-linked, localized to the X-chromosome as follows:

Hyperkinetic[1]	*(Hk*[1]*)*	30.9
Hyperkinetic[2]	*(Hk*[2]*)*	30.4
ether à go go	*(eag)*	50.0
Shaker[5]	*(Sh*[5]*)*	58.2

(When written with a small *s* shaker refers to the whole class of mutants).

Although originally described as semi-dominant the hyperkinetic shaking is recessive. Sh^5 remains a strong dominant and in addition to leg-shaking etherized males and females scissor their wings. *Ether à go go* is strongly temperature sensitive; the shaking increases with rising temperature.

GENETIC BACKGROUND

Each mutant stock was originally established from only one male, thus from only one X-chromosome, in which the mutant gene was present. Subsequently, the autosomes and chromatin[1] material of the X-chromosome to the left and right of the mutant locus were replaced, by a series of appropriate crosses, with *Canton-S* chromatin. The genetic backgrounds of the mutant and control stocks are, therefore, identical so that observed behavioural differences may be attributed to the action of the mutant gene in question, and not to modifiers or background differences (Ikeda and Kaplan 1970a; Kaplan and Trout 1974). Modifiers, of course, accumulate with time. To offset this, the mutant stocks were periodically crossed back to the control *Canton-S* stock.

BUZZING ACTIVITY LEVEL

There is always more activity going on in cultures of shakers than in those of wild-type flies. Most of the activity stems from short flights and hopping movements which involve the beating of wings. Accordingly, activity levels were measured by placing a vial containing flies near a microphone, isolated from external light and sound. The number of buzzes was monitored electronically. Under these conditions it was found that shaker flies unetherized, produce more buzzes over a period of time than the reference *Canton-S* wild-type control stock (Kaplan and Trout 1969). The activity increases with

[1]Chromatin is the basic substance of the chromosomes and includes both proteins and DNA. In essence the term means chromosome material.

age, reaching a plateau at about five days. Hk^1 and Sh^5 are the two most active stocks; Hk^2 and *eag* lie midway between Hk^1 and the wild-type.

It was also found that the flight of one fly may set off activity in others. Indeed, shakers react to the presence of other flies; the number of buzzes per fly doubles when more than one is present (Kaplan and Trout 1968).

The way in which activity is measured influences the definition of 'more' or 'less' active. In an open field test shakers turn out to be less active than normal flies (Burnet, Connolly and Mallinson 1974).

QUANTIFYING OF SHAKING BEHAVIOUR

Subjectively, the impression obtained from viewing the several mutants through a dissecting microscope was that each mutant had its characteristic shaking pattern. It was, therefore, desirable to obtain an objective measure of the several phenotypes. To do this the image of the moving right midleg of 5-day-old females was focused upon a ground glass viewing screen using the optical system of a compound microscope (Figure 6.1). During the measurements flies were kept in a stoppered test tube in an atmosphere of 3 per cent ether. The shaking

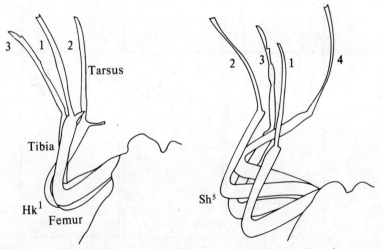

Figure 6.1 Silhouettes of right midlegs of two flies, projected upon a microscope screen as when monitoring leg shaking. Drawn from frames of high-speed film and superimposed to illustrate the difference in leg movement between Hk^1 and Sh^5. Original photographs from Trout, W. E. and Kaplan, W. D. 1973.

was monitored and recorded electronically by several different techniques, details of which may be found in Trout and Kaplan (1973).

Figure 6.1 is a superimposition of several consecutive frames of a motion picture film photographed at 128 frames per second. The difference in pattern between the *Hk* and *Sh*[5] mutants may be clearly seen. All segments of the *Sh*[5] midleg are involved in shaking whereas the femur of *Hk* remains fairly quiet.

Figure 6.2 gives a visual impression of the difference in shaking patterns of *Hk*[1] and *Sh*[5] although the quantitative aspects, with the method used, are not highly accurate (see legend, Figure 6.2).

From more accurate methods during which the tibia was monitored and the femur immobilized, it was determined that the shaking patterns provide three types of data: the number of shakes per minute, the number of shaking episodes per minute and the percentage of time spent shaking. For the *Hk* locus these parameters are highly correlated ($r > 0.9$). Thus, *Hk*[1] with a higher number of shakes per minute than *Hk*[2] has fewer but longer shaking episodes and a greater percentage of time spent shaking.

Hk[1] has a cycling pattern with periods of silence between the waxing and waning. *Hk*[2] is similar but, with shorter bursts of shaking,

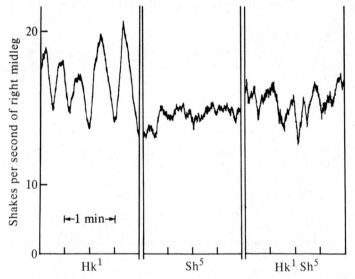

Figure 6.2 Shaking patterns of *Hk*[1], *Sh*[5], and the double mutant, *Hk*[1] *Sh*[5], obtained by monitoring the shaking rate of the end of unrestrained midleg, thereby summing the movements of all leg segments, including the continuous movements of the tarsus. Reproduced with permission as for Figure 6.1.

its average rate is lower. Sh^5 has an even rate with short bursts superimposed, imparting a jerkiness to the basic pattern. It is active 100 per cent of the time. Hk^1 shakes an average of 420 times per minute; Hk^2, 222 times; and Sh^5, 312. Because of temperature sensitivity and the constraints imposed under the experimental conditions used for tibial monitoring, *eag* rates were not measureable.

DOUBLE MUTANTS

By appropriate crosses which insert two mutant genes into one chromosome it is possible to obtain double mutants of Hk^1 and Sh^5 and vary the number of Hk^1 and Sh^5 genes with respect to each other. The resultant interacting phenotypes make it possible to determine whether the mutant genes at the two loci act similarly or in different ways (Trout and Kaplan 1973). The same may be achieved for Hk^2 and Sh^5.

Figure 6.2 shows the shaking pattern obtained from a female homozygous for both Hk^1 and Sh^5. The characteristics of both mutants are present; the cycling and silent periods of Hk^1 with the short bursts of Sh^5 superimposed. However, the effect of the inter-action is not simply additive. Instead, the mutants mutually inhibit each other resulting in a more normal phenotype (Trout and Kaplan 1973). That this double mutant is indeed more normal, rather than merely weak, is shown by the fact that it lives longer than either Hk^1 or Sh^5 homozygotes, which have half the lifespan of normal flies (Trout and Kaplan 1970). Moreover, the wing scissoring of Sh^5 is reduced in Hk^1Sh^5.

Not all shaker interactions lead to a more normal phenotype than either reactant possesses. Sh^5 is epistatic[1] to Hk^2; Hk^2Sh^5 has the same shaking pattern as Sh^5 by itself. Hk^1eag is an extremely weak fly that shakes without etherization and $eagSh^5$, in addition to perpetual shaking has lost the ability to fly (Wong *et al.* 1974).

For all shakers the rates increase with age reaching a plateau five days after hatching from the pupa, and shaking is decreased with increasing ether concentration. The optimal concentration is 3 per cent. The change with age is typical of many age-related phenomena in *D. melanogaster*. The same curve has been obtained for buzzing activity level and the jump response (see below) and for oxygen consumption in both normal and shaker flies (Trout and Kaplan

---

[1]Epistasis is non-additive interaction between two or more different loci.

1970). Chadwick (1953) investigating wing-beat frequency in *Drosophila* observed a similar change in motor output with age. All of these changes must reflect a maturation process generally found in insects (Chapman 1971), which should be taken into account in any behavioural study.

GENE DOSAGE

Until the molecular basis of the shaker phenotype has been determined one can only speculate on how the mutant genes are acting. However, by creating a fly carrying Hk^1 (or Hk^2) in one X-chromosome and a second X from which a piece of chromosome which includes the Hk locus has been deleted one can determine whether the mutant effect is due to the absence of the normal gene product or to one that has been altered.

Since the deficiency chromosome carries no hyperkinetic gene, mutant or normal, the deficiency heterozygotes, Hk^1/Df and Hk^2/Df, have only one gene at the Hk locus, a mutant one. If either Hk^1 or Hk^2 produced no functional gene product the phenotypes of Hk^1/Hk^1 and Hk^1/Df would be identical and Hk^2/Df should have the same phenotype as Hk^2/Hk^2. However, in both cases the shaking phenotypes of the deficiency heterozygotes are more extreme than their respective mutant homozygotes (Trout and Kaplan 1973). This indicates that the mutant genes are, indeed, coding for a functional gene product but one that is less efficient, in smaller quantity, or with a different action, than normal. Two doses of the mutant gene make for greater normality than one. The deficiency homozygote is lethal so that one cannot measure the effect of the complete absence of the locus, but since the deficiency removes more than the Hk gene the lethality cannot be attributed to that locus alone. The effect of the deficiency which was used in the above experiments is specific for the Hk alleles. It has no influence upon the Sh^5 mutant.

NEUROLOGICAL BASIS OF LEG-SHAKING

Recording extracellularly it was found that areas furnishing rhythmic mutant patterns of nerve impulses were limited to three small paired regions of the ventral thoracic ganglion corresponding to the areas that govern the movements of the pro-meso- and metathoracic legs. The discharges were found to be correlated with leg-shaking behaviour (Ikeda and Kaplan 1970a).

Removal of heads and complete deafferentiation of the thoracic ganglion had no influence upon the mutant firing patterns indicating that the neuronal firing was controlled endogenously in the thoracic ganglion.

After the areas of mutant motor activity were located it was possible to obtain intracellular recordings from single motor neurons. Two types of neurons were encountered. In the presence of ether, type I neurons discharged action potentials without any sign of prepotential. In the case of type II neurons, an action potential was always preceded by a slowly rising depolarization. Type I neurons were encountered about three times more frequently than type II (Ikeda and Kaplan 1970a).

When antidromic stimulation was applied to a leg nerve the invading spike potential could be recorded at the soma of type I neurons in the corresponding motor region; type II neurons showed no response. Destruction of the type I neuron after obtaining an intracellular recording was not followed by any change in activity by other neurons observed extracellularly at the leg nerve. However, when the type II neuron was destroyed the specific mutant motor output disappeared. This suggests that the activity of type I neurons is controlled by the type II neuron acting as a pacemaker (Ikeda and Kaplan 1974).

Tracings obtained from intracellular recordings of pacemaker neurons reveal a pattern that changes with time, the frequency waxing and waning within a range of 2 to 16 per second. The waxing and waning and quiet periods observed agree with the leg shaking measurements obtained by Trout and Kaplan (1973).

The concept of the command interneuron turning on or off an endogenously, genetically determined firing pattern of a pacemaker neuron may serve as a model for the basic mechanism of the central nervous system. According to this concept the central nervous system is not simply an input-output mechanism but contains elements which possess their own preprogrammed endogenous activities. This kind of system was investigated by Ikeda and Wiersma (1964) and Wiersma and Ikeda (1964) and is discussed by Ikeda (1976).

The hyperkinetic mutants of *Drosophila* may have revealed an endogenously patterned activity under the control of a command interneuron. The leg shaking of Hk^1 was released only under the influence of diethyl ether which paralyses wild-type *Canton-S* flies. Since, under normal circumstances, Hk^1 flies do not show any motor disorders, it may be reasoned that the activity of the pacemaker neuron of Hk^1 is ordinarily suppressed by some other neuron. The endogenous activity of the pacemaker neuron, however, may be released by blocking the suppressive action of the command neuron, as in the presence of ether (Ikeda 1976).

STUDIES ON MOSAIC FLIES

Genetic mosaicism[1] was used to test the possibility that the observed physiological effects were secondary to the activity of cells in other regions of the thorax or a circulating humoral agent.

It is possible by a relatively simple technique to generate gynandromorphs, flies mosaic for male and female tissue. The crosses may be set up in such a way that the male tissue carries Hk^1

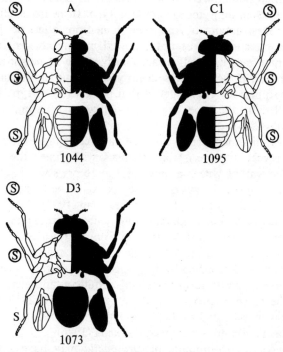

Figure 6.3 Gynandric patterns. Male tissue shown in white, female in black. Legs marked S shake. Rhythmic bursts obtained from motor regions corresponding to legs with circled S. Adapted from Ikeda, K. and Kaplan, W. D. 1970b.

[1] Mosaicism refers to the presence in an individual of two or more cell genotypes. Animals so constituted may be called gynandromorphs if they contain male and female tissue as the basis for the mosaicism.

hemizygously along with markers for eye and body colour, whereas in the female tissue Hk^1 and the markers are heterozygous (Ikeda and Kaplan, 1970b). Because Hk^1 shaking and the markers are recessive the female tissue may be distinguished from the male phenotypically. Furthermore, because of the nature of *Drosophila* embryology the line establishing the male-female demarcation may vary in position resulting in a wide variety of mosaic types.

Figure 6.3 illustrates three representative mosaic types. From Figure 6.4 may be seen the electrophysiological tracing obtained from comparable areas of male (mutant) and female (normal) tissue (Ikeda and Kaplan 1970b).

In the control experiments and male-female comparisons within a single mosaic the lack of a pattern similar to Hk^1 should ideally be shown in a neuron identical to the mutant one. Because of the small size of the motor neurons (1-3 μ), insertion of the electrode into identical cells of different preparations could not be verified. A secondary choice, extracellular recordings, as shown in the lower tracings of Figure 6.4A, B and C, was employed to show that the rhythmic activity pattern of the mutant was never detected in the controls (Ikeda and Kaplan 1970b).

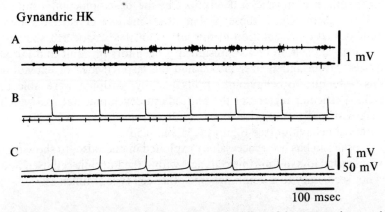

Gynandric HK

A

B

C

1 mV

1 mV
50 mV

100 msec

Figure 6.4 Electrical activities in the thoracic ganglion of three gynandromorph types, mosaic for Hk^1. (A) Simultaneous extracellular recording from pair of prothoracic regions: *upper trace*, male side; *lower trace*, female. Gynandromorph type as Figure 6.3A. (B) Simultaneous recordings from pair of metathoracic motor regions; *upper trace*, intracellular recording from type I neuron on male side; *lower trace*, extracellular recording from region on female side. (C) Simultaneous recordings from pair of mesothoracic motor regions; *upper trace*, intracellular recording from type II neuron on male side; *lower trace*, extracellular recording from region on female side. Adapted from Ikeda, K. and Kaplan, W. D. 1970b.

The mosaic studies clearly demonstrate that the expression of Hk^1 is autonomous in the genetic sense, that the leg movements of the two sides of the fly are governed independently, that the genotype of the head and abdomen have no influence upon the motor areas and that nothing circulating in the body fluids may mediate the expression of the mutant or wild-type gene, either with respect to the shaking or the firing pattern of the motor neurons.

From mosaics of a more complicated type, where a single male leg is associated with an otherwise female thorax (Kaplan 1972), it is possible to conclude that each motor region acts independently of the others and that the genotype of leg cuticle and motor neurons may occasionally differ.

External markers may be identified easily but the genotype of the internal nervous tissue cannot be determined by inspection. Hotta and Benzer (1972) proposed a method for determining which internal tissues have been made defective by behavioural mutations.

Their method involved the construction of morphogenetic fate maps (Sturtevant 1929; Poulson 1950) establishing embryonic relationships among the tissues of *Drosophila*. Sturtevant recognized that the probability that any two structures may be of different genotype in a large number of mosaics is determined by the 'developmental distance' between them. Using these probabilities one can construct a two-dimensional representation of the surface of the blastoderm showing the relative position of the presumed progenitors of adult and larval tissues. Hotta and Benzer (1972) had the inspired idea of extending this technique to behavioural traits and by so doing were able to define particular regions of the blastoderm developmental foci which were assumed to give rise to the adult structure responsible for the observed behaviour (see Figures 6.5a and 6.5b).

Mosaicism has been successfully exploited in mice also, to show that an inherited loss of Purkinje cells acts within the Purkinje cell itself and is not secondary to a lesion in some other cell type (Mullen 1977).

KINETOGENIC RESPONSE OF HYPERKINETIC FLIES

Hk^1 and Hk^2 show an unusual response to movement. When an object moves above a vial containing these mutant flies, they jump and fall over. The response may be measured quite simply by the experimenter moving his hand above a vial containing a single fly and scoring the number of positive responses in fifty trials. Hk^1

(a)

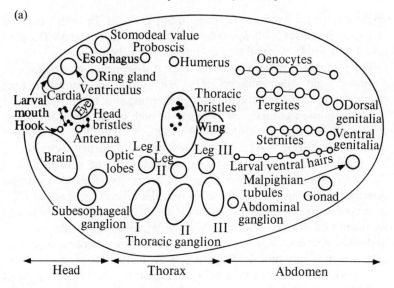

Figure 6.5(a) Fate map of *Drosophila* embryo, showing right half of blastoderm seen from inside. Approximate locations of primordia of various larval and adult structures are shown, as determined via mosaic mapping by various authors. (b) Fate map sites of the behavioural foci for the hyperkinetic mutant *Hk*[1]. There is a separate focus for each leg; they fall in the region of the blastoderm which, according to embryological studies, gives rise to the ventral nervous system. (a) Reproduced with permission from Hotta, Y. and Benzer, S., *Proc. Nat. Acad. Sci.* 1976; (b) *ibid*, 1972.

(b)

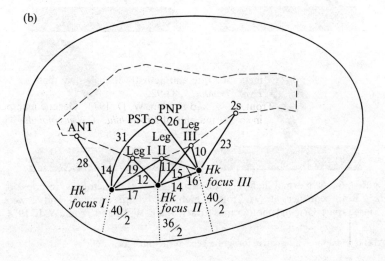

responds, on the average, 42 times in 50; Hk^2, 24. In both cases the response increases with age, plateauing at about five days (Kaplan and Trout 1969). Normal flies do not show this behaviour.

The jump phenotype is recessive since it disappears in hybrids with *Canton-S* and other shakers. Hk^1/Hk^2, however, shows a high response; the two genes are non-complementing and, therefore, allelic.[1]

The response was analyzed by means of high speed cinematography. Figure 6.6 is a comparison of the moment of take-off of a *Canton-S* and Hk^1 fly. Frames A1 and A2 show that the normal fly raises its wings while all six legs are still in contact with the substrate. The fly then pushes off with its midlegs and brings its wings forward and downward. Frames B1 and B2 show that the takeoff sequence of Hk^1, in response to movement, is different from the normal pattern. The fly pushes off with its midlegs while the wings are still held over the abdomen and does not beat its wings until it has become airborne, after which it may tumble (Kaplan and Trout 1974).

Hyperkinetic flies can take off spontaneously into normal flight at which time the launching pattern is observed to be normal.

Although Sh^5 does not show a consistent kinetogenic response,

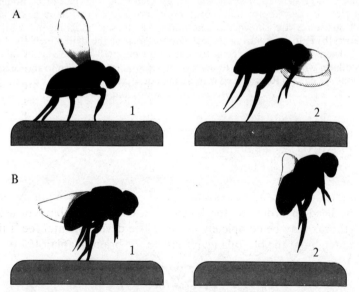

Figure 6.6   A. Normal flight take-off of *Canton S*. B. Kinetogenic response of Hk^1. Both sequences drawn from a high-speed film; frames 1 and 2 were 2.5 msec apart. Original photographs from Kaplan, W. D. and Trout, W. E. 1974.

[1] Allelic refers to an alternative form of a gene at the same locus; alleles.

occasionally a fly will respond to movement as much as 20 times out of 50. When combined with Hk^1 in a double mutant, instead of the response being enhanced, it is found to be reduced. The addition of one Sh^5 gene to Hk^1/Hk^1 or Hk^2/Hk^2 reduces the response by about 35 per cent. Two doses of Sh^5 are roughly twice as effective as one. This means that Sh^5 genes have a quantitative effect on Hk^1 and Hk^2 homozygotes, making them more nearly normal with respect to response to movement, just as in the case of shaking.

Genetic background was found to have little influence upon the jumping phenotype. When tested in four different backgrounds the response of Hk^1 and Hk^2 remained the same (Kaplan and Trout 1974).

According to Hoyle (1964) almost any sensory input to the insect nervous system is capable of producing a detectable response in the motor nervous system, which is insufficient to produce an overt behaviour. In the case of Hk^1 movement may elicit an overt response. Dethier (1964) has pointed out that the head determines the onset and duration of locomotion. In some way the hyperkinetic mutation has upset the balance usually present. Normal flies, although capable of detecting movement, maintain whatever physiological state exists at the time. In the mutant the balance between excitatory and inhibitory elements has been upset as a result of the change in the neuronal properties or in the threshold of the behaviour pattern.

In conducting experiments to measure the jump response, we have, in effect, a shadow moving above the flies. It is possible, therefore, that the flies respond to a decrease or an increase in light intensity. Turning an incandescent light on and off does not elicit the response. However, a rapidly flashing, high intensity strobe light does call forth the kinetogenic response (Kaplan 1972).

With only one mutant gene, Hk^2, present in the deficiency heterozygote, Hk^2/Df, the jump phenotype becomes more abnormal, about 40 times in 50 trials as compared to about 24 for Hk^2/Hk^2.

Studies with mosaics have shown that there must be mutant tissue in the head in order for the kinetogenic response to be expressed. The thorax may be completely normal. The developmental focus lies in the region of the blastula giving rise to the brain (Kaplan 1976).

THE COMBINATION OF Hk^1 WITH OTHER BEHAVIOURAL MUTANTS

The use of double mutants may be a valuable approach to behavioural studies. In the presence of ether we have an endogenous oscillating system in specific motor neurons of Hk^1 flies that can serve as a test system in the investigation of other mutants.

The sex-linked temperature-sensitive paralytic mutant, $para^{ts}$ moves normally at 22°C but is quickly paralysed at 29.5°C. Paralysis is usually complete. Upon return to 22°C mobility is recovered within five seconds (Suzuki *et al.* 1971). The nature of the paralysis is still unknown.

When combined with $para^{ts}$ the legs of Hk^1, at 22°C, shake in the presence of ether but are inhibited at 29.5°C. However, at 29.5°C, a paralysed fly responds to a high intensity flashing light. The fly pushes off with the midlegs and beats its wings several times. The escape, however, is short-lived; the fly travels only 2-3 cm before sinking back into paralysis (Williamson *et al.* 1974).

Obviously, the sensory, neuronal and muscular elements are functional. A degree of motor competence in paralysed *para* flies has also been demonstrated by the production of leg jerks through electrical stimulation (Siddiqi and Benzer 1976).

Experiments with picrotoxin, which blocks the inhibitory transmitter, γ-aminobutyric acid (Usherwood and Grundfest 1965) suggest that *para*-induced paralysis is brought about by an augmented inhibition of motor units (Williamson *et al., op. cit.*).

Hk^1 has been combined with several visual mutants showing clearly defined morphological abnormalities in order to determine which anomalies block the kinetogenic response (Kaplan 1976). The data suggest a focus lying within the lamina, the most distal region of the optic lobe (Figure 6.7). The mutant sev^{LY3} (*sevenless*) removes the central retinula cell number 7 from each omatidium of the compound eye. The mutant $rdgB^{KS222}$ (*retinula degeneration*) shows complete degeneration of cell bodies and rhabdomeres (photoreceptive structures) of cells 1–6, whereas in ora^{JK84} (*outer rhabdomeres absent*), only rhabdomeres, of cells 1–6 fail to develop (Hotta and Benzer 1970; Koenig and Merriam 1977).

Rhabdomeres of cells 1–6 are larger than those of cells 7–8 and have different synaptic connections within the optic lobe. The two groups are believed to have different functions (Heisenberg and Buchner 1977). Cells 1–6 make synaptic connections within the lamina, whereas axons from cells 7–8 bypass that structure and connect directly to the medulla. The double mutant, $Hk^1 sev^{LY3}$, permits the expression of the kinetogenic response. In $Hk^1 rdgB^{KS222}$ and $Hk^1 ora^{JK84}$ the response is blocked. The focus of the jump response, therefore, lies within the lamina or an interneuronal pathway arising in that region.

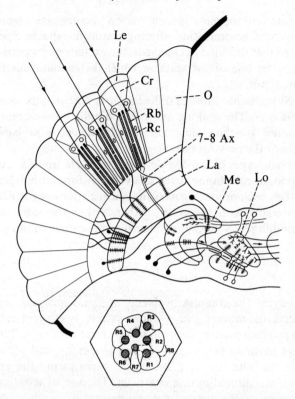

Figure 6.7 Schematic drawing of the dipteran eye and optic ganglia: 7-8 AX, axons from retinula cells 7 and 8. Cr, crystalline cone; La, lamina; Le, lenslet; Lo, lobula; Me, medulla; Rb, rhabdomere; Rc, receptor or retinula cell. Adapted with permission from Heisenberg, M. and Buchner, E. 1977, *J. Comp. Physiol. A, 117*, 127-62.

SUMMARY

In the absence of biochemical and additional physiological data on shaker mutants and their interactions a provisional explanation has been offered for the behavioural phenotypes described. The *Hk* mutants produce different amounts of a normal gene product or abnormal end products of differing efficiency and the observed phenotypes are related to the total amount or efficiency of this product: the less product, the greater the abnormality. This end product may be a membrane component, which, when inadequate, increases the excitability of neurons, thus altering neural thresholds. Sperry (1958) suggested that this kind of change in the excitatory properties of nerve cells may be one of the ways in which behavioural alterations are brought about.

The Sh^5 mutant although different from Hk^1 may be thought of in the same way. The shaking maps to individual motor centres within the thoracic ganglion and like Hk^1 the defect is probably general throughout the nervous system.

The phenotypes of the double mutants of Hk and Sh^5 suggest that the supposed membrane defects have been formed independently of each other, each producing its own typical pattern of oscillation which then interacts with the other, either within the same neurons or between differently oscillating neurons in the same motor pathway.

ENVOI

For studying the complex problems of behaviour and neurobiology in general, the mutant gene offers an extremely efficient microsurgical tool to produce precise blocks in behavioural pathways. Temperature-sensitive mutants permit turning the blocks on and off at will and provide the ultimate in a biological experiment: the control and experimental animal in one organism. The use of mosaics offers the opportunity of grafting normal and mutant parts while retaining the structural integrity of the intact animal. By so doing, the primary focus of the behavioural defect is revealed and the interrelationships of the individual units may be established.

There is many a developmental pathway between a gene and the ultimate expression of its behavioural effect. The many genetic manipulations available in *Drosophila* combined with biochemical, histological and physiological techniques, or with techniques yet unknown, may help to isolate the individual steps. These are exciting prospects for the future.

ACKNOWLEDGEMENT

The many contributions of my colleagues, Kazuo Ikeda, William Trout, Patrick Wong and Rodney Williamson are enthusiastically acknowledged. The author's work is supported by U.S.P.H.S. Grant NS-08014 and in part by the Helen Reddy and Jeff Wald Research Fund.

REFERENCES

Benzer, S. 1967. 'Behavioral mutants of *Drosophila* isolated by countercurrent distribution.' *Proc. Nat. Acad. Sci. 58*, 1112-19.

Burnet, B. and Connolly, K. 1974. 'Activity and sexual behaviour in *Drosophila melanogaster.*' In J. H. F. van Abeelen (ed.) *The genetics of behaviour.* Amsterdam: North-Holland Publishing Company.

Burnet, B., Connolly, K. and Mallinson, M. 1974. 'Activity and sexual behavior of neurological mutants in *Drosophila melanogaster.*' *Behav. Genet. 4*, 227-35.

Chadwick, L. E. 1953. 'The motion of the wings.' In K. D. Roeder (ed.) *Insect physiology.* New York: Wiley.

Chapman, R. F. 1971. *The insects: structure and function,* 2nd ed. New York: Elsevier.

Connolly, K. 1966. 'Locomotor activity in *Drosophila.* II. Selection for active and inactive strains.' *Anim. Behav. 14*, 444-9.

Dethier, J. G. 1964. 'Microscopic brains.' *Science 143*, 1138-45.

Dobzhansky, Th. and Spassky, B. 1969. 'Artificial and natural selection for two behavioral traits in *Drosophila pseudoobscura.*' *Proc. Nat. Acad. Sci. 62*, 75-80.

Ewing, A. W. 1963. 'Attempts to select for spontaneous activity in *Drosophila melanogaster.*' *Anim. Behav. 11*, 369-78.

Hall, J. C. 1977. 'Portions of the central nervous system controlling reproductive behavior in *Drosophila.*' *Behav. Genet. 7*, 291-312.

Heisenberg, M. and Buchner, E. 1977. 'The role of retinula cell types in visual behavior of *Drosophila melanogaster.*' *J. comp. Physiol. A 117*, 127-62.

Hirsch, J. 1967. 'Behavior-genetic analysis at the chromosome level of organization.' In J. Hirsch (ed.) *Behavior-genetic analysis.* New York: McGraw-Hill.

Hotta, Y. and Benzer, S. 1970. 'Genetic dissection of the *Drosophila* nervous system by means of mosaics.' *Proc. Nat. Acad. Sci. 67*, 1156-63.

Hotta, Y. and Benzer, S. 1972. 'Mapping of behaviour in *Drosophila* mosaics.' *Nature 240*, 527-35.

Hotta, Y. and Benzer, S. 1976. 'Courtship in *Drosophila* mosaics: sex-specific foci for sequential action patterns.' *Proc. Nat. Acad. Sci. 73*, 4154-8.

Hoyle, G. 1964. 'Exploration of neuronal mechanisms underlying behavior in insects.' In R. F. Reiss (ed.) *Neuronal theory and modeling.* Stanford: Stanford University Press.

Ikeda, K. 1976. 'Genetically patterned neural activity.' In J. C. Fentress (ed.) *Simpler networks and behavior.* Sunderland: Sinauer Assoc., Inc.

Ikeda, K. and Kaplan, W. D. 1970a. 'Patterned neural activity of a mutant *Drosophila melanogaster.*' *Proc. Nat. Acad. Sci. 66*, 765-72.

Ikeda, K. and Kaplan, W. D. 1970b. 'Unilaterally patterned neural activity of gynandromorphs, mosaic for a neurological mutant of *Drosophila melanogaster.*' *Proc. Nat. Acad. Sci. 67*, 1480-7.

Ikeda, K. and Kaplan, W. D. 1974. 'Neurophysiological genetics in *D. melanogaster.*' *Amer. Zool. 14*, 1055-66.

Ikeda, K. and Wiersma, C. A. G. 1964. 'Autogenic rhythmicity in the abdominal ganglia of the crayfish: the control of swimmeret movements.' *Comp. Biochem. Physiol. 12*, 107-15.

Kaplan, W. D. 1972. 'Genetic and behavioral studies of *Drosophila* neurological mutants.' In J. A. Kiger, Jr. (ed.) *The biology of behavior.* Corvallis: Oregon State University Press.

Kaplan, W. D. 1976. 'The use of double mutants in the investigation of visual mutants of *Drosophila.*' *Genetics 83*, s38-s39 (abstr.).

Kaplan, W. D. and Trout, W. E. 1968. 'Activity and reactivity of shaker flies.' *Genetics 60*, 191 (abstr.).

Kaplan, W. D. and Trout, W. E. 1969. 'The behaviour of four neurological mutants of *Drosophila.*' *Genetics 61*, 399-409.

Kaplan, W. D. and Trout, W. E. 1974. 'Genetic manipulation of an abnormal jump response in *Drosophila.*' *Genetics 77*, 721-39.

Koenig, J. and Merriam, J. R. 1977. 'Autosomal ERG mutants.' *Drosoph. Inf. Serv. 52*, 50.

Manning, A. 1961. 'Selection for mating speed in *Drosophila melanogaster* based on the behaviour of one sex.' *Anim. Behav. 11*, 369-78.

Manning, A. 1965. '*Drosophila* and the evolution of behaviour.' In J. D. Carthy and C. L. Duddington (eds) *Viewpoints in biology.* London: Butterworths.

Mullen, R. J. 1977. 'Site of *pcd* gene action and Purkinje cell mosaicism in cerebella of chimaeric mice.' *Nature 270*, 245-7.

Pak, W. L. and Pinto, L. H. 1976. 'Genetic approach to the study of the nervous system.' *Ann. Rev. Biophys. Bioengin. 5*, 397-447.

Poulson, D. F. 1950. 'Histogenesis, organogenesis and differentiation in the embryo of *Drosophila melanogaster Meigen.*' In M. Demerec (ed.) *Biology of Drosophila.* New York: John Wiley and Sons, Inc.

Siddiqi, O. and Benzer, S. 1976. 'Neurophysiological defects in temperature-sensitive paralytic mutants of *Drosophila melanogaster.*' *Proc. Nat. Acad. Sci. 73*, 3253-7.

Sperry, R. W. 1958. 'Developmental basis of behavior.' In A. Roe and G. G. Simpson (eds) *Behavior and evolution.* New Haven: Yale University Press.

Sturtevant, A. H. 1929. 'The claret mutant type of *Drosophila simulans*: a study of chromosome elimination and of cell lineage.' *Z. wiss. Zool. 135*, 323-56.

Suzuki, D. T., Grigliatti, T. and Williamson, R. 1971. 'Temperature sensitive mutations in *D. melanogaster*. VII. A mutation (*para^{ts}*) causing reversible adult paralysis.' *Proc. Nat. Acad. Sci. 68*, 890-3.

Trout, W. E. and Kaplan, W. D. 1970. 'A relation between longevity, metabolic rate and activity in shaker mutants of *Drosophila melanogaster.*' *Exp. Gerontol. 5*, 83-92.

Trout, W. E. and Kaplan, W. D. 1973. 'Genetic manipulation of motor output in shaker mutants of *Drosophila.*' *J. Neurobiol. 4*, 495-512.

Usherwood, P. N. R. and Grundfest, H. 1965. 'Peripheral inhibition in skeletal muscle of insects.' *J. Neurophys. 28*, 497-518.

Wiersma, C. A. G. and Ikeda, K. 1964. 'Interneurons commanding swimmeret movements in the crayfish, *Procambarus Clarki* (Girard).' *Comp. Biochem. Physiol. 12*, 509-25.

Wilcock, J. 1969. 'Gene action and behavior: an evaluation of major gene pleiotropism.' *Psychol. Bull. 72*, 1-29.

Williamson, R. L., Kaplan, W. D. and Dagan, D. 1974. 'A fly's leap from paralysis.' *Nature 252*, 224-6.

Wong, P. T., Ikeda, K. and Kaplan, W. D. 1974. 'Genetic control of flight motor function in *Drosophila melanogaster*.' *Soc. Neurosci.* Ann. Meet., 4th, 484 (abstr.).

FURTHER READING

Dudai, Y., Jan, Y-N., Byers, D., Quinn, W. C. and Benzer, S. 1976. '*dunce*, a mutant of *Drosophila* deficient in learning.' *Proc. Nat. Acad. Sci.* *73*, 1684-8.

Hall, J. C., Gelbart, W. M. and Kankel, D. R. 1976. 'Mosaic systems.' In E. Novitski and M. Ashburner (eds) *Genetics and biology of Drosophila Ia.* London: Academic Press.

Harris, W. A., Stark, W. S. and Walker, J. A. 1976. 'Genetic dissection of the photoreceptor system in the compound eye of *Drosophila melanogaster*.' *J. Physiol. 256*, 415-39.

Heisenberg, M. and Götz, K. G. 1975. 'The use of mutations for the partial degradation of vision in *Drosophila melanogaster*.' *J. Comp. Physiol. 98*, 217-41.

Hotta, Y. and Benzer, S. 1973. 'Mapping of behavior of *Drosophila* mosaics.' In F. H. Ruddle (ed.) *Genetic mechanisms of development*. New York: Academic Press.

Kankel, D. R. and Hall, J. C. 1976. 'Fate mapping of nervous system and other internal tissues in genetic mosaics of *Drosophila melanogaster*.' *Dev. Biol. 48*, 1-24.

Pak, W. L. 1975. 'Mutations affecting the vision of *Drosophila melanogaster*.' In R. C. King (ed.) *Handbook of genetics 3*, New York: Plenum.

Chapter 7

Young Children's Capacity to Communicate

MARGARET MARTLEW

Consider the following conversation between two four year old children who were talking about abstract shapes drawn on wooden blocks. Child A described a shape in a metaphorical manner, 'It's a bird.' Child B held up a block for confirmation that his selected block was the correct one. 'Is this it?' he asked. 'No,' responded Child A. Here, apparently, is an exchange of messages exemplifying structured, coherent discourse, with utterances contingent on the form and content of the preceding utterance, while relevant use is made also of contextual clues by appropriate ellipsis. *But* a screen separated the children so they could neither see each other nor each other's blocks. Although apparently adhering to discourse conventions the children failed to encode messages to take account both of the listener and the situation.

These children were engaged in a referential communication task devised by Glucksberg, Krauss and Weisberg (1966). The child acting as speaker had to name an abstract shape, the referent, to enable the listener to discriminate the same shape from a set of other abstract shapes (Figure 7.1). This experiment represents a method frequently adopted for investigating young children's communication skills. It is laboratory centred, using structured situations and concentrating on referential processes in communication. The general conclusion drawn is that the child's capacity to communicate effectively is largely a function of age (Krauss and Glucksberg 1969). There are a number of reasons for this which relate both to what the child is talking about or to whom he is talking. For example, the younger the child, the poorer his ability to make initial discriminatory comparisons and so select the salient attributes of the referent/non-referent (Asher 1976;

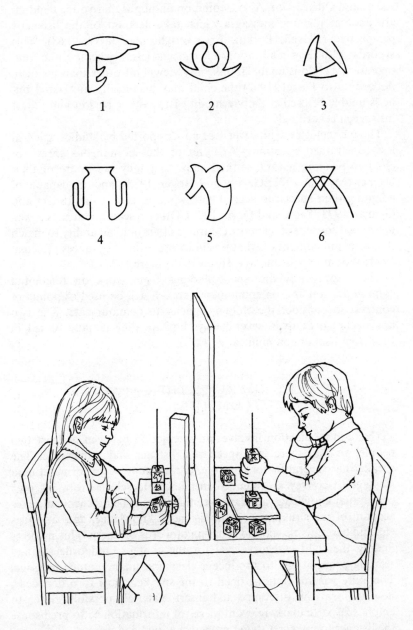

Figure 7.1 Experimental setting for referential communication task and the abstract shapes drawn on blocks and used in the study. After Glucksberg, Krauss and Weisberg 1966.

Asher and Oden 1976). Also a common finding is that young children are poor at forming messages which take account of the listener's perspective (Flavell, Botkin, Fry, Wright and Jarvis 1968). This accords with Piaget's notion of egocentricism whereby the pre-operational child is unable to take any viewpoint other than his own. According to Piaget (1962) the child may be socially motivated but he is unable to predict the viewpoint of the other person and adjust his speech accordingly.

These conclusions, however, are not supported by studies made in less constrained situations. Analyses of the spontaneous speech of children in more natural settings show that they are aware of their listener (Mueller 1972; Garvey and Hogan 1973), and are capable of adapting their speech to accord with whoever is listening (Shatz and Gelman 1973; Sachs and Devin 1976). Other research indicates a well developed concept of reference (Maratsos 1976) and an ability to match the form and content of what is said to preceding utterances (Keenan 1974; Bloom, Rocissano and Hood 1976; Dore 1977).

These apparently discrepant findings from work on referential communication and on spontaneous speech will be used as points of contrast to consider the child's capacity to communicate. The two approaches overlap in several ways but are differentially biased in their appraisal of communication skills.

WHAT UNDERLIES THE CAPACITY TO COMMUNICATE

Verbal communication involves an interaction between at least two people, so that there is a speaker, a listener and a message. The speaker has several factors to take into account when formulating a message to convey an intended meaning. He selects from his own conceptual knowledge in relation to the content being encoded, takes account of the situation and the listener's knowledge, age, attitudes etc. and bases his choice and ordering of words on these. This involves finding the right category level for the content, and ordering and relating propositions to produce a clear and unambiguous message. There are various options open to the speaker: how to order ideas, how to form the utterance and insert material, possibly either to emphasize particularly relevant pieces of information or to predispose the listener to interpret the utterance in a qualified way.

Speakers also have options whether their utterance is to have the force of an assertion, a command, a request etc. This, the illocutionary force of the utterance, is the speech act which the speaker intends to carry out (Searle 1969). The form of the utterance may not always match the intended meaning. Saying 'It's cold in here,' the speaker may be using the declarative with the force of a request, the intended but indirect meaning being that the listener should close the window. When formulating an utterance the speaker relies on the listener's ability to make inferences about the intended meaning based on shared linguistic and contextual knowledge. To communicate efficiently speakers and listeners adhere to co-operative principles and the basic conventions of discourse (Gordon and Lakoff 1975).

The speaker's capacity to communicate can be assessed in terms of his intention and whether his utterance reflects this (Grice 1975). This may be regarded as sufficient without taking into account whether the listener comprehends on the grounds that he might be deliberately unhelpful or recalcitrant (Gelman and Shatz 1977). Generally, however, the effectiveness of the speaker's message is assessed on whether it ensures that the listener does comprehend (Piaget 1926). Comprehension involves the listener inferring the speaker's intended meaning by decoding what he hears using linguistic, pragmatic and extra-linguistic means. If the message is not comprehensible, then the listener evaluates its deficiencies and requests further information. Using this feedback the speaker modifies his original message to meet with the listener's expressed needs. The appropriateness of an utterance depends on how well it relates to the situation.

HOW IS COMMUNICATIVE CAPACITY TO BE ASSESSED?

The two approaches, broadly defined as referential and spontaneous speech studies, emphasize different aspects of what is involved when a speaker formulates a message. Referential communication stresses the cognitive processes underlying communication, the propositional content of utterances and verification procedures. Assertions have to be formed and understood about objects, people, events and relationships between these. The verification processes involved are not assessments of propositions as true or false in themselves, as there is a tendency to accept what is said as true. It is the verification occurring when a proposition is matched to an external referent. The referential meaning of a word is generally highly specific, constrained to represent the particular entity being talked about in a given situation. In their review of referential communication skills, Glucksberg,

Krauss and Higgins (1975) argue that the central aspect of language acquisition is the acquisition of denotative as opposed to referential meanings. Denotative meanings are the generic ideas or concepts represented by a word. Learning how to use words for referential purposes is seen as essential to the acquisition of communicative competence as it necessitates selecting appropriate words in particular situations. Referential communication they claim is the simplest to conceptualize and the most basic communicative function.

Searle (1969) posits the speech act as the basic unit of communication and spontaneous speech studies tend to examine speech acts, interpreted in various ways, formal changes in speech and discourse conventions. As the illocutionary force of an utterance is based on a knowledge of when to use demands, requests, threats etc., it is possible that a social code rather than a conceptual one can be the basis of an appropriate utterance. Language is acquired in the context of social interaction and illocutionary acts are likely to play an important part in early communication (Dore 1975; Bates, Camaiono and Volterra 1975).

This oversimplified dichotomy of the research on communicative skills in young children is made in order to highlight the differences inherent in two approaches. Each has methodological drawbacks. The bizarre nature and cognitively overtaxing complexity of some tasks in the referential studies may be affected by aspects of a child's behaviour other than his communicative capacities. Spontaneous speech studies contend with problems of the validity of inferences made by adult observers concerning the intended meaning of utterances or the occurrence/non-occurrence of a speech event. The child is not forced, as he is in an experimental setting, to produce responses directly contingent on the propositional content of the previous utterances. He can choose to reformulate a message or change a topic, or make use of habitual gestural or extralinguistic cues.

The processes underlying communication make a tortuous knot, the unravelling of which may be distorted by any failure to appreciate that the processes are inter-related and that this inter-relationship is an important part of what the child is learning. Assessment of young children's communicative capacity will be considered from three perspectives.

The Child's Ability to Formulate Messages and Take Account of the Listener

No one would dispute that children below the age of seven talk to adults and other children for a variety of purposes. The interest centres on the young child's capacity to formulate messages which will enable a particular listener to understand what he means. Referential communication tasks show that young children's messages are generally inadequate, failing to provide relevant clues and being too subjective or ambiguous to admit listener comprehension (Glucksberg, Krauss and Higgins 1975). These inadequacies could be a function of the child's inability to take the listener's perspective or of task requirements creating a breakdown in the initial encoding stages. Structured referential tasks tend to adopt one of two methods to elicit messages from children; either (i) the description of abstract shapes (Glucksberg, Krauss and Weisberg 1966) or, (ii) the finding of a word clue to differentiate a designated target word in word pairs. For example, in the word pair river/*sea*, an appropriate clue word for the target word *sea* would be *waves* (Rosenberg and Cohen 1966). Using the latter model, Asher and Parke (1975) propose that communication failure occurs in the comparison stage when children have to distinguish two similar words. They found when only sampling was required, because the referent and non-referent were unrelated (river/*glove*), that second, fourth and sixth graders all gave word clues which differentiated the two words. When a comparison was needed (river/*sea*) second graders (7-8 years) were significantly worse than sixth graders (12-13 years). Also, children who were poor at encoding failed to make comparisons even for themselves (Asher and Oden 1976). When presented with their own communications two weeks later they could not fully interpret them.

This supports the view that communication failure is initially task related. It goes against the notion of the child being egocentric and communicating only for himself. Also it is contrary to evidence concerning the child's ability to interpret his own subjective descriptions of abstract shapes (Glucksberg, Krauss and Weisberg 1966). But it is doubtful whether tasks which create communication failure in the initial processing stages give a useful picture of the young child's capacity to communicate. Furthermore an examination of adults' performance on tasks, such as giving coherent directions, could well reveal similar limitations.

Egocentricism has been cited as a major factor contributing to children's poor performance on communication tasks (Flavell, Botkin, Fry, Wright and Jarvis 1968). Egocentricism is a diffuse notion which is subject to problems of interpretation when trying to decide how far the child communicates only for his own benefit or is only able to take his own perspective. When the young child has to cope with complex verbal or visual tasks his performance is poor compared to

that of older children, so other cognitive factors are compounded
with listener related needs (Piaget 1926). Children's performance on
simple visual role taking tasks shows they are aware of the listener's
perspective (Shantz 1970; Masangkay, McClusky, McIntyre, Sims-
Knight, Vaughn and Flavell 1974). Although children do at times talk
only to communicate with themselves, this does not preclude a
potential for social speech (Vygotsky 1962). Mueller (1972)
demonstrated children's awareness of their listener by examining
responses to utterances. An analysis of speech exchanges between
children from 3:6 to 5:6 years showed only 15 per cent of the utterances
evoked no response, 62 per cent successfully elicited replies and the
remaining 23 per cent received visual acknowledgement. Similar results
were recorded by Garvey and Hogan (1973). Even though they
discerned more egocentric speech in the younger children than
Mueller did, they demonstrated that genuinely social speech existed.

Children can also adapt what they say to take account of the
listener's needs. In a simple game situation even three-year-olds
could give more explicit descriptions to a 'blind' as opposed to a
sighted adult (Maratsos 1973). In a more natural setting, Menig-
Peterson (1975) found that various events (a guinea-pig escaping from
a cage or orange juice 'accidentally' spilt by an adult) elicited different
descriptions from children recounting the event a week later to an
adult who had, or had not, witnessed them. There were errors and
inaccuracies in the children's reports but the descriptions were
modified to fit the respective listener's knowledge. Children appear to
have an awareness of different perspectives but lack the cognitive
capacity to cope with certain task demands. Egocentricism may not be
a quality specific to children but may occur throughout life (Looft
1972).

Taking account of the listener's needs presumes an awareness that
other people can have different viewpoints. In four stages outlining
the development of interpersonal inferences Flavell (1974) proposes
that this awareness marks the first stage which he terms 'existence'.
This is followed by a recognition that the situation requires inferences
about the other person's experience (need) and the ability to act upon
this (inference). Finally there is the capacity to use this information
for some situationally appropriate interpersonal end (application). At
this level the child can perceive the role of the other person and so
adapt his message to meet the needs of his listener. Selman (1971)
proposes similar changes in role taking skills. Before about the age of
six, even though the child may know the other person has a different
viewpoint, he may be unable to specify what it is. After this he is able

to make inferences about the intentions and thoughts of another but not till about ten years can he simultaneously be aware of both his own and the other's perspective.

Evidence for a relationship between communication skills and standard egocentrism tasks is equivocal. Shatz and Gelman (1973) found that although only 37 per cent of 4-year-olds tested on egocentricism tasks performed successfully, their spontaneous speech differed depending on whether they were talking to 2-year-olds, peers or adults. Significantly more short, simple utterances with more repetitions and attention words were used to 2-year-olds. Other studies show that children are able to adapt the form and function of their speech (Sachs and Devin 1976), to use a variety of speech registers to convey different meanings in different social contexts (Weeks 1971) and to switch codes, whining to mothers, for example, but engaging in verbal play with peers (Gleason 1973). These studies provide no evidence on how content is adapted to meet listener needs, whereas this is the criterion basis of referential studies. The formal and functional aspects of speech provide the basis for adaptation in spontaneous speech. It is largely on these measures that children are shown to formulate messages which take account of listener needs. Satisfaction '. . . with evidence that suggests the speaker has attempted to meet the mind of the listener' (Gelman and Shatz 1977) reduces the requirement for comprehension of the propositional content.

Somewhat paradoxically however, Hoy (1975), replicating the Glucksberg, Krauss and Weisberg (1966) study, found when children were used as listeners they could make 'correct guesses' and interpret many of the speaker's messages despite their poor quality.

The Child's Awareness of the Role of the Message

'If children fail to understand one another, it is because they think that they do understand one another. The explainer believes from the start that the reproducer will grasp everything.' (Piaget 1926). This proposal assumes that the young child is unaware that the role of the message is to convey meaning. It suggests a failure to recognize that the message has to be evaluated for comprehensibility by the speaker when producing it and by the listener before he can respond. An optimal message has to take account of both the context and the listener so that discriminatory words based on criterion attributes enable the listener to respond appropriately. The directive 'Look at the long legged bird,' gives no positive indication of the intended referent in a group comprising a flamingo, a stork or a bikini clad beauty queen. Nor can an appropriate response be made to the suggestion 'We'll play the same game as before,' by someone not previously there.

Children may be aware that their message is inadequate but be unable to change it. Attempts to train children to communicate more effectively by making them evaluate the quality of messages have met with mixed results (Fry 1969; Shantz and Wilson 1972). Asher (1976) finding second graders could not evaluate whether messages were good or poor attributed this to an inability to make adequate comparisons when word pairs were used as stimuli.

Robinson and Robinson (1976a and b) proposed that young children do not have even a rudimentary notion of the role of the message and its relation to communication failure. When deliberately given messages of poor quality and asked who was to blame for the resulting breakdown in communication, almost all 5:6-6:6-year-olds blamed the listener, while older children tended to blame the speaker. An intermediate group most frequently blamed the experimenter (speaker for half the trials). Reinterpreting their results however, they concluded that listener 'blamers' did have some understanding of the message as they were able to indicate inappropriateness and make corrections (Robinson and Robinson 1977). They concluded that the development of general classificatory skills and not the acquisition of understanding about the nature of communication was responsible for these differences. Robinson and Robinson (in press) posit tentative proposals for the development of the awareness of the role of the message. First the child assumes all messages are good, then recognizes that some are better than others on the basis of their likelihood of communicating successfully. The ability to see poor messages as sources of communication failure develops from this. Initially when the child realizes the speaker's message can be responsible for communication failure he tends to over apply the rule of blaming the speaker. He is then able to consistently consider the properties of the message and its concomitant outcome.

If children make appropriate responses to utterances, can this be taken as evidence that they can evaluate the quality of the message? Some children can show an extraordinary awareness of the way language is used (Gleitman, Gleitman and Shipley 1972). Generally it may be that utterances classified as appropriate responses in studies of children's spontaneous speech reflect an evaluation of the function of the message rather than the propositional content. As Keenan and Klein (1974) point out, 'A relevant response can be constructed at a fairly low level of processing . . . If the child does process the previous speaker's utterance at the semantic level the presence of salient objects in the environment usually serves as a focus for joint attention'. The twins they studied, age 2:9 years, frequently adapted their utterances to the content as well as the form of the previous speaker's utterance. Content however in this instance consisted largely of fragments of songs or rhymes which were imitated or expanded by the listener. Bloom, Rocissano and Hood (1976) suggest that imitation is frequently used, particularly in complex situations, as it provides an easy way for the young child to process linguistic form and maintain the topic of the conversation. They were examining the sources of contextual contingency in adult-child discourse and proposed that certain rules of discourse function independently of understanding. The child knows when to speak and when he is being spoken to, and this constitutes the basis of the child's performance. The major development they noted was an increase in messages which shared and added to information contained in the previous utterance. However Dore (1977) found that children between 2:10 and 3:3 years talking in a nursery were able to understand the content of utterances and act appropriately. They showed full comprehension of both propositional and pragmatic intentions in their responses to questions of various types. Young children know a great deal about question/response routines, being aware for instance of the subtleties of contingent analysis (Garvey 1977):

Child 1.   This is a nice place.   Child 2.   What's a nice place?
                                                                         This room?

Children's developing ability to analyze the semantic content of utterances appears to stem from a willingness to co-operate in verbal interactions, the child's initial concept of the message being that it functions to sustain the interaction. The listener is relied upon to use various strategies to solve the comprehension problem. If he fails to do so, the young child may well start a new topic (Bloom, Rocissano and Hood 1976). This may or may not indicate a developing awareness that the speaker's message is responsible for communication failure but the evidence suggests that there are different levels of awareness of the role of the message. The question now is whether children are able to act on an awareness of message failure and what measures they can take to rectify it.

The Young Child's Ability to Provide Feedback

A skilled speaker can utilize cues from a listener indicating that a message is inadequate, evaluate what additional information is needed and adjust his utterance accordingly. The skilled listener is able to provide cues having recognized insufficiencies in the message. Karabenick and Miller (1977) found that although 5-year-old children showed some awareness of a need to provide feedback, their attempts to do so were inappropriate. In an earlier study Glucksberg and Krauss (1967) failed to encourage kindergarten children and first graders to change their descriptions of abstract shapes. They had three conditions using different forms of request for feedback: (i) 'Tell me more about it.' (ii) 'I don't understand what you mean.' (iii) These two requests were combined. The children however either repeated their initial descriptions or remained silent.

But young children are capable of reorientating their message if it is made absolutely clear to them what is being asked. Peterson, Danner and Flavell (1972) gave children of 4 and 7 years the implicit feedback used by Glucksberg and Krauss but included an explicit condition. All the children altered their message in the explicit condition but only 7-year-olds did in the implicit one. Fishbein and Osborne (1971) also found that corrective feedback can improve performance if given at the appropriate level.

In studies of spontaneous speech the ability to adapt speech can be inferred from the provision of feedback in response to the needs of the listener. Repetitions for instance, although dismissed as inadequate feedback in the studies cited above, may be taken as the 4-year-old's response to the 2-year-old's need to have information reinforced before he can act. Precise evidence for definite feedback however is sparse. Gelman and Shatz (1977) found clarifications of previous utterances occurred very infrequently in 4-year-olds' speech to adults and not at all to 2-year-olds. Children may, however, according to Sachs and Devin (1976) have some abstract notion of appropriateness that is not dependent on listener cues. Children can adapt their speech without feedback as they found when 2-5 year olds were asked to talk to a baby doll. Bates (1975) suggests that young children talking to other young children tend not to insist upon uninterpretable messages being clarified, they fail to react to non-verbal or implicit clues. This means that children receiving their linguistic input largely from peers rather than adults are at a disadvantage. However, as adults frequently respond to intended meanings in inadequately formulated messages this is debatable.

According to the way in which communicative capacity is measured, different assessments can be made of the young child's competence. Appraisal of his performance as good or poor can be accounted for in several ways: as a function of age or task complexity; or whether referential skills are tested in structured settings or discourse ability investigated in natural settings. Children can formulate messages to take account of the situation and the listener's perspective; they have some awareness of the role of the message and are able to give feedback. Younger children however are limited in the contexts in which they can show these abilities and their performance varies from that of older children.

THE DEVELOPMENT OF COMMUNICATION

Referential Aspects of Language Use

The development of referential communication is essentially linked to the child's conceptual development, his classification skills and the development of word meaning (Clark 1973; Nelson 1974; Leonard 1977). The child has to be aware that entities can be identified by attaching various words to them which have to be selected at the level appropriate to the situation.

As Olson (1970) points out, the critical information for making referential decisions is cognitive, based on the speaker's knowledge of the referent and his ability to differentiate it from a set of alternatives. The name chosen for any particular referent can be correctly indicated by words at different levels in category hierarchies. A spaniel, for instance, might be termed animal, dog, spaniel or cocker-spaniel though the word generally chosen will be the one most frequently used. This Brown (1958) calls the *level of usual utility*, that is the most frequent name for a thing is that name which most usually discriminates the referent from potentially confusable non-referents. Children have to learn to select the level of word appropriate to a particular context so that they not only perceive the object with its defining word at the level of usual utility but can alter the category level if this is insufficient as a discriminating referent. Brown suggested that the child initially uses words given to him by adults and attaches his concepts to these. Following Rosch, Mervis, Gray, Johnson and Boyes-Braem (1976) investigations into linguistic reference and concept formation Brown now proposes that the child attaches his own word onto what is most perceptually salient (Brown 1977). The concept comes first and the word attaches to the 'basic object level,' that is the level of greatest physical distinctness and utility for the widest variety of situations. However, as Schlesinger (1977) points out children have to discover the boundaries of words. After constructing a map of the world through extra-linguistic experience the child utilizes his linguistic input to draw the borders between adjacent categories. The young child's initial difficulties in making appropriate reference may stem from a restricted appraisal of word and concept boundaries due to his limited experience as much as from a limited capacity for making comparisons. Children make comparisons even when they are over-generalizing words. Although 'dog' may be used for several four legged animals, children can correctly select the picture of a dog from other animal referents.

A child acquires concepts generally in situations where the object, event or relationship is observable, where direct reference is possible. He is not often called upon to make indirect reference. Baron (1977) hypothesized that children initially begin to recognize that names are separable from what they represent then realize that not knowing a name does not inevitably create a breakdown in communication. They can adopt other strategies either by using descriptions or making up new names.

Even in the preverbal stage children display deictic and referential abilities (Bruner 1973). Brown (1973) assessed the semantic appropriateness of children's use of the definite and indefinite article to denote what was being referred to in both verbal and non-verbal contexts. His evidence indicates that their appropriate use becomes stable at about 2:6-3:6 years. Specific reference largely occurred in relation to entities present in the immediate environment while non-specific reference through use of the indefinite article occurred for objects or people not in sight. Maratsos (1976) points out that the child learning to use the definite and indefinite article correctly has to formulate a semantic system which is both abstract and sensitive to discourse conventions. This includes taking account of the listener's view of particular referents. This, however, appears to come later than the child taking into account his own knowledge of class membership and recursive use in the linguistic system. He suggests that semantic acquisition of great analytical complexity takes place with great rapidity in the early years and is much more rapid than the acquisition of lexical semantics.

The pre-operational child appears to have an awareness of reference which is quite complex and develops strategies to cope with indirect reference. He lacks, however, the ability to match words with concepts that will enable a listener to identify referents when the stimuli are too abstract or arbitrary and the task is cognitively overtaxing. His experience is limited and his restricted conceptual and word boundaries force him to make seemingly egocentric encodings based on his own limited knowledge and experience.

Social Aspects of Speech

The child's capacity to communicate involves other uses of language than the encoding and interpreting of the propositional content of utterances. Language is acquired in a communicative context (Nelson 1973; Bruner 1973; Lewis and Rosenblum 1977). Linguistic behaviour can be seen to have its origins in a more general communicative system stemming from mother/infant interaction patterns (Lewis and Freedle 1973). Even at 12 weeks mother and infant affect each other's behaviour in a way that is non-random, sequential and determined by the situation. Bruner (1973) claims that the semantic system derives from social interaction. By the time the child can use words referentially he knows a considerable amount about the nature of indicating. Reference stems from the joint attention of the mother and child centring on objects, while ritualized games (peek-a-boo) lead to 'learning the nature of semantic roles by taking roles in reciprocal interactions'.

Garvey (1974) also focuses on games as important for the development of communication. She proposes children initially lack the skills and talents to interact therefore interaction is initially centred in games. As the child becomes able to sustain interactions, play becomes less important and he can use just verbal means. As routines and repetitions are found in child/child but not in mother/child discourse, Bloom, Rocissano and Hood (1976) conclude that adults give monitored support which facilitates the development of participation in conversations. Young children appear to have a surprisingly well developed pragmatic competence in their use of language. Though they may not encode the precise propositional content of utterances and rely heavily on context for interpreting linguistic cues, they are able to make utterances contingent on both the form and content of preceding utterances (Dore 1977; Garvey 1977). This is apparent in quite subtle ways. Ervin-Tripp (1977) finds evidence that children can differentiate and interpret various forms of directives as requests, for example; imperatives (Give me the scissors), imbedded imperatives (Could you give me a match) and hints (It's cold in here with the window open). Sinclair and Coulthard (1975) framed general rules for 9-year-olds' appreciation of directions in the classroom. They found a well established awareness of such rules as interpreting declaratives (Someone is talking) or interrogatives (Are you chewing?) as commands to stop if referring to a prohibited activity.

CONCLUSIONS

Referential studies may underestimate the young child's capacity to communicate. The contrived situations and difficult cognitive tasks show performance to be a function of age and task complexity affecting several levels of processing. Referential tasks tend to show what children cannot do, whereas spontaneous speech studies, based largely on an appreciation of the rules of discourse, describe what children can do. Spontaneous speech studies show that children can make their utterances contingent on the content as well as the form and function of a previous speaker's utterance, but the way the ideas are expressed is not explored with the same rigour as in referential tasks. A great deal remains to be learnt about the integration of the processes involved in communication particularly how the child develops the ability to find non-egocentric ways of talking about objects and events which are unfamiliar and/or not present in the immediate environment. The interesting question is how much this relies on the more socially orientated features of communication for its development.

Attempts to discover what the children know as speakers and how and why they develop their capacity to communicate benefit from having many methods and approaches. Consider for example the sophisticated awareness of language in this 4-year-old's corrective feedback (Gleitman, Gleitman and Shipley 1972) particularly in view of the observed poor performance generally found:

> Mother: Hold on tight.
> Child: Isn't it *tightly*?

Combining knowledge gained from several areas of research helps to expose the questions that need to be asked particularly in an area where findings can be apparently so discrepant.

REFERENCES

Asher, S. R. 1976. 'Children's ability to appraise their own and another person's communication performance.' *Develop. Psychol. 12*, 24-32.

Asher, S. R. and Oden, S. L. 1976. 'Children's failure to communicate: an assessment of comparison and egocentricism explanations.' *Develop. Psychol. 12*, 132-9.

Asher, S. R. and Parke, R. D. 1975. 'Influence of sampling and comparison processes on the development of communication effectiveness. *J. Educ. Psychol. 67*, 64-75.

Baron, N. S. 1977. 'The acquisition of indirect reference: functional motivations for continued language learning in children.' *Lingua 42*, 349-64.

Bates, E. 1975. 'Peer relations and the acquisition of language.' In M. Lewis and L. A. Rosenblum (eds) *Friendship and peer relations*. New York: Wiley.

Bates, E., Camaiono, L. and Volterra, V. 1975. 'The acquisition of performatives prior to speech.' *Merrill-Palmer Quart. 21*, 205-26.

Bloom, L., Rocissano, L. and Hood, L. 1976. 'Adult-child discourse: developmental interaction between information processing and linguistic knowledge.' *Cog. Psychol. 8*, 521-2.

Brown, R. 1958. 'How shall a thing be called?' *Psychol. Rev. 65*, 14-21.

Brown, R. 1973. *A first language*. London: George Allen and Unwin.

Brown, R. 1977. Introduction to C. E. Snow and C. A. Ferguson (eds) *Talking to children: language input and acquisition*. Cambridge: Cambridge University Press.

Bruner, J. S. 1973. 'From communication to language – a psychological perspective.' *Cognition 3*, 255-87.

Clark, E. 1973. 'What's in a word? On the child's acquisition of semantics in his first language.' In T. Moore (ed.) *Cognitive development and the acquisition of language*. New York: Academic Press.

Dore, J. 1975. Holophrases, speech acts and language universals. *J. Child Lang. 2*, 21-39.

Dore, J. 1977. '"On them Sheriff": A pragmatic analyses of children's responses.' In S. Ervin-Tripp and C. Mitchell-Kernan (eds) *Child discourse*. New York: Academic Press.

Ervin-Tripp, S. 1977. 'Wait for me, roller skate!' In S. Ervin-Tripp and C. Mitchell-Kernan (eds) *Child discourse*. New York: Academic Press.

Fishbein, H. D. and Osborne, M. 1971. 'The effects of feedback variations on referential communication of children.' *Merrill-Palmer Quart. 17*, 243-50.

Flavell, J. H. 1974. 'The development of inferences about others.' In T. Mischel (ed.) *Understanding other persons*. Oxford: Blackwell, Basil and Mott.

Flavell, J. H., Botkin, P. T., Fry, C. L., Wright, J. W. and Jarvis, P. E. 1968. *The development of role taking and communicative skills in young children*. New York: Wiley.

Fry, C. L. 1969. 'Training children to communicate with listeners who have varying listener requirements.' *J. genet. Psychol. 114*, 153-66.

Garvey, C. 1974. 'Some properties of social play.' *Merrill-Palmer Quart. 20*, 163-80.

Garvey, C. 1977. 'The contingent query: a dependent act in conversation.' In M. Lewis and L. A. Rosenblum (eds) *Interaction, conversation and the development of language*. New York: Wiley.

Garvey, C. and Hogan, R. 1973. 'Social speech and social interaction: egocentricism revisited.' *Child Develop. 44*, 562-8.

Gelman, R. and Shatz, M. 1977. 'Appropriate speech adjustments: the operation of conversational constraints on talk to two-year-olds.' In M. Lewis and L. A. Rosenblum (eds) *Interaction, conversation and the development of language*. New York: Wiley.

Gleason, J. B. 1973. 'Code switching in children's language.' In T. E. Moore (ed.) *Cognitive development and the acquisition of language*. New York: Academic Press.

Gleitman, L. R., Gleitman, H. and Shipley, E. F. 1972. 'The emergence of the child as grammarian.' *Cognition 1*, 137-64.

Glucksberg, S. and Krauss, R. 1967. 'What do people say after they have learned to talk?' *Merrill-Palmer Quart. 13*, 309-16.

Glucksberg, S., Krauss, R. M. and Higgins, E. T. 1975. 'The development of referential communication skills.' In F. Horowitz (ed.) *Review of child development research 4*, Chicago: University of Chicago Press.

Glucksberg, S., Krauss, R. M. and Weisberg, R. 1966. 'Referential communication in nursery school children: method and some preliminary findings.' *J. Exp. Child Psychol. 3*, 333-42.

Gordon, D. and Lakoff, G. 1975. 'Conversational postulates.' In P. Cole and J. L. Morgan (eds) *Syntax and semantics 3: Speech acts.* New York: Academic Press.

Grice, H. P. 1975. 'Logic and conversation.' In P. Cole and J. L. Morgan (eds) *Syntax and semantics 3: Speech acts.* New York: Academic Press.

Hoy, E. A. 1975. 'Measurement of egocentricism in young children's communication.' *Develop. Psychol. 11*, 392-7.

Karabenick, J. D. and Miller, S. A. 1977. 'The effects of age, sex and listener feedback on grade school children's referential communication.' *Child Develop. 48*, 678-83.

Keenan, E. O. 1974. 'Conversational competence in children.' *J. Child Lang. 1*, 163-83.

Keenan, E. and Klein, E. 1974. 'Coherency in children's discourse.' Paper presented at the Summer Meeting of the Linguistic Society of America, Amherst, Massachusetts.

Krauss, R. M. and Glucksberg, S. 1969. 'The development of communication: competence as a function of age.' *Child Develop. 40*, 255-6.

Leonard, L. B. 1977. *Meaning in child language.* New York: Grune and Stratton.

Lewis, M. and Freedle, R. 1973. 'Mother and infant dyad: the cradle of meaning.' In P. Pliner, L. Krames and T. Alloway (eds) *Communication and affect: language and thought.* New York: Academic Press.

Lewis, M. and Rosenblum, L. A. 1977. (eds) *Interaction, conversation and the development of language.* New York: Wiley.

Looft, W. 1972. 'Egocentricism and social interaction across the lifespan.' *Psychol. Bull. 78*, 73-92.

Maratsos, M. 1973. 'Non-egocentric communicative abilities in preschool children.' *Child Develop. 44*, 697-700.

Maratsos, M. P. 1976. *The use of definite and indefinite reference in young children: an experimental study in semantic acquisition.* Cambridge: Cambridge University Press.

Masangkay, Z., McClusky, K., McIntyre, C., Sims-Knight, J., Vaughn, B. and Flavell, J. H. 1974. 'The early development of inferences about the visual percepts of others.' *Child Develop. 45*, 357-66.

Menig-Peterson, C. L. 1975. 'The modification of communicative behaviour in preschool aged children as a function of the listener's perspective.' *Child Develop. 46*, 1015-18.

Mueller, E. 1972. 'The maintenance of verbal exchanges between young children.' *Child Develop. 43*, 930-8.

Nelson, K. 1973. 'Structure and strategy in learning to talk.' *Monogr. soc. res. Child Develop. 38*.

Nelson, K. 1974. 'Concept, word and sentence: interrelationships in acquisition and development.' *Psychol. Rev. 81*, 267-85.

Olson, D. R. 1970. 'Language and thought: aspects of a cognitive theory of semantics.' *Psychol. Rev. 77*, 257-73.

Peterson, C. L., Danner, F. W. and Flavell, J. H. 1972. 'Developmental changes in children's response to three indications of communicative failure.' *Child Develop. 43*, 1463-8.

Piaget, J. 1926. *The language and thought of the child.* London: Routledge, and Kegan Paul.

Piaget, J. 1962. *Comments on Vygotsky's critical remarks concerning the language and thought of the child and judgement and reasoning in the child.* Cambridge, Mass.: MIT Press.

Robinson, E. J. and Robinson, W. P. 1976a. 'The young child's understanding of communication.' *Develop. Psychol. 13*, 328-33.

Robinson, E. J. and Robinson, W. P. 1976b. 'Developmental changes in the child's explanation of communication failure.' *Austr. J. Psychol. 28*, 155-65.

Robinson, E. J. and Robinson, W. P. 1977. 'The young child's explanations of communication failure: a reinterpretation of results.' *Percep. and Mot. Skills 44*, 363-6.

Robinson, E. J. and Robinson, W. P. (in press). 'Development in the understanding of causes of success and failure in verbal communication.' *Cognition* (in press).

Rosch, E., Mervis, C. B., Gray, W. D., Johnson, D. M. and Boyes-Braem, P. 1976. 'Basic objects in natural categories.' *Cog. Psychol. 8*, 382-439.

Rosenberg, S. and Cohen, B. D. 1966. 'Referential processes of speakers and listeners.' *Psychol. Rev. 73*, 208-31.

Sachs, J. and Devin, J. 1976. 'Young children's use of age-appropriate speech styles in social interaction and role-playing.' *J. Child Lang. 3*, 81-98.

Schlesinger, I. M. 1977. 'The role of cognitive development and linguistic input in language acquisition.' *J. Child Lang. 4*, 153-69.

Searle, J. 1969. *Speech acts.* Cambridge: Cambridge University Press.

Selman, R. 1971. 'Taking another's perspective: role taking development in early childhood.' *Child Develop. 42*, 171-83.

Shantz, C. U. 1970. 'Assessment of spatial egocentricism through expectancy violation.' *Psychon. Sci. 18*, 93-4.

Shantz, C. and Wilson, K. 1972. 'Training communication skills in young children.' *Child Develop. 43*, 693-8.

Shatz, M. and Gelman, R. 1973. 'The development of communication skills: modifications in the speech of young children as a function of the listener.' *Monogr. soc. res. Child Develop. 38*.

Sinclair, J. and Coulthard, R. M. 1975. *Towards an analysis of discourse: the English used by teachers and pupils.* London: Oxford University Press.

Vygotsky, L. 1962. *Thought and language.* Cambridge, Mass.: MIT Press.

Weeks, T. E. 1971. 'Speech registers in young children.' *Child Develop. 42*, 1119-31.

Chapter 8

The theory of colour vision

J. D. MOLLON

In 1900 more than sixty theories of colour vision were extant and no psychologist of stature could afford to be without a Theory of his own. Parsons, in his *Colour vision* of 1915, saw fit to review eleven Theories. Judd, in Steven's *Handbook* of 1951, listed eight. The textbooks and the examiners of the 1960s distinguished two survivors, those eponymously coupled with Helmholtz and Hering. Now at last it is possible to speak of the theory of colour vision. The details of the system remain the subject of vigorous controversies, but the debates are those of sober men who share common assumptions, common standards of stimulus control and common criteria for the acceptability of data.

TRICHROMACY

The most fundamental fact about human colour vision remains the fact of *trichromacy*: if we take three, suitably chosen wavelengths, it will be possible, by mixing them together, to match any other wavelength or mixture of wavelengths. In a colour-matching experiment of this kind, we are not required to use one particular set of three 'primaries', but it is convenient to space them along the visible spectrum and essential that no one of them is matchable by a mixture of the remaining two. Thus by just three variables we can specify the visual effect of any given wavelength or mixture of wavelengths. Sometimes, it is true, one of the variables will have to be negative: that is to say, when matching the saturated hue of a monochromatic[1] stimulus we shall often have to take one of our primary lights and add it to the light that is to be matched.

---

[1] Monochromatic light is light of a single wavelength. In practice, a narrow band of wavelengths is meant.

Although it is often said that trichromacy was first stated in 1757 by Lomonosov, the 'Russian Leonardo', the fact was explicitly known much earlier in the eighteenth century. For in 1719 a ne'er-do-well but ingenious engraver, J. C. Le Blon, arrived in London seeking capital to exploit his method of 'printing paintings' by a three-colour process. Shortly afterwards (probably in 1723, although the book is undated) he set out the principles in his neglected monograph, *Il coloritto* (Figure 8.1). Le Blon had no talent for business and

I.

Of *Preliminaries.*

COLORITTO, or the *Harmony* of Colouring, is the *Art* of *Mixing* COLOURS, in order to reprefent naturally, in all Degrees of *painted* Light and Shade, the fame FLESH, or the Colour of any other Object, that is reprefented in the true or *pure* Light.

PAINTING can reprefent all *vifible* Objects with three Colours, *Tellow, Red,* and *Blue* ; for all other Colours can be compos'd of thefe *Three,* which I call *Primitive* ; for Example,

> *Tellow*
> and   } make an *Orange Colour.*
> *Red*

> *Red*
> and   } make a *Purple* and *Violet Colour.*
> *Blue*

> *Blue*
> and   } make a *Green Colour.*
> *Tellow*

And a *Mixture* of thofe *Three* Original Colours makes a *Black,* and all *other* Colours whatfoever ; as I have demonftrated by my Invention of *Printing* Pictures *and* Figures *with their* natural *Colours.*

I am only fpeaking of *Material* Colours, or thofe ufed by *Painters* ; for a *Mixture* of *all* the primitive *impalpable* Colours, that cannot be felt, will not produce *Black,* but the very Contrary, *White*; as the Great Sir ISAAC NEWTON has demonftrated in his Opticks.

> *White,* is a Concentering, or an *Excefs* of Lights.
> *Black,* is a deep Hiding, or *Privation* of Lights.

But

Figure 8.1 A page from *Il coloritto* by J. C. Le Blon (c. 1723). Notice that the rules that Le Blon gives are for mixing pigments, but that he grasps the difference between this 'substractive' mixture and the 'additive' mixture of lights. For the difference between additive and subtractive mixture see Marriott (1976).

died in poverty in Paris in 1741. The fact of trichromacy became a commonplace in the second half of the eighteenth century, but it was almost universally regarded as a fact of physics rather than as a fact of human physiology. The confusion lingered on among leading scientists until as late as 1850 and it is still common among non-specialists.

Trichromacy is certainly a fact of physiology and almost certainly it has its basis in the existence of just three classes of retinal cone, with peak sensitivities at different points in the spectrum (Figure 8.2).

PRINCIPLE OF UNIVARIANCE

Any single cone, or any single class of cone, is in itself colour blind. Its response is governed by what W. A. H. Rushton has called the *Principle of Univariance:* the stimulus may vary in intensity and in wavelength but the response of a cone is thought to vary along only one dimension – the extent of its electrical polarization. Once a photon has been absorbed, all information about its energy level (or wavelength) is lost – although as wavelength is varied the *probability* of a given photon's being absorbed will vary according to the spectral sensitivity function[1] of the photopigment that the cone contains. Thus a change in intensity or a change in wavelength may produce the same change in the polarization of the cone. The Principle of Univariance means that it is wrong to say 'cones discriminate colour'; but by comparing the outputs of the individually colour-blind cones the visual system is nevertheless able to discriminate wavelength.

SPECTRAL SENSITIVITY FUNCTIONS

Ideally, to specify the visual effect of a light, we should take as our three variables the rates of absorption of photons in the three classes of cone, rather than the intensities of our three standard wavelengths. Unhappily the spectral sensitivity functions of the cones cannot be derived from the results of colour-matching experiments alone. Many methods of obtaining these crucial functions have been proposed. No method is entirely satisfactory. In most of the psychophysical procedures the principle has been to ensure that the observer's response depended on only one class of cone – either by using colour-blind

[1]The *spectral sensitivity function* is the curve relating sensitivity to wavelength. See, for example, Figure 8.2a.

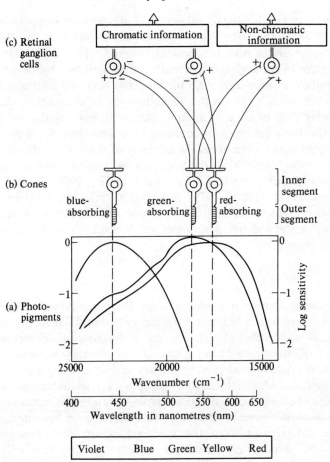

Figure 8.2 The initial stages of colour vision. a The probable spectral sensitivities of the three types of cone. Notice that the abscissa is plotted in terms of frequency (the reciprocal of wavelength), since spectral sensitivity functions of different pigments have nearly the same form when so plotted. The curves shown are based on the field-sensitivity data of Stiles (see text) and represent sensitivity at the cornea of the eye, when, that is, allowance has been made for absorption by the media of the eye and the macular pigment. b The three classes of cone. Notice that the so-called 'blue' cones have their peak sensitivity in the violet and the so-called 'red' cones have their peak sensitivity in the yellow-green. c Schematic representations of ganglion cells and their connections from different classes of cone. The two left-hand cells receive 'opponent' inputs from different classes of cone and thus potentially transmit colour information; the right-hand cell receives inputs of the same sign from red- and green-sensitive cones. Several other combinations of inputs have been reported in ganglion cells: for clarity, only three typical cells are represented here.

observers, or by adapting the other classes of cone with monochromatic fields to which the first class of cone is little sensitive, or by selecting retinal positions or stimulus parameters that favour a particular class of cones, or by combining two or more of these devices. One of the most systematically and widely used methods has been the field-sensitivity method of W. S. Stiles. In this procedure the experimenter isolates a particular class of cone by suitable choice of wavelengths for a test flash and for a background adapting field, and then, for a range of field wavelengths, determines the intensity of the field needed to raise the detection threshold of the test flash by a fixed amount. Several accounts of Stiles' method are available (Stiles 1978; Enoch 1972; Marriott 1976; Mollon 1979) and it is therefore not reviewed in detail here. Instead we outline two recently introduced methods, one psychophysical and one densitometric, chosen because they illustrate general principles.

Silent Substitution ·

This general method has been used by Rushton, Powell and White (1973 a, b), who refer to it as the 'exchange threshold' method; and by Cavonius and Estévez (1975), who call it the 'spectral compensation' method. Rushton (1975) has given an introductory account of the particular procedure adopted by himself and his collaborators.

In methods of this kind the Principle of Univariance (*v. supra*) provides the basis of a novel means of isolating the response of a single class of cones. Most of the experiments have been performed in the red-green part of the spectrum where the blue-sensitive mechanism makes little significant contribution and thus only one further mechanism has to be eliminated. The threshold event is not a simple increment (as in the method of Stiles) but the transition between two wavelengths that have been equated for their effects on one of the two remaining mechanisms. The Principle of Univariance means that if two wavelengths are adjusted in intensity so that they lead to the same rate of quantum catch[1] in, say, the green cones, then the transition between the two wavelengths will be invisible to the green cones and so detectable only by the red cones: for the green cones the substitution is silent. The method may appear circular to the reader, since it seems to require that we know in advance the spectral sensitivity of at least one class of cone, but for the method to work it is enough to know the sensitivities only roughly at the outset – it

---

[1]'Rate of quantum catch' is Rushton's term for the rate at which photons are absorbed by a class of cone.

is only necessary that one class of cone should be much more sensitive to the transition than is the other class. Rushton *et al.* in fact take as their starting points the spectral sensitivities of those types of colour-blind observer (dichromats) who appear to have only one effective class of cone in the red-green range – red cones in the case of 'deuteranopes' and green cones in the case of 'protanopes'.

The second stage in Rushton's procedure closely resembles the field-sensitivity method of Stiles: the threshold for detecting the transition is measured on a green field (540 nm) and on a red field (640 nm) and the experimenter estimates how intense the red field must be to raise the threshold by the same amount as does the green field. When red and green fields are equated in this way it is assumed they are producing equal rates of absorption in the class of cones that has been detecting the transition. At this stage the method, like that of Stiles, is critically dependent on the assumption that sensitivity of the isolated class of cones depends only on the rate at which quanta are absorbed from the field by that class of cone – and is independent of the signals from the other classes of cone. Stiles himself demonstrated that this critical assumption is correct to a first approximation, but there is now good evidence that it is not always exactly true.

If we wish, the equation established by the second stage can now be used to arrange a silent substitution for this class of cone and the field sensitivity of the other class can then be measured. By an iterative process we are therefore able to check the validities of the spectral sensitivities assumed at the outset (see Figure 8.3).

The third stage of Rushton's procedure is to establish the spectral sensitivity of a given class of cone at wavelengths other than the two (540 and 640 nm) used in the second stage. Of course, it would be possible simply to extend the measurements of field sensitivity, finding at each wavelength the intensity of a field needed to bring the transition to threshold, but in fact Rushton and his collaborators now introduce an elegant twist to the method.

By mixing together the 540-nm and 640-nm lights it is possible to match any intermediate wavelength, λ. Rushton *et al.* set the intensities of the 540-nm and 640-nm lights so that they have equal effects on one of the classes of cone and they arrange these two beams to be orthogonally polarized. The mixing is then achieved by means of a rotatable polarizer, which at one extreme position transmits only green light and at the other, transmits only red. At intermediate positions, varying ratios of red and green are transmitted and the light appears yellow-green, yellow or orange, but the total number of photons

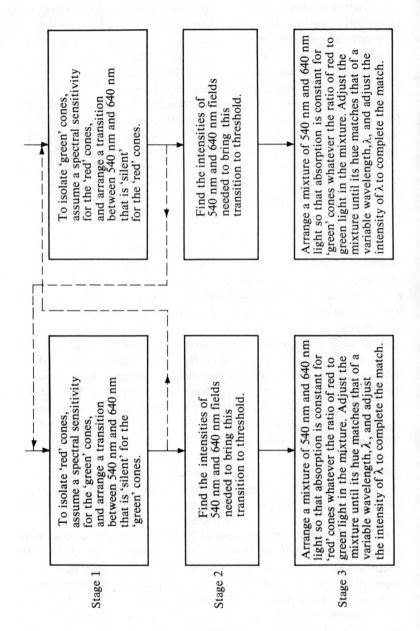

Figure 8.3 A schematic representation of the 'exchange threshold' method used by Rushton, Powell and White (1973a, b) to estimate the spectral sensitivities of 'red' and 'green' cones.

absorbed by the selected cones will remain constant. The observer is shown stripes illuminated by this red-green mixture and is asked to make them match interdigitated stripes that are illuminated with the single wavelength, λ. To make the hues identical he adjusts the red-green mixture (by rotating the polarizer) but to make the brightnesses identical he is allowed only to adjust the intensity of λ. Now, when the two sets of stripes appear identical the absorptions in all three classes of cone must have been equated. For each value of λ that we use we shall have found the intensity that leads to the same rate of absorption in our chosen class of cone as does the red-green mixture – and the reader will recall that the absorption from the latter is constant, whatever the ratio. These settings of intensity directly give us the spectral sensitivity of these cones, for sensitivity is defined as the reciprocal of the intensity required to produce a criterion effect. The *hue* of the stripes will have been varying as we varied λ, but this is because rates of absorption in other classes of cone have been varying: we have held constant the absorption in only one class of cone.

It is not merely for reasons of elegance that Rushton *et al.* introduce this third stage in their method: provided the hues of two stimuli are the same, matches of brightness can be made with greater precision and more speedily, than thresholds can be measured.

Measurements by the 'exchange threshold' method agree with other estimates (such as those of Stiles) in placing the peak sensitivities of the so-called 'green' and 'red' cones at $\sim$540 nm and $\sim$570 nm respectively. The method has not yet been extended to wavelengths shorter than 540 nm, where the blue-sensitive mechanism becomes significant, but in principle it is always possible to make a silent substitution for two mechanisms simultaneously – by passing between two lights that are confusable by dichromats.

Microspectrophotometry

Direct measurements of the pigments in individual primate cones were first published in 1964, by Brown and Wald and by Marks, Dobelle and MacNichol. In this technically formidable procedure of 'microspectrophotometry' a tiny monochromatic beam is passed through individual receptors in freshly dissected tissue. Cells are first centred in the measuring-beam with the help of an infra-red converter (to avoid bleaching). The light absorbed at each visible wavelength is then measured. Since light will be absorbed by material other than the photopigment, the experimenter either passes a reference beam through adjacent tissue and uses this as a baseline or else takes the difference between absorption in the receptor before bleaching and absorption after bleaching. The former procedure yields an *absorption spectrum*, the latter a *difference spectrum*; neither is necessarily the same as the *action spectrum*, the actual effectiveness of different wavelengths in producing a given physiological or psychophysical effect.

Unhappily, the early microspectrophotometric measurements were very noisy and only preliminary records (for a total of about twenty human and monkey cones) were ever published before these exciting experiments were abandoned. Because the density of the pigment was at the time thought to be low, the measuring beam (about 2 μm in diameter) was passed axially along the outer segment of the receptor, which has a length of about 30 μm and a diameter of only 1-2 μm: thus the measuring beam is likely to leak into adjacent cones and rods and the results will thereby be distorted. The difficulties of the technique are reviewed by Liebman (1972), who concludes that the measurements '. . . cannot be regarded as accurate to better than 20-30 nm'.

Recently, however, a fresh attempt has been made to obtain satisfactory microspectrophotometric measurements of primate cones. The instrument was one designed by Liebman and the measuring beam was passed *transversely* through the isolated outer segments of individual receptors. The density of pigment proves to be much higher than was previously thought: from the transverse data it is estimated that the optical density[1] would be 0.5 for light of the optimum wavelength passing axially along a 35-μm outer segment. Results for a large sample of cones from rhesus monkeys have been obtained by Bowmaker, Dartnall, Lythgoe and Mollon (1978) and for a human eye by Bowmaker and Dartnall (1979). For the rhesus monkeys, the peak sensitivities of the 'green' and 'red' cones lay at 536 $\pm$ 3.5 nm and at 564.5 nm $\pm$ 2.5 nm; for the human cones these values were 534 nm and 564 nm respectively. Blue-sensitive cones appear to be very rare; none was recorded in the sample of 82 rhesus cones and only 3 in the sample of 27 human cones. For man (and for cynomolgus macaque monkeys, which are closely related to rhesus monkeys) the 'blue' cones have their peak sensitivities in the extreme violet at about 420 nm – a value much shorter than that given by the early microspectrophotometric results.

Microspectrophotometric estimates of peak sensitivities for the three

---

[1]Optical density is expressed as the logarithm of the ratio of incident light to transmitted light.

classes of cone appear to coincide well with psychophysical estimates. The values for the 'blue' cones are brought into much closer coincidence when we allow for absorption by the lens of the eye, which is increasing steeply at short wavelengths. However, the comparison of absorption spectra with psychophysical action spectra is not to be made lightly: not only must we make assumptions about absorption by the macular pigment[1] and by the media of the eye, but we must also ignore the contribution of photoproducts to the microspectrophotometric measurements. A comparison that does overcome the first of these two difficulties is presented in Figure 8.4:

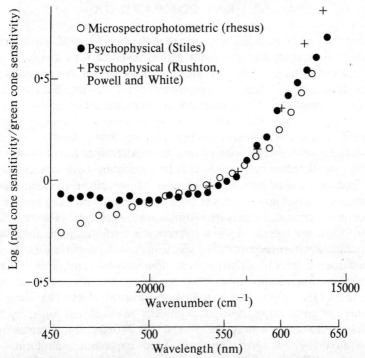

Figure 8.4   A comparison between microspectrophotometric and psychophysical estimates of the sensitivities of 'red' and 'green' cones. The microspectrophotometric results are for rhesus monkeys and are taken from the study of Bowmaker, Dartnall, Lythgoe and Mollon (1978); the psychophysical results are for man and are taken from Stiles (1978) and from Rushton, Powell and White (1973b). What is plotted in this figure is the logarithm of the ratio of the sensitivity of the 'red' cones to that of the 'green' cones. By plotting *ratios* of sensitivities in this way we can compare the psychophysical and microspectrophotometric data without making assumptions about absorption by the ocular media.

[1] An inert blue-absorbing pigment in the foveal region of the retina.

here the ratio of the sensitivities of the red and green psychophysical mechanisms is compared with the ratio of the sensitivities of 'green' and 'red' rhesus cones. This is a somewhat more secure comparison, since it is reasonable (though not entirely safe) to assume that absorption by the macular pigment and the media will affect green and red cones equally. The agreement is very pleasing – except at wavelengths less than 470 nm, where the microspectrophotometric data may be distorted by non-transparent products of bleaching.

NEURAL COMPARISON

Since the different classes of cone are individually colour blind, there cannot be colour vision without neural machinery to compare the outputs of different classes of cone. The necessity of this comparison has traditionally been obscured by controversies between the proponents of the trichromatic (three-cone) theory of colour vision and proponents of the rival 'opponent process' theory of Hering – controversies that are today redundant.

Differences between rates of quantum catch in different classes of cone are detected in a way closely analogous to the way local differences in illumination are detected. Many cells in the retina and the lateral geniculate nucleus (LGN) of the rhesus monkey appear to receive antagonistic inputs from different types of cone (Figure 8.2c): they show an increase in firing rate when their receptive fields are stimulated with one part of the spectrum and a decrease (below any spontaneous level of activity) when stimulated by another part of the spectrum. Such cells, called *colour opponent*, were first demonstrated in the LGN by De Valois (1965). A detailed electrophysiological survey of colour-opponent ganglion cells has been published by De Monasterio and Gouras (1975) and De Monasterio, Gouras and Tolhurst (1975 a, b), who have used chromatic adaptation to separate different types of cone input to a given cell and have then measured spectral sensitivity in an attenuated version of Stiles' technique (see above). They report almost all possible combinations of excitatory and inhibitory inputs from the three classes of cone. Most common were ganglion cells receiving opposed input from 'red' and 'green' cones, but many cells were 'trichromatic', having inputs from all three types of cone, two being opposed to the remaining one. Inputs from 'blue' cones were demonstrated only in 'trichromatic' cells.

Other cells in the retina and LGN are chromatically *non-opponent*:

they appear to receive inputs of the same sign from more than one class of cone. According to Gouras and his collaborators, such non-opponent ganglion cells have larger receptive fields and their responses are transient, whereas sustained responses characterize colour-opponent cells. Whether, as has often been suggested, the non-opponent cells signal brightness is an open question.

THE ODDITY OF THE BLUE MECHANISM

The trichromatic scheme is not an entirely tidy one, for it is no longer possible to neglect a catalogue of properties in which the blue-sensitive cone mechanism, as defined psychophysically by Stiles' method, differs from the red and green mechanisms.

Whereas genetic anomalies of the blue mechanism are rare, this mechanism seems disproportionately vulnerable to diseases that affect the retina, such as retinitis pigmentosa and diabetes mellitus. Even in its normal state its absolute sensitivity is low: the Weber fraction $(\Delta I/I)$, the percentage increment in intensity that can just be detected, is five times greater for the blue cones than for the red and green. This is the size of the discrepancy for Stiles' standard 1-deg, 200-msec flash, but if the target is made very small or very brief the difference in sensitivities increases and our vision becomes *tritanopic*, resembling that of the rare individuals who congenitally lack the blue-sensitive cones. The reason that the Weber fractions differ only by a factor of five when the target is large and long is that larger space and time constants provide some compensation for the basic insensitivity of the blue system. Thus the blue-sensitive mechanism shows much more extensive spatial integration than the red and green; its spatial resolution is correspondingly poor. Its time constants have been found to be longer, whether they are measured by the critical flicker-fusion-frequency, by reaction times or by the critical duration for Bloch's Law[1] (Mollon and Krauskopf 1973).

The basic insensitivity of the blue mechanism and several of the associated properties could be explained (directly or indirectly) if blue cones were relatively rare. That this is so is suggested by the

---

[1]The temporal summation of the visual system is expressed by Bloch's Law, which states that the psychophysical effect of a brief flash depends on the product of its intensity and duration. Thus a flash of intensity 1 (in arbitrary units) and duration 1 msec will be as detectable as a flash of intensity 0.1 and duration 10 msec. Bloch's Law holds (approximately) for flashes of less than a 'critical duration'; the latter, in the light-adapted eye, has a value of about 100 msec for the blue-sensitive mechanism and about 30 msec for the other cone mechanisms.

microspectrophotometric results and also by the results of Marc and Sperling (1977), who used a staining technique to identify particular classes of cone in the baboon retina.

A second group of anomalies is associated with the light- and dark-adaptation of the blue mechanism. One striking example is *transient tritanopia*: when the eye has been adapted to a long-wavelength field and the latter is then extinguished, the threshold for the blue mechanism does not recover according to the normal dark adaptation curve but rather the threshold actually rises and for several seconds does not return to the value that obtained when the adapting field was actually present (Mollon and Polden 1977). Typical results are shown in Figure 8.5a. It is significant that yellow or red adapting fields produce transient tritanopia but not white fields (Augenstein and Pugh 1977).

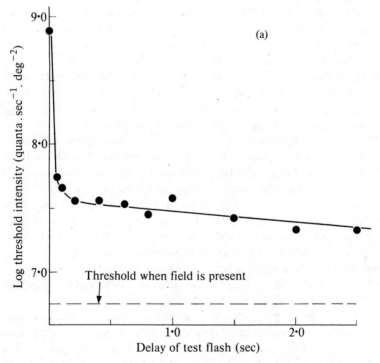

Figure 8.5 Two anomalies of the blue-sensitive mechanism of the eye. a *Transient tritanopia*. The data points show the threshold for a violet (445-nm) test flash in the first 2.5 sec after a yellow adapting field had been turned off. The dashed line shows the level of the threshold when the steady yellow field was present. The wavelength of the yellow field was 580 nm and its intensity $10^{9\cdot6}$ quanta.sec^{-1}.deg^{-2}. Unpublished data. Conditions as described in Mollon and Polden (1977). b *Negative masking*. The threshold for violet

Another anomaly is the *negative masking* of the blue mechanism, described by Polden and Mollon (1979) and representing a strange reversal of Weber's Law. The threshold is first found for a violet increment on a blue field of 473 nm. The size, duration and retinal position are chosen to favour detection by the blue mechanism. Yellow light of 575 nm is then added to the blue background. The wavelengths 473 nm and 575 nm are *complementaries*: when mixed in the correct proportions they yield white. The amount of added yellow is such as to render the composite field white. Although the field is now much brighter, the threshold for the violet target actually falls, by as much as 0.4 $\log_{10}$ units (Figure 8.5b).

These two strange phenomena and a number of related ones could be explained by two assumptions. First, near-threshold signals from

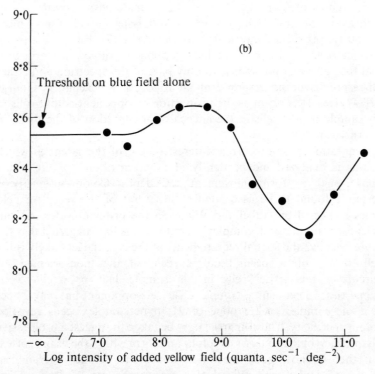

(420-nm) flashes is first measured on a blue (473-nm) field; this value is represented by the leftmost data point. Yellow light is then added and the threshold falls, being minimum when the composite field appears white. The intensity of the fixed blue field was $10^{9.7}$ quanta.sec^{-1}.deg^{-2}. (Replotted from Polden and Mollon, 1979). Note that the ordinates of the two graphs in this figure are in the same units but are plotted to different scales.

the blue cones are detected only by the colour-opponent channels of the visual system. Secondly, the opponent channel is at its most sensitive when it is in its neutral state (that is, when our sensation is neither bluish nor yellowish). A version of this theory is developed formally by Pugh and Mollon (1979).

CENTRAL ANALYSIS OF COLOUR. INDEPENDENCE OF CHROMATIC AND SPATIAL ATTRIBUTES

Electrophysiology

The idea has been prevalent in the literature that colour information is under-represented in Area 17 of the primate visual cortex[1] – in contrast to the LGN, which is rich in colour-specific cells (and which, of course, provides the primary input to Area 17). But in fact many cells in Area 17 do prove to have 'opponent-colour' properties, in that they give an on-response to only part of the spectrum and either off-responses or no response at all to other wavelengths: Gouras (1974) gives 41 per cent as the proportion of opponent-colour cells in his sample of 317 cells in the cortical representation of the fovea in the rhesus monkey.

A question of some current interest is that of the extent to which colour is analyzed independently of other attributes of the visual image, such as form, movement and depth. Colour-specificity is certainly found to be associated with several of the receptive field types identified by Hubel and Wiesel in the primate cortex – 'non-oriented', 'simple' and 'complex'[2] – but Gouras has suggested that the more selective the spatial requirements of the cell, the less likely is the cell to be colour-specific: 60 per cent of the 'non-oriented' or 'circularly symmetric' cells in his sample had opponent-colour properties; 75 per cent of 'simple' cells were opponent but only 24 per cent of 'complex' cells; none of 21 'hypercomplex' cells revealed colour specificity. These figures might be taken to suggest a progressive dissociation of the analyses of colour and form within the visual cortex, but there is now good reason to doubt the detailed hierarchical model of Hubel and Wiesel (for discussion, see Mollon 1977a;

[1] The terms 'Area 17' (of Brodmann), 'striate cortex', 'Visual Area 1' (of Hubel and Wiesel) and 'V1' are used interchangeably in the literature. The relationship of the different visual areas is illustrated in Figure 8.6.

[2] The reader who is unfamiliar with these terms may turn to Hubel and Wiesel (1977) or, for secondary accounts, to Blakemore (1975) or Mollon (1977a).

Hoffmann 1977): in particular, many 'complex' cells and some 'hypercomplex' cells may draw their input not from simple cells, as Hubel and Wiesel originally proposed, but directly from lateral geniculate units of a type that respond transiently and do not show opponent colour properties.

Bearing on our question in a further way is the work of Zeki (1973, 1977), who has identified two areas in the prestriate cortex of the rhesus monkey that appear to be specialized for the analysis of colour. The first of these 'Visual Area IV' lies on the anterior bank of the lunate sulcus; the second lies on the posterior bank of the superior temporal sulcus (see Figure 8.6). Electrophysiological recording

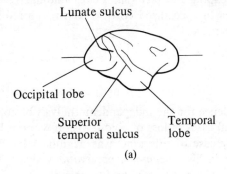

Lunate sulcus

Occipital lobe

Superior
temporal sulcus

Temporal
lobe

(a)

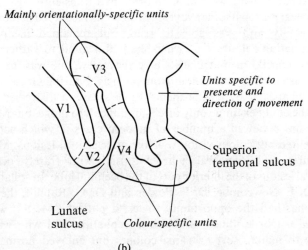

Mainly orientationally-specific units

V3

V1

V2   V4

*Units specific to
presence and
direction of movement*

Superior
temporal sulcus

Lunate
sulcus   *Colour-specific units*

(b)

Figure 8.6   a A lateral view of the brain of the rhesus monkey, showing the positions of the lunate sulcus and the superior temporal sulcus. b A horizontal section through the prestriate cortex. The section has been made at the level of the horizontal line in a. (After Zeki 1977).

revealed colour specificity in over 56 per cent of units in these two areas (Zeki 1978). Some cells had very narrow action spectra. Most cells were binocularly driven, the colour preference and receptive field properties being similar for the two eyes. A few cells had an orientational preference, but most of the colour-specific cells were not selective either for orientation or for direction of motion. In Areas 18 and 19 ('V2' and 'V3') on the other hand, colour-specific cells are rare while orientational preferences are common. Similarly, in the *medial* part of the posterior bank of the superior temporal sulcus (see Figure 8.6) there is a region where cells are specialized for detecting the presence and direction of movement but are not concerned with colour. There is no escaping the fact that Zeki's findings recall the nineteenth century idea of specialized cortical 'centres' for different attributes of the visual image.

Pathology

Another source of evidence for the independent analysis of colour is provided by rare clinical cases of loss of colour vision without loss of visual acuity. An early case of this kind was examined by Robert Boyle and is described in his *Uncommon observations about vitiated sight* (1688): a gentlewoman of 18 or 20 had transiently lost her sight (for unclear reasons) some five years earlier, had recovered demonstrably good acuity and was able to read, but remained incapable of discriminating colours. '. . . when she had a mind to gather Violets, tho' she kneel'd in that Place where they grew, she was not able to distinguish them by the Colour from the neighbouring Grass, but only by the Shape, or by feeling them.' Boyle's case, a distressed woman whom he could examine only briefly, is difficult to judge, but Mcadows (1974) has reviewed a number of modern cases in which acuity was unimpaired but colour vision was lost after central lesions. Meadows associates such 'cerebral achromatopsia' with (rarely occurring) bilateral lesions of the inferior part of the occipital lobe. In collaboration with Dr F. Newcombe, Dr P. Polden and Dr G. Ratcliff, the present writer has had the opportunity to test a patient ('M. S.') who had suffered a febrile illness, probably encephalitis, and who was quite unable to match, sort or name colours but enjoyed normal visual acuity. M. S. was a good psychophysical observer and by systematic measurements we were able to show that his retina must contain three functional cone mechanisms, that these have the normal spectral sensitivities and that each can independently control his behaviour in a verbal detection task. We used the psychophysical method of W. S. Stiles, in which the detection threshold for a test flash of one colour is measured on fields of the same or different colour. The existence of such a case nicely brings out the implications of the Principle of Univariance: M. S. can respond to signals from any of the three classes of colour-blind cone, but lacks the machinery to compare the signals from different classes of cone.

It would be tempting to suppose that M. S. has lost the homologue of the colour areas demonstrated in the rhesus monkey by Zeki. An alternative possibility is that fibres carrying colour information are disproportionately vulnerable in encephalitis: at any level of the visual system there is a wide variation in the size of cell bodies and in the diameters of axons and it is established that these differences correlate with differences in the information carried; so it is plausible that one class of cell may be more susceptible than another to a disease or toxin, as in fact, for example, large fibres are more susceptible to anoxia.

Colour-contingent After-effects

A very odd perceptual phenomenon reported by McCollough in 1965 has also been taken to bear on the question of independence of analysis. The reader may secure a McCollough Effect for himself by observing for about four minutes the red and green pattern printed on the back cover of this book. (Detailed guidance is given at the end of this chapter.) Notice that the red gratings are all of one orientation and the green gratings all of the orthogonal orientation. If afterwards the black and white pattern (Figure 8.7) is observed, it will appear pink where the grating is tilted right and pale green where the grating is tilted left. These illusory colours are 'contingent', in that they are seen only when a second stimulus dimension has a particular value. The most widely favoured explanation of the McCollough Effect attributes it to the presence in our visual system of neurons specific to both colour and orientation. We are to suppose that our perception of the colour of a black and white grating depends on the relative activity in a population of neurons all specific to the same orientation but differing in the colour to which they most strongly respond. If then we selectively adapt those neurons specific to, say, red bars of a given orientation, these units will later not make their normal contribution when a corresponding black and white grating is observed and so the grating will be perceived as pale green.

The McCollough Effect has proved to be only one of a large number of contingent after-effects: there are, for example, colour after-effects

Figure 8.7 Colour-contingent ´ after-effects. Black and white pattern for
observation as described in the text.

contingent on the direction of movement and on spatial frequency, as
well as after-effects of tilt and movement that are contingent on
colour. In each case the after-effect is attributed to the presence of
multiple specific neurons. However, a distinct hypothesis notes the
resemblance of these phenomena to Pavlovian conditioning: contingent
after-effects may persist for hours, days and even months, they show
spontaneous recovery and their decay depends on the frequency of
test trials during 'extinction'. We might suppose that the unconditioned
response of the visual system to an excess of redness in the world is

to turn down the gain in the red-sensitive channels; a correlated visual attribute (in our example, the vertical contour) then becomes the conditioned stimulus for this response.

CONCLUSION

There is good evidence that the analysis of chromatic information is to some extent independent of the analysis of other attributes of the visual image. But the fact remains that man is able to relate colours to forms in a complex scene and we have nothing more than guesses as to how this synthesis is achieved.

To obtain the McCollough Effect

Place the cover of the book in strong light (direct sunlight is excellent; northern daylight is adequate) and gaze at the red and green pattern for about four minutes from your usual reading distance. Do not let your eye rest on any one point for very long and try to look as frequently at red as at green areas. Resist the temptation to tilt your head (or the book) to one or other side. The book should be perpendicular to your line of sight.

After four minutes, rest your eyes for a few moments to allow any conventional after-images to dissipate. If now you look at the black and white pattern printed on page 146 you should see illusory colours that vary according to the orientation of the tilted lines: where the lines are tilted to the right you will see pinks and where they are tilted to the left you will see pale greens. Don't expect the illusory hues to be very strong: the effect is scientifically, rather than phenomenally, striking. Try tilting the book, or your head, 90 degrees to one side: the apparent colours should exchange positions.

One of the most curious aspects of the McCollough Effect is its persistence, particularly if you restrict the amount of your exposure to the black and white test pattern. Try testing yourself again after half-an-hour. Or adapt to the coloured pattern before retiring and test yourself the following morning. If you gaze at the coloured figure for, say, a quarter of an hour, you may produce an effect that survives for days or weeks.

To obtain the basic effect some readers will need to look at the coloured pattern for a little longer than four minutes, some for a little less. Since the phenomena, once established, is very stable, it does no harm to glance occasionally at the uncoloured pattern.

REFERENCES

Augenstein, E. J. and Pugh, E. N. Jr. 1977. 'The dynamics of the π_1 colour mechanism: further evidence for two sites of adaptation.' *J. Physiol. 272*, 247-81.

Blakemore, C. 1975. 'Central visual processing.' In M. S. Gazzaniga and C. Blakemore (eds) *Fundamentals of psychobiology*. New York: Academic Press.

Bowmaker, J. K. and Dartnall, H. J. A. 1979. 'Human visual pigments.' In preparation.

Bowmaker, J. K., Dartnall, H. J. A., Lythgoe, J. N. and Mollon, J. D. 1978. 'The visual pigments of rods and cones in the rhesus monkey, *Macaca mulatta*.' *J. Physiol. 274*, 329-48.

Boynton, R. M. 1971. 'Color vision.' In J. W. Kling and L. A. Riggs (eds) *Experimental psychology*. New York: Holt, Rinehart and Winston.

Brindley, G. S. 1970. *Physiology of the retina and visual pathway*. London: Arnold.

Cavonius, C. R. and Estévez, O. 1975. 'Contrast sensitivity of individual colour mechanisms of human vision.' *J. Physiol. 248*, 649-62.

Cornsweet, T. N. 1970. *Visual perception*. New York and London: Academic Press.

De Monasterio, F. M. and Gouras, P. 1975. 'Functional properties of ganglion cells of the rhesus monkey retina.' *J. Physiol. 251*, 167-95. .

De Monasterio, F. M., Gouras, P. and Tolhurst, D. J. 1975a. 'Trichromatic colour opponency in ganglion cells of the rhesus monkey retina.' *J. Physiol. 251*, 197-216.

De Monasterio, F. M., Gouras, P., and Tolhurst, D. J. 1975b. 'Concealed colour opponency in ganglion cells of the rhesus monkey retina.' *J. Physiol. 251*, 217-29.

De Valois, R. L. 1965. 'Analysis and coding of color vision in the primate visual system.' *Cold Spring Harbor Symp. Quant. Biol. 30*, 567-79.

Enoch, J. M. 1972. 'The two-color threshold technique of Stiles and derived component color mechanisms.' In D. Jameson and L. M. Hurvich (eds) *Handbook of sensory physiology VII/4*. Berlin: Springer-Verlag.

Gouras, P. 1974. 'Opponent-colour cells in different layers of foveal striate cortex.' *J. Physiol. 238*, 583-602.

Hoffmann, K. P. 1977. 'The projection of X, Y and W cells.' In H. Spekreijse and L. H. van der Tweel *Spatial contrast*. Amsterdam, Oxford, New York: North-Holland Publishing Company.

Hubel, D. H. and Weisel, T. N. 1977. 'Functional architecture of macaque monkey visual cortex.' *Proc. Roy. Soc. B., 198*, 1-59.

Judd, D. B. 1951. In Stevens, S. S. *Handbook of experimental psychology*. London: Chapman and Hall.

Liebman, P. A. 1972. 'Microspectrophotometry of photoreceptors.' In H. J. A. Dartnall (ed.) *Handbook of sensory physiology VII/1*. Berlin: Springer-Verlag.

Meadows, J. C. 1974. 'Disturbed perception of colours associated with localized cerebral lesions.' *Brain 97*, 615-32.

Marc, R. E. and Sperling, H. G. 1977. 'Chromatic organisation of primate cones.' *Science 196*, 454-6.

Marriott, F. H. C. 1976. 'The two-colour threshold technique of Stiles.' In H. Davson (ed.) *The eye 2A*. New York and London: Academic Press.

McCollough, C. 1965. 'Colour adaptation of edge-detectors in the human visual system.' *Science 149*, 1115-6.

Mollon, J. D. 1977a. In K. von Fieandt and I. K. Moustgaard *The perceptual world*. London: Academic Press.

Mollon, J. D. 1977b. In H. Spekreijse and L. H. van der Tweel *Spatial contrast*. Amsterdam, Oxford, New York: North-Holland Publishing Company.

Mollon, J. D. 1977c. 'The oddity of blue.' *Nature 268*, 587-8.

Mollon, J. D. 1979. 'Colour vision.' In H. B. Barlow and J. D. Mollon (eds) *The senses*. Cambridge: Cambridge University Press.

Mollon, J. D. and Krauskopf, J. 1973. 'Reaction time as a measure of the temporal response properties of individual colour mechanisms.' *Vision Res. 13*, 27-40.

Mollon, J. D. and Polden, P. G. 1977. 'An anomaly in the response of the eye to light of short wavelengths.' *Phil. Trans. Roy. Soc., B. 278*, 207-40.

Parsons, J. H. 1915. *An introduction to the study of colour vision*. Cambridge: Cambridge University Press.

Polden, P. G. and Mollon, J. D. 1979. 'Negative masking of blue flashes.' In preparation.

Pugh, E. N. and Mollon, J. D. 1979. 'A theory of the π_1 and π_3 colour mechanisms of Stiles.' *Vision Res*. in press.

Rushton, W. A. H. 1972. 'Pigments and signals in colour vision.' *J. Physiol. 220*, 1-31P.

Rushton, W. A. H. 1975. 'Visual pigments and color-blindness.' *Sci. Amer.* March, 64-74.

Rushton, W. A. H., Powell, D. P. and White, K. D. 1973a. 'Exchange thresholds in dichromats.' *Vision Res. 13*, 1993-2002.

Rushton, W. A. H., Powell, D. P. and White, K. D. 1973b. 'The spectral sensitivity of "red" and "green" cones in the normal eye.' *Vision Res. 13*, 2003-15.

Stiles, W. S. 1978. *Mechanisms of colour vision*. London: Academic Press.

Stromeyer, C. S. 1978. In R. Held and H. Leibowitz (eds) *Handbook of sensory physiology VIII*. Berlin: Springer-Verlag.

Willmer, E. N. 1961. 'Human colour vision and the perception of blue.' *J. Theoret. Biol. 2*, 141-79.

Zeki, S. M. 1973. 'Colour coding in Rhesus monkey prestriate cortex.' *Brain Res. 53*, 422.

Zeki, S. M. 1977. 'Colour coding in the superior temporal sulcus of rhesus monkey visual cortex.' *Proc. Roy. Soc., B. 197*, 195-223.

Zeki, S. M. 1978. 'Uniformity and diversity of structure and function in Rhesus monkey prestriate visual cortex.' *J. Physiol. 277*, 273-290.

FURTHER READING

The reviews of colour vision by Cornsweet (1970), Boynton (1971) and Rushton (1972, 1975) are recommended. An intellectual account is given by Brindley (1970). The papers of W. S. Stiles have recently been gathered together from their several obscure hiding places (Stiles 1978).

For further discussion of the anomalies of the blue mechanism, see Willmer (1961), Mollon (1977c), Pugh and Mollon (1979). The extent to which different attributes of the visual image are analyzed independently is further discussed by the present author elsewhere (Mollon 1977 a, b). The McCollough Effect is reviewed by Stromeyer (1978).

Chapter 9

Effects of electrical stimulation of the brain on behaviour

E. T. ROLLS

Electrical stimulation at some sites in the brain is rewarding, in that animals including man will work to obtain the stimulation. In other brain regions, electrical stimulation can produce analgesia comparable to that produced by morphine. These and other effects of electrical stimulation of the brain are described below.

BRAIN-STIMULATION REWARD

The discovery that rats would learn to stimulate electrically some regions of the brain was reported by Olds and Milner (1954). Olds noticed that rats would return to a corner of an open field apparatus where stimulation had just been given. He stimulated the rat whenever it went to the corner and found that the animals rapidly learned to go there to obtain stimulation. Olds and Milner (1954) went on to show that rats would work to obtain the stimulation, by making delivery of it contingent on other types of behaviour, such as pressing a lever in a Skinner box or crossing a shock grid.

The electrical stimulation is usually delivered through electrodes insulated to within 0.1-0.5 mm of the tip and permanently implanted so that the tip is in a defined location in the brain. The stimulation usually consists of pulses at a frequency of 50-100 Hz delivered in a train 300-500 ms long. At self-stimulation sites the animal will repeatedly perform the operant response to obtain one train of stimulation for each response. The rate of lever pressing provides a measure of the self-stimulation behaviour. The phenomenon can be called brain-stimulation reward because the animal will work to obtain the stimulation, and it has been found in all vertebrates tested. For example, it occurs in the goldfish, pigeon, rat, cat, dog, monkey and man (Rolls 1975).

The Nature of the Reward Produced

One way in which the reward value of brain stimulation can be tested in animals is by altering the drive (e.g. the hunger) of the animal to determine how this influences the reward produced by the stimulation. At some brain sites, for example in the lateral hypothalamus, a reduction of hunger may decrease self-stimulation rate (Hoebel 1969, 1976). As reducing hunger reduces both food reward, as the animal will no longer work for food, and brain-stimulation reward of some brain sites, it is suggested that the stimulation at these sites is rewarding because it mimics the effect of food for a hungry animal (Hoebel 1969; Rolls 1975). It is important to note that this effect is not just a general effect on performance of, for example, drowsiness, because a reduction of hunger may reduce self-stimulation at some sites but not at others (Rolls 1975). Further, at some sites hunger may facilitate self-stimulation, while at other sites thirst may facilitate self-stimulation. For example, in an experiment by Gallistel and Beagley (1971), rats chose stimulation on one electrode if they were hungry and on a different electrode if they were thirsty. One interesting and useful feature of this experiment is that a choice rather than a rate measure of the reward value of the brain stimulation was used. The advantage of the choice measure is that any general effect such as arousal or drowsiness produced by the treatment which could affect response rate has a minimal effect on the outcome of the experiment. The experiment shows that at some sites brain-stimulation reward can be equivalent to a specific natural reward, such as food for a hungry animal or water for a thirsty animal. Support for this view that brain-stimulation reward can mimic the effects of a natural reward such as food comes from neurophysiological experiments described below in which brain-stimulation reward and food reward have both been shown to activate cells in the hypothalamus. At other sites natural drives such as hunger and thirst do not modulate self-stimulation, so that some other reward process must underly the reward produced (Rolls 1975).

A different type of evidence on the nature of the reward produced by electrical stimulation of the brain comes from direct reports of the sensations elicited by the stimulation in man. During the invest-igation of or treatment of epilepsy, tumours or Parkinson's disease, electrical stimulation has been given to localized brain regions to evaluate the functioning of particular regions. Sem-Jacobsen (1968, 1976) reported on the effects of stimulation at 2 639 sites in 82 patients. Pleasant smells were evoked by the stimulation at nine sites, and unpleasant at six. Pleasant tastes were evoked at three sites, and unpleasant at one. Sexual responses were elicited at two sites. This type of finding is consistent with the food-related and other effects of the stimulation at some sites inferred from experiments with animals. The relative paucity of reports of this type in man may be because temporal and frontal sites are usually investigated and the electrodes do not normally reach the basal regions such as the hypothalamus which are often investigated in animals. More common in man are reports that mood changes are elicited by stimulation at some sites. In Sem-Jacobsen's series, at 360 points the patients became relaxed, at ease, had a feeling of well-being and/or were a little sleepy (classed as Positive I). At 31 sites the patients in addition showed enjoyment, frequently smiled and might want more stimulation (Positive II). At 8 sites (in seven patients) the patients laughed out loud, enjoyed themselves, positively liked the stimulation and wanted more (Positive III). These and other reports of mood changes were produced by the stimulation. Thus at some brain sites in man electrical stimulation may produce mood changes, stimulation may be desired and this may be associated with self-stimulation (see further Heath 1954, 1963, 1972; Bishop *et al.* 1963; Delgado 1976; Sem-Jacobsen 1976; Valenstein 1974).

The evidence available from animals and man thus suggests that the nature of the reward produced at different self-stimulation sites depends on the site: at some sites the stimulation may be equivalent to a specific natural reward such as food for a hungry animal; at other sites the stimulation may produce more general changes in mood and may thus be desired. At other sites it is possible that the stimulation taps into reinforcement processes (see Rolls 1975; Olds 1976, pp 22-24). This analysis makes it clear that self-stimulation may occur for any one of a number of reasons and that a single basis for self-stimulation should not be expected.

It is now to the bases of self-stimulation that we turn. We will be concerned not only with the neural mechanisms of brain-stimulation reward at different sites, but also with what can be learned about reward processes in the brain from studies of brain-stimulation reward. For example, one question before us will be how it happens that animals will only work for food (i.e. find it rewarding) when they are hungry. Another question will be how studies of the pharmacology of brain-stimulation reward relate to our understanding of the control of mood.

The Location of Self-stimulation Sites in the Brain

To understand the neural mechanisms of brain-stimulation reward it is first necessary to know where self-stimulation sites are located. One group is located along the general course of the medial forebrain bundle, passing lateral to the midline from the ventral tegmental area of the midbrain posteriorly, through the lateral hypothalamus, preoptic area and nucleus accumbens, towards the prefrontal cortex (orbitofrontal cortex in the monkey) anteriorly (Figure 9.1). Many cell groups and neural pathways follow this path or much of this general course. For example, there is the medial forebrain bundle itself, interconnecting forebrain and brainstem regions with hypothalamic and other diencephalic systems. There are fibres

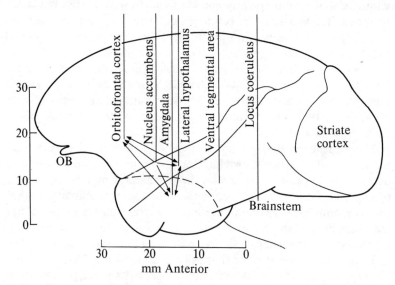

Figure 9.1   Lateral view of the rhesus monkey brain showing examples of self-stimulation sites extending in a trajectory from the orbitofrontal cortex through the nucleus accumbens, hypothalamus and ventral tegmental area (region of the A9 and A10 dopamine-containing cells) to the brainstem, where self-stimulation can be obtained, for example near (but not necessarily off) the locus coeruleus. The amygdala electrode is an example of a limbic self-stimulation site. OB – olfactory bulb.

connected to neurones in prefrontal self-stimulation sites, which pass many self-stimulation sites in their course through the brain (Routtenberg, Gardner and Huang 1971; Rolls and Cooper 1973, 1974). Also there are ascending catecholamine fibres (German and Bowden 1974; Rolls 1975), for example the noradrenaline containing fibres of the locus coerulus, which is classified as cell group A 6. Self-stimulation occurs with electrodes placed near the locus coerulus (Crow, Spear and Arbuthnott 1972). In addition there are dopamine containing fibres in the substantia nigra (cell group A 9) coursing to the striatum, and in the meso-limbic and mesocortical systems ascending from cell group A 10 in the ventral tegmental region. It is likely that many neural systems are activated by electrodes in this group of sites and it is possible that stimulation of any one of a number of systems in this region may support self-stimulation (see previous section above). A second group of self-stimulation sites is in limbic and related areas such as the amygdala, nucleus accumbens septi, hippocampus and prefrontal (orbitofrontal in the monkey) cortex. This group of sites is highly interconnected neurophysiologically with the first group lying along the general course of the medial forebrain bundle (Rolls 1974; see below).

The Effects of Brain Lesions on Intracranial Self-stimulation

Lateral or posterior hypothalamic self-stimulation rate is decreased (but not abolished) by small lesions in or near the medial forebrain bundle, particularly if the lesions are caudal to the self-stimulation electrode (Olds and Olds 1969; Boyd and Gardner 1967). Ipsilateral but not contralateral lesions are effective. Thus a unilaterally organized system which can be disrupted particularly by posterior lesions at least modulates hypothalamic self-stimulation. Lesions which destroy most of the locus coeruleus do not abolish self-stimulation from regions anterior to it through which its fibres pass, so that it is unlikely that the cells of the locus coeruleus support self-stimulation even from these sites (Clavier and Routtenberg 1976; Clavier 1976). It is interesting to note that self-stimulation can occur after ablation of most of the forebrain. Huston and Borbely (1973) were able to show this, by requiring only a simple response, of tail raising (or lowering) which their forebrain-ablated rats were able to learn in order to obtain posterior hypothalamic stimulation (although extinction was impaired). This finding underlines the view that self-stimulation can occur because of the activation of one of a number of systems, and suggests that the basic mechanisms for rewarded behaviour must be represented at a low level in the brain. Forebrain areas may be related to reward not because they are essential for rewarded behaviour, but because they are concerned with relating complex sensory inputs to reward and with executing complex motor responses to obtain reward (see below).

The neurophysiology of reward

By recording from single neurones while stimulation is delivered at the threshold current to self-stimulation electrodes[1], it is possible to determine which neural systems are actually activated by brain-stimulation reward. In the rat it is clear that during hypothalamic self-stimulation, neurones in the prefrontal cortex, amygdala and some areas of the brainstem, as well as in the hypothalamus itself, are activated (see Rolls 1974, 1975, 1976a; Ito 1976). In the monkey it has been found that neurones in the lateral hypothalamus, orbitofrontal cortex and amygdala are activated during self-stimulation of any one of these sites or of the nucleus accumbens, Figure 9.1 (see Rolls 1974, 1975). Thus in the monkey, there is a highly interconnected set of structures, stimulation in any one of which will support self-stimulation and will activate neurones in the other structures. Mainly in the monkey, it has been possible to record in the alert, behaving animal from neurones activated by brain-stimulation reward, and to determine whether these neurones are also activated by natural rewards such as food given to the hungry animal or during learning. When recording in the lateral hypothalamus and substantia innominata (which is lateral to the lateral hypothalamus) from neurones activated by brain-stimulation reward, it was found that some neurones (approximately 13 per cent in one sample of 764 neurones) altered their activity in relation to feeding (Rolls 1975, 1976b, 1979). Some of these neurones altered their activity only during the ingestion of some substances, so that their activity appeared to be associated with the taste of food. Many more of these neurones (approximately 11 per cent of the total sample) altered their activity before ingestion started, while the animal was looking at the food (Rolls *et al.* 1976). The activity of this second set of neurones only occurred on the sight of food if the monkey was hungry (Burton *et al.* 1976), and becomes associated with the sight of food during learning (Mora *et al.* 1976). Thus the activity of these neurones is associated with the sight and/or taste of food in the hungry animal, that is with the presentation of

---

[1]'The threshold current for self-stimulation is the minimum amount of current for a given stimulation pulse width required to produce self-stimulation at a given self-stimulation site.'

food reward. To determine whether the activity of these neurones precedes and could thus mediate, the responses of the hungry animal to food reward, their latency of activation was measured using a shutter which opened to reveal a food or a non-food related visual stimulus (Rolls *et al.* 1979). The latency for different neurones was 150-200 ms, and compared with a latency of 250-300 ms for the earliest electrical activity associated with the motor responses of a lick made to obtain food when the food-related visual stimulus was shown, Figure 9.2. Thus the motor response to the food could not result in the food-related activity of the hypothalamic neurones and it is possible that these neurones activated both by food reward and brain-stimulation reward are involved in the reactions of the animal to food. These responses to the food reward include the initiation of

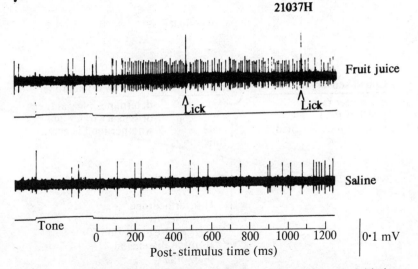

Figure 9.2 Activity of a hypothalamic food-related neurone during the initiation of feeding. Following the tone which signals the trial, the shutter opened at time 0 to reveal (upper trace) a food-related visual stimulus, which indicated that the monkey could lick a tube to obtain fruit juice. The hypothalamic neuron responded to the sight of the food approximately 150 ms after the shutter opened and preceded the lick contact (which occurred at approximately 480 ms after the shutter opened, as shown) and its associated EMG (not shown here). On a non-food trial (lower trace), the shutter opened to reveal a saline-related visual stimulus which indicated that if the monkey licked, hypertonic saline which is aversive, would be obtained. There was no neuronal response to this stimulus and, correctly, there was no lick. The activity of this type of neurone is associated with food reward. It precedes and can be used to predict the response which the monkey makes to food and non-food visual stimuli.

feeding behaviour, as well as endocrine and autonomic responses to the food, Figure 9.3.

A fuller understanding of reward-related processes will require not only an analysis of the function of neurones activated by brain-stimulation reward in other brain areas (for example the amygdala and orbitofrontal cortex), but also of the input and output connections of neurons with reward-related activity. In this context (see Figure 9.4) it has been shown that neurones in a dorso-lateral region of the amygdala, which anatomically could connect the visual inferotemporal cortex (a region of visual association cortex) with the lateral hypothalamus and substantia innominata, respond to visual inputs with shortest latencies of 110-150 ms, and independently of whether

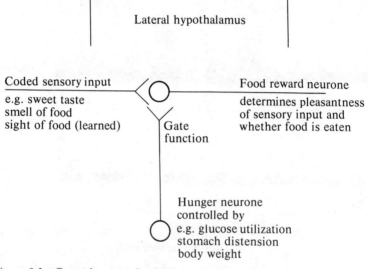

Figure 9.3   Control system for feeding consistent with experiments on brain-stimulation reward (see text). The effects of coded sensory input on lateral hypothalamic reward neurones are gated by neurones which signal hunger. The input is coded beyond the receptor level so that, for example, the sight of a food which has been learned but not of a non-food object is signalled. The gating (which could be pre- or post-synaptic and which may or may not be in the hypothalamus) by hunger neurones is performed on the basis of factors such as glucose utilization, stomach distension, gut signals and body weight. Activity in the food-reward neurons could determine the pleasantness of the sensory input and whether feeding will continue. The initiation of food-seeking behaviour depends on activity in the 'hunger' neurons. Self-stimulation of the lateral hypothalamus could occur because of excitation of either the coded sensory input neurones, in which case modulation by hunger would occur, or because of excitation of the food-reward neurons.

the visual stimuli have been associated with food during learning (Sanghera *et al.* 1979). Visual responses in the inferotemporal cortex in the same test situation occur with shortest latencies of 100-140 ms, and also are not dependent on the food-related association of the visual stimuli (Rolls *et al.* 1977). In the globus pallidus some neurones are active in relation to movements made to obtain food or non-food objects (Rolls *et al.* 1976), and fire after hypothalamic food-related neurones during the initiation of feeding. Thus in this type of analysis the neural processes which underlie reward behaviour such as feeding are traced through input stages to reward-related stages and then to output stages which initiate the movements. At present, it appears that a food reward related stage is in the lateral hypothalamus and substantia innominata. These neurones are also activated by brain-stimulation reward of some sites, so that the electrical stimulation activates a system normally activated by food reward. Self-stimulation of these sites may occur because the stimulation mimics the effects of the food reward on these neurones (Rolls 1975). Self-stimulation of some other sites may occur because other neural systems concerned with different reward processes are activated but the function of such neural systems is not yet understood.

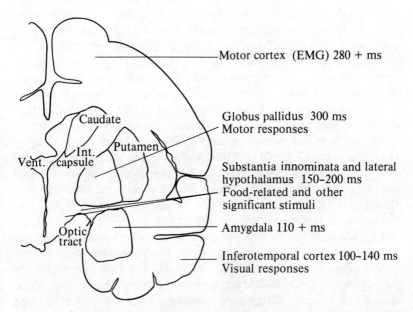

Figure 9.4 Activity in some brain areas related to different processes involved in feeding (see text).

The Pharmacology of Brain-stimulation Reward

It is well known that pharmacological manipulations of the catecholamine transmitters in the brain (noradrenaline and dopamine) alter
self-stimulation rates (Rolls 1975). For example, amphetamine, which
enhances the release of noradrenaline and dopamine from axon
terminals at synapses, increases hypothalamic self-stimulation rate.
Drugs which decrease catecholamine levels (e.g. α-methyl-p-tyrosine)
or which block catecholamine receptors (e.g. the 'neuroleptic' or
'anti-psychotic' drugs chlorpromazine and spiroperidol), reduce self-
stimulation rates. Stein (1967, 1969), noting these points, and that
many self-stimulation sites occurred along the course of the dorsal
noradrenergic bundle from its origin in the locus coeruleus (cell group
A 6) through the hypothalamus towards its termination in the
neocortex, formulated the noradrenergic theory of reward. According
to this theory, activation of noradrenergic axons in this pathway
by electrical stimulation at self-stimulation sites and the consequent
release of noradrenaline at its terminals, mediates brain-stimulation
reward (Stein 1967, 1969; Crow 1976). Evidence against this theory
comes from several sources. Roll (1970) found that animals treated
with disulfiram, which depletes the brain of noradrenaline, could
self-stimulate if aroused, but were usually too drowsy to do so.
Rolls *et al.*, (1974) came to a similar conclusion when they found
that the doses of disulfiram required to reduce hypothalamic self-
stimulation rates produced a major attenuation of spontaneous
locomotor activity. Interestingly, the dopamine receptor blocking
agents pimozide or spiroperidol (used following an earlier study by
Wauquier and Niemegeers 1972) produced a much greater attenuation
of self-stimulation rate than of locomotor activity, suggesting that
dopamine was more closely related to brain-stimulation reward at
these sites than was noradrenaline. Clavier and Routtenberg's finding
(1976; see also Clavier 1976) that lesions to the locus coeruleus did
not attenuate self-stimulation along the course of the dorsal
noradrenergic bundle also argues strongly against the noradrenergic
theory of reward, unless it is held that the small percentage of neurones
remaining in this structure after the lesions is sufficient to maintain
self-stimulation. An experiment sometimes quoted in support of the
noradrenergic theory of reward is one by Shaw and Rolls (1976).
Hypothalamic self-stimulation attenuated by the depletion of
noradrenaline with disulfiram was not restored by agents which
directly activated adrenergic receptors such as clonidine and
naphthazoline administered intraventricularly. Thus it was not sufficient
for self-stimulation to occur to restore adrenergic activation present

at the postsynaptic receptor. It was necessary for the receptor activation to be elicited when the neurones afferent to the synapses were active. In the experiment, agents such as methylphenidate and phenylephrine which acted to mobilize noradrenaline from a reserve pool for use as a transmitter did restore self-stimulation in these animals. For details see Shaw and Rolls (1976). The experiment thus suggests that the release of noradrenaline contingent on neuronal activity in the presynaptic neurones is necessary for self-stimulation of these sites, but it does not suggest that this necessary contingent release of noradrenaline mediates reward. It could be necessary for some other function related to the animal's performance. Thus the evidence which now supports the noradrenergic theory of reward is weak.

There is better evidence that dopamine is involved in self-stimulation of some brain sites. Following the observation described above, that dopamine-receptor blockade with spiroperidol attenuated hypothalamic self-stimulation without producing an arousal deficit (Rolls, Kelly and Shaw 1974), it was shown that spiroperidol attenuated self-stimulation at different sites in the rat (Rolls *et al.* 1974). It was also shown that spiroperidol attenuated self-stimulation even when the motor response required to obtain the stimulation was made simple in order to minimize the effect of motor impairment (Mora, Sanguinetti, Rolls and Shaw 1975). Spiroperidol also attenuates self-stimulation in the monkey (Mora, Rolls, Burton and Shaw 1976). These findings were consistent with the observation that self-stimulation in the rat can be obtained in the ventral mesencephalon near the A 10 dopamine-containing cell bodies (Crow, Spear and Arbuthnott 1972). However, strong supporting evidence is needed in view of the situation emphasized by Rolls and his colleagues that it is difficult to exclude the possibility that dopamine-receptor blockade interferes with self-stimulation by producing a motor impairment (see also Fibiger 1978). Evidence supporting a role for dopamine in brain-stimulation reward came from experiments with apomorphine, which directly stimulates dopamine receptors. It was found that apomorphine attenuates self-stimulation of the prefrontal cortex in the rat and of the comparable region in the monkey, the orbitofrontal cortex (Mora, Phillips, Koolhaas and Rolls 1976). Both areas are rich in dopamine-containing terminals of the meso-cortical (A 10) dopamine system. An attenuation of self-stimulation by the dopamine-receptor stimulant apomorphine would be predicted in a system in which the release of dopamine influenced the reward produced by stimulation of the prefrontal cortex.

In these experiments, self-stimulation with electrodes in the caudate nucleus was not attenuated by the apomorphine, so that this self-stimulation could not depend on dopamine (even though dopamine is present in this region), and the attenuation of prefrontal self-stimulation produced by the apomorphine could not have been due to a general disruption of behaviour. In a further investigation of the role of dopamine in brain-stimulation reward in the prefrontal cortex, it has been found that the administration of apomorphine intravenously decreases the firing rate of neurones in the medial prefrontal cortex of the rat (Mora, Sweeney, Rolls and Sanguinetti 1976) (as does the local iontophoretic administration of dopamine – Bunney and Aghajanian 1976), and that dopamine is released from this region during electrical stimulation of medial prefrontal reward sites (Mora and Myers 1977). This evidence thus suggests that the mesocortical dopamine system can influence brain-stimulation reward of the prefrontal cortex in the rat and the corresponding orbitofrontal cortex in the monkey, but dopamine may not be essential for self-stimulation of the prefrontal cortex, as lesions of the dopaminergic fibres which ascend to the prefrontal cortex may not abolish prefrontal self-stimulation (Phillips and Fibiger 1978). In relation to the role of dopamine in reward in the prefrontal cortex, it is of interest that a main pharmacological effect of neuroleptic drugs (which are used in treating schizophrenia) is the blockade of dopamine receptors (Anden *et al*. 1970), and that a dopamine disorder could play a role in schizophrenia (see Snyder *et al*. 1974).

Thus the present evidence implicating noradrenaline in brain-stimulation reward is weak. There is better evidence that dopamine is involved in brain-stimulation reward of some sites, for example the prefrontal (orbitofrontal) cortex, but it is not involved in self-stimulation at all sites. Future analyses of the pharmacology of brain-stimulation reward will need to show that reward, rather than performance, is affected by experimental variables. Effects on self-stimulation rate are difficult to interpret unless (as shown above) controls for side effects on performance are included. Also, as emphasized by Fibiger (1978), drug effects may depend on the initial rate of bar pressing shown by the animal. But to equalize initial self-stimulation rates at different sites does not help, because although the self-stimulation rate at some sites may be low, stimulation at these sites may be preferred to stimulation at other sites (Valenstein 1964), and this could influence the effects of drugs. With rate measures, it is at least necessary to determine how the rate of bar pressing is affected by the stimulation current intensity and to determine how this relation is affected by experimental variables. Other measures of reward are time spent in the side of the box in which stimulation is given and a runway in which reward can be measured independently of performance (Edmonds and Gallistel 1977; see further Valenstein 1964).

STIMULUS-BOUND MOTIVATIONAL BEHAVIOUR

Electrical stimulation at some brain sites can elicit feeding, drinking and other consummatory types of behaviour (see Valenstein, Cox and Kakolewski 1970). The behaviour may be called 'stimulation-bound' because it occurs during the electrical stimulation or 'stimulus-bound' because the behaviour is associated with a particular goal object, for example food pellets. If small stimulation electrodes are used relatively specific behaviours are elicited, such as drinking with electrodes near the zona incerta and feeding with electrodes in the lateral hypothalamus (Olds *et al.* 1971; Huang and Mogenson 1972). A frequently observed feature of such behaviour is plasticity, that is stimulus-bound feeding may develop into stimulus-bound drinking if food is removed from the environment and replaced with water (Valenstein *et al.* 1970). It is as if the stimulation activates the animal at least partly non-specifically, and the behaviour which is elicited depends on which environmental stimuli are available for the animal to respond to. For example, food to chew or water to lap. This type of interpretation receives support from the observation that a mild continuous tail-pinch (with for example a paper clip) leads to 'stimulus-bound' types of behaviour such as eating in the rat (Antelman and Szechtman 1975). Because of such findings, it is difficult to interpret stimulus-bound behaviour produced by brain stimulation as a proof of activation of a hunger or thirst mechanism: rather it could be a more general type of behavioural activation. It is worth noting that although stimulus-bound behaviour may not represent activation of a specific drive (e.g. hunger), there is evidence that reward elicited by electrical stimulation can be relatively specific. For example, it may be equivalent to food for a hungry animal or water for a thirsty animal (Rolls 1975).

ANALGESIA PRODUCED BY ELECTRICAL STIMULATION OF THE BRAIN

Electrical stimulation of some regions of the brain can lead to analgesia in animals ranging from rats to man and can be equivalent in its pain-reducing properties to large doses of morphine (Liebeskind and Paul 1977). These analgesic effects may last for hours after only seconds of stimulation. The analgesia is often for only part of the body, so that a strong pinch to one side but not to the other may be ignored. This shows that the stimulation-produced analgesia is not simply some general interference with the animal's ability to respond to stimulation. The effective stimulation sites are in the medial brainstem, and extend from the rostral medulla (nucleus raphe magnus), through the midbrain central gray matter, towards the hypothalamus. There is no clear relation with reward mechanisms, because at some sites analgesia and self-stimulation are found and at others the stimulation is aversive but is followed by analgesia. It has been shown that naloxone, a specific morphine antagonist, reverses, at least partly, stimulation-produced analgesia in both the rat and man (Akil, Mayer and Liesbeskind 1976; Adams 1976). The endogenous morphine-like peptide enkephalin (Hughes 1975; Hughes *et al.* 1975) injected intraventricularly yields analgesia (Beluzzi *et al.* 1976), and central gray matter stimulation releases this substance or a peptide similar to it (Stein, Wise and Beluzzi, unpublished results, Liebeskind *et al.* 1976). Further, there are stereospecific opiate binding sites in the central gray matter, and elsewhere in the brain (Kuhar *et al.* 1973). These findings raise the possibility that stimulation-produced analgesia is effective because it causes the release of a naturally occurring morphine-like substance which acts on opiate receptors in the central gray matter and elsewhere to provide analgesia.

CONCLUSIONS AND SUMMARY

Animals including man will learn to stimulate electrically certain areas of the brain. At some sites the stimulation may be equivalent to a natural reward such as food for a hungry animal, in that hunger increases working for brain-stimulation reward at these (but not at other) sites. It has been found in the monkey that one population of neurones activated by the brain-stimulation reward at these sites is in the region of the lateral hypothalamus and substantia innominata. Some of these neurones are also activated by the sight and/or taste of food if the monkey is hungry, that is when the food is rewarding. The latency of the responses of these neurones to the sight of food is 150-200 ms. This is longer than the responses of sensory neurons to visual stimuli in the inferotemporal cortex and dorso-lateral amygdala, but shorter than the latency, as shown by electrographic recording, of the motor responses of the animals to the sight of food. Thus it is possible that these hypothalamic neurones mediate some of the reactions of the hungry animal to food reward, such as the initiation of feeding and/or autonomic and endocrine responses. In this way reward-related processes can be identified and studied by analyzing the operations (from sensory input through central control processes to motor output) which are involved in the responses of animals to rewarding stimuli. Self-stimulation of some sites may occur because neurones whose activity is associated with food reward are activated by stimulation at these sites. At other sites, brain-stimulation reward may be produced because the stimulation mimics other types of natural reward or, as shown by verbal reports in man, because it is associated with moods such as pleasure or happiness.

The evidence that noradrenergic neurones mediate reward is weak. There is better evidence that dopamine is involved in brain-stimulation reward of some sites, for example the prefrontal (orbitofrontal) cortex. This subject is of great interest in view of the known effects of neuroleptic drugs on dopamine systems.

Stimulation at some other sites in the brain produces analgesia which can be equivalent in its pain-reducing properties to large doses of morphine. Stimulation-produced analgesia is at least partly reversed by naloxone, a specific morphine antagonist, and may release the morphine-like peptide enkephalin (or a similar peptide). Thus the stimulation may activate an endogenous mechanism capable of controlling pain by the release of a peptide which acts on stereospecific opiate binding sites known to be present in some of the regions in which electrical stimulation produces analgesia.

REFERENCES

Adams, J. E. 1976. 'Naloxone reversal of analgesia produced by brain stimulation in the human.' *Pain 2*, 161-6.

Akil, H., Mayer, D. J. and Liebeskind, J. C. 1976. 'Antagonism of stimulation-produced analgesia by naloxone, a narcotic antagonist.' *Science 191*, 961-2.

Anden, N. E., Butcher, S. G., Corrodi, H., Fuxe, K. and Ungerstedt, U. 1970. 'Receptor activity and turnover of dopamine and noradrenaline after neuroleptics.' *Eur. J. Pharm. 11*, 303-14.

Antelman, S. M. and Szechtman, H. 1975 'Tail pinch induces eating in sated rats which appears to depend on nigrostriatal dopamine.' *Science 189*, 731-3.

Beluzzi, J. D., Grant, N., Garsky, V., Sarantakis, D., Wise, C. D. and

Stein, L. 1976. 'Analgesia induced *in vivo* by central administration of enkephalin in rat.' *Nature 260*, 625-6.

Bishop, M. P., Elder, S. T. and Heath, R. G. 1963. 'Intracranial self-stimulation in man.' *Science 140*, 394-5.

Bunney, B. S. and Aghajanian, G. K. 1976. 'Dopamine and norepinephrine innervated cells in the rat prefrontal cortex: pharmacological differentiation using micro-iontophoretic techniques.' *Life Sci. 19*, 1783-92.

Boyd, E. S. and Gardner, L. C. 1967. 'Effect of some brain lesions on intracranial self-stimulation in the rat.' *Amer. J. Physiol. 213*, 1044-52.

Burton, M. J., Rolls, E. T. and Mora, F. 1976. 'Effects of hunger on the responses of neurones in the lateral hypothalamus to the sight and taste of food.' *Exp. Neurol. 51*, 668-77.

Clavier, R. M. 1976. 'Brain stem self-stimulation: catecholamine or non-catecholamine mediation?' In A. Wauquier and E. T. Rolls (eds) *Brain-stimulation reward*. Amsterdam: North-Holland.

Clavier, R. M. and Routtenberg, A. 1976. 'Brain stem self-stimulation attenuated by lesions of medial forebrain bundle but not by lesions of locus coeruleus or the caudal ventral norepinephrine bundle.' *Brain Res. 101*, 251-71.

Crow, T. J. 1976. 'Specific monoamine systems as reward pathways.' In A. Wauquier and E. T. Rolls (eds) *Brain-stimulation reward*. Amsterdam: North-Holland.

Crow, T. J., Spear, P. J. and Arbuthnott, G. W. 1972. 'Intracranial self-stimulation with electrodes in the region of the locus coeruleus.' *Brain Res. 36*, 275-87.

Delgado, J. M. R. 1976. 'New orientations in brain stimulation in man.' In A. Wauquier and E. T. Rolls' (eds) *Brain-stimulation reward*. Amsterdam: North-Holland.

Edmonds, D. E. and Gallistel, C. R. 1977. 'Reward vs. performance in self-stimulation: electrode-specific effects of AMPT on reward.' *J. comp. physiol. Psychol. 91*, 962-74.

Fibiger, H. C. 1978. 'Drugs and reinforcement mechanisms: a critical review of the catecholamine theory.' *Review of Pharmacology and Toxicology 18*,

Gallistel, C. R. and Beagley, G. 1971. 'Specificity of brain-stimulation reward in the rat.' *J. comp. physiol. Psychol. 76*, 199-205.

German, D. C. and Bowden, D. M. 1974. 'Catecholamine systems as the neural substrate for intracranial self-stimulation: a hypothesis.' *Brain Res. 73*, 381-419.

Heath, R. G. 1954. *Studies in schizophrenia. A multidisciplinary approach to mind-brain relationship*. Cambridge: Harvard University Press.

Heath, R. G. 1963. 'Electrical self-stimulation of the brain in man.' *Amer. J. Psychiat. 120*, 571-7.

Heath, R. G. 1972. 'Pleasure and brain activity: deep and surface encephalograms during orgasm.' *J. Nerv. Ment. Dis. 154*, 3-18.

Hoebel, B. G. 1969. 'Feeding and self-stimulation.' *Ann. N.Y. Acad. of Sci. 157*, 758-78.

Hoebel, B. G. 1976. 'Brain-stimulation reward and aversion in relation to behavior.' In A. Wauquier and E. T. Rolls (eds) *Brain-stimulation reward*. Amsterdam: North-Holland.

Huang, Y. H. and Mogenson, G. J. 1972. 'Neural pathways mediating drinking and feeding in rats.' *Exp. Neurol. 37*, 269-86.

Hughes, J. 1975. 'Isolation of an endogenous compound from the brain with pharmacological properties similar to morphine.' *Brain Res. 88*, 293-308.

Hughes, J., Smith, T. W., Kosterlitz, H. W., Fothergill, L. A., Morgan, B. A. and Morris, H. R. 1975. 'Identification of two related pentapeptides from the brain with potent opiate antagonist activity.' *Nature 258*, 577-9.

Huston, J. P. and Borbely, A. A. 1973. 'Operant conditioning in forebrain ablated rats by use of rewarding hypothalamic stimulation.' *Brain Res. 50*: 467-72.

Ito, M.1976. 'Mapping unit responses to rewarding stimulation.' In A. Wauquier and E. T. Rolls (eds) *Brain-stimulation reward*. Amsterdam: North-Holland.

Kuhar, M. J., Pert, C. B. and Snyder, S. H. 1973. 'Regional distribution of opiate receptor binding in monkey and human brain.' *Nature 245*, 447-50.

Liebeskind, J. C., Giesler, G. J. and Urca, G. 1976. 'Evidence pertaining to an endogenous mechanism of pain inhibition in the central nervous system.' In Y. Zotterman (ed.) *Sensory Functions of the skin,* 561-73. Oxford: Pergamon.

Liebeskind, J. C. and Paul, L. A. 1977. 'Psychological and physiological mechanisms of pain.' *Ann. Rev. Psychol. 88*, 41-60.

Mora, F., Sanguinetti, A. M., Rolls, E. T. and Shaw, S. G. 1975. 'Differential effects on self-stimulation and motor behaviour produced by micro-intracranial injections of a dopamine-receptor blocking agent.' *Neuroscience Letters 1*, 179-84

Mora, F., Rolls, E. T. and Burton, M. J. 1976. 'Modulation during learning of the responses of neurones in the lateral hypothalamus to the sight of food.' *Exp. Neurol. 53*, 508-19.

Mora, F., Rolls, E. T., Burton, M. J., and Shaw, S. G. 1976. 'Effects of dopamine-receptor blockade on self-stimulation in the monkey.' *Pharm. Biochem. and Behav. 4*, 211-16.

Mora, F., Phillips, A. G., Koolhaas, J. M. and Rolls, E. T. 1976. 'Prefrontal cortex and neostriatum. Self-stimulation in the rat: differential effects produced by apomorphine.' *Brain Res. Bull. 1*, 421-4.

Mora, F., Sweeney, K. F., Rolls, E. T. and Sanguinetti, A. M. 1976. 'Evidence for a dopaminergic inhibition of neurons in the prefrontal cortex of the rat.' *Neuroscience Abstracts 2*, 713.

Mora, F. and Myers, R. 1977. 'Brain self-stimulation: direct evidence for the involvement of dopamine in the prefrontal cortex.' *Science 197*, 1387-9.

Olds, J. 1976. *Drives and reinforcements*. New York: Raven Press.

Olds, J. and Milner, P. 1954. 'Positive reinforcement produced by electrical stimulation of septal area and other regions of the rat brain.' *J. comp. physiol. Psychol. 47*, 419-27.

Olds, J., Allan, W. S. and Briese, A. E. 1971. 'Differentiation of hypothalamic drive and reward centres.' *Amer. J. Physiol. 221*, 368-75.

Olds, M. E. and Olds, J. 1969. 'Effects of lesions in medial forebrain bundle on self-stimulation behaviour.' *Amer. J. Physiol. 217*, 1253-64.

Phillips, A. G. and Fibiger, H. C. 1978. 'The role of dopamine in mediating self-stimulation in the ventral tegmentum, nucleus accumbens and medial prefrontal cortex.' *Can. J. Psychol. 32*, 58-66.

Roll, S. K. 1970. 'Intracranial self-stimulation and wakefulness: effects of manipulating ambient brain catecholamines.' *Science 168*, 1370-2.

Rolls, E. T. 1974. 'The neural basis of brain-stimulation reward.' *Prog. Neurobiol. 3*, 71-160.

Rolls, E. T. 1975. *The brain and reward*. Oxford: Pergamon Press.

Rolls, E. T. 1976a. 'The neurophysiological basis of brain-stimulation reward.' In *Brain-stimulation reward*. A Wauquier and E. T. Rolls (eds), 65-7, Amsterdam: North-Holland.

Rolls, E. T. 1976b. 'Neurophysiology of feeding.' *Life Sci. Res. Rep. 2*, 21-42.

Rolls, E. T. 1979. 'Activity of hypothalamic and related neurons in the alert animal.' In *Handbook of the hypothalamus*, P. J. Morgane and J. Panksepp (eds). New York: Dekker.

Rolls, E. T., Kelly, P. H. and Shaw, S. G. 1974. 'Noradrenaline, dopamine and brain-stimulation reward.' *Pharm. Biochem. and Behav. 2*, 735-40.

Rolls, E. T., Rolls, B. J., Kelly, P. H., Shaw, S. G. and Dale, R. 1974. 'The relative attenuation of self-stimulation, eating and drinking produced by dopamine-receptor blockade.' *Psychopharm. (Berl.) 38*, 219-310.

Rolls, E. T. and Cooper, S. J. 1973. 'Activation of neurones in the prefrontal cortex by brain-stimulation reward in the rat.' *Brain Res. 60*, 351-68.

Rolls, E. T. and Cooper, S. J. 1974. 'Connection between the prefrontal cortex and pontine brain-stimulation reward sites in the rat.' *Exp. Neurol. 42*, 687-99.

Rolls, E. T., Burton, M. J. and Mora, F. 1976. 'Hypothalamic neuronal responses associated with the sight of food.' *Brain Res. 111*, 53-66.

Rolls, E. T., Judge, S. J. and Sanghera, M. 1977. 'Activity of neurones in the inferotemporal cortex of the alert monkey.' *Brain Res. 130*, 229-38.

Rolls, E. T., Sanghera, M. K. and Roper-Hall, A. 1979. The latency of activation of neurons in the lateral hypothalamus and substantia innominata during feeding in the monkey. *Brain Res.* in press.

Routtenberg, A., Gardner, E. I. and Huang, Y. H. 1971. 'Self-stimulation pathways in the monkey, Macaca mulatta.' *Exp. Neurol. 33*, 213-24.

Sanghera, M. K., Rolls, E. T. and Roper-Hall, A. 1979. Visual responses of neurons in the dorsolateral amygdala of the alert monkey. *Expl. Neurol.* in press.

Sem-Jacobsen, C. W. 1968. *Depth-electrographic stimulation of the human brain and behavior: from fourteen years of studies and treatment of Parkinson's disease and mental disorders with implanted electrodes,* Springfield, Ill: C. C. Thomas.

Sem-Jacobsen, C. W. 1976. 'Electrical stimulation and self-stimulation in man with chronic implanted electrodes. Interpretation and pitfalls of results.' In A. Wauquier and E. T. Rolls (eds) *Brain-stimulation reward*. Amsterdam: North-Holland.

Shaw, S. G. and Rolls, E. T. 1976. 'Is the release of noradrenaline necessary for self-stimulation?' *Pharm. Biochem. and Behav. 4*, 375-9.

Snyder, S. H., Banerjee, S. P., Yamamura, H. I. and Greenberg, D. 1974. 'Drugs, neurotransmitters and schizophrenia.' *Science 184*, 1243-53.

Stein, L. 1967. 'Psychopharmacological substrates of mental depression.' In S. Garattini and M. N. G. Dukes (eds) *Anti-depressant drugs*. Amsterdam: Excerpta Medica Foundation.

Stein, L. 1969. 'Chemistry of purposive behavior.' In J. Tapp (ed.) *Reinforcement and behavior*, 328-35. New York: Academic Press.

Valenstein, E. S. 1964. 'Problems of measurement and interpretation with reinforcing brain stimulation.' *Psychol. Rev. 71*, 415-37.

Valenstein, E. S. 1974. *Brain control. A critical examination of brain stimulation and psychosurgery.* New York: Wiley.

Valenstein, E. S., Cox, V. C. and Kakolewski, J. W. 1970. 'A re-examination of the role of the hypothalamus in motivation.' *Psychol. Rev. 77*, 16-31.

Wauquier, A. and Niemegeers, C. J. E. 1972. 'Intra-cranial self-stimulation in rats as a function of various stimulus parameters: II, influence of haloperidol, pimozide and pipamperone on medial forebrain stimulation with monopolar electrodes.' *Psychopharm. 27*, 191-202.

Chapter 10

Human Factors Engineering

WILLIAM B. ROUSE

Human factors engineering is concerned with designing and evaluating the interface between people and machines. Psychologists, physiologists and engineers participate in this field. Their goal is to produce machines that achieve the objectives for which they were designed while assuring at the same time the safety of their operators. It is also important that the individuals using the machines find their interactions with these machines to be rewarding at least in the sense that they do not feel confused, powerless and unappreciated.

The word engineering in 'human factors engineering' connotes the applied nature of the field. This does not mean that human factors researchers do not develop their share of theories. Instead, it serves to point out that a real world problem (e.g. building an automobile) is usually the motivating force behind human factors research and that the primary result of such research is a contribution to the solution of the problem.

For the sake of discussion, it is convenient to divide human factors into three fairly distinct areas. These can be denoted by their orientation and include psychological, physiological and systems engineering. This categorization will serve to illustrate the breadth of interests within human factors engineering.

The psychologically orientated area of human factors is concerned with the design and evaluation of displays, controls and workspaces from the point of view of a person's ability to perceive displayed information and to use it in making appropriate decisions and carrying out subsequent action. Further, they are interested in the problems of selecting and training people to operate the systems produced.

The physiologically orientated specialists within human factors are usually concerned with topics such as stress due to heat or vibration, and the ability of people to lift, push, pull, etc., and with safety in industrial environments.

Within the systems engineering orientated area of human factors, research is concerned with predicting the behaviour of complex man-machine systems such as aircraft, spacecraft, and factories. The results of such research are often in terms of sets of equations which express how humans make and execute decisions within the appropriate man-machine system. The set of equations, which is called a 'model', represents the abilities of both human and machine in the same terms and thereby allows one to predict how well the overall man-machine system will perform.

The above categorization has served to emphasize that the area of human factors engineering is the concern not only of psychologists but also physiologists and engineers. The diversity of training among these professions leads to the literature of human factors having great methodological diversity ranging from fairly uncontrolled empirical field studies to mathematical treatises where no empirical data are ever collected. On the other hand, while methodologies are diverse, the problems of interest form the common threads of research among psychologists, physiologists and engineers.

HUMAN FACTORS IN SYSTEMS DESIGN

While human factors engineers are often involved in solving problems with existing man-machine systems, it is more useful to explain the role of human factors in the process of designing new systems. The first step in systems design is defining the objectives of the system. For example, one may desire a method of getting people from the earth to the moon. While various esoteric solutions to this problem might be envisaged, it is quite likely that the final design concept would involve some type of vehicle. Thus, the objective would become that of getting a vehicle from the earth to the moon and back to earth again. The next step in the process is defining more specifically what the system would have to do. For example, it would have to be capable of escaping the earth's gravitational force, accurately travelling over 500,000 kilometers, safely landing on the moon, etc. The vehicle system would have to accomplish all this within several constraints including size, weight and of course cost.

At this point, one would define the detailed functions which the vehicle system would have to perform. Three levels of functions are readily discernible. The first level includes those functions necessary for normal system operations, examples include propulsion, guidance and navigation. The second level includes functions necessary when the system malfunctions. For example, fault detection, diagnosis and correction. The third level of system functions involves management of the system. This includes overall evaluation of the success of the current operating procedures utilized within the system and determination of possible new operating procedures that will lead to improved system performance.

Once system functions have been defined they must be allocated between humans and machines. For many functions, allocation is easy; for example, propulsion of the vehicle can not be allocated to the human. On the other hand, tasks that require recognizing complex patterns or flexibly responding to unforeseen situations must usually be allocated to the human. Economics may also dictate whether human or machine performs a particular function. In some cases, machines are less expensive (e.g. manufacturing inexpensive plastic parts) while in other cases, it is less expensive to utilize humans (e.g. picking delicate fruits and vegetables).

If the above considerations were all that was important one could simply allocate to the machine every function which it could economically perform. The human would be allocated everything else. But there are two main difficulties here. First, the resulting functions allocated to the human may result in his having too little to do (underload) or too much to do (overload). Second, the human may end up with an incoherent set of bits and pieces which can lead to poor performance and to a lack of job satisfaction. While the solution to this problem is to determine an appropriate number of coherent functions for the human to perform, this is far from straightforward. The problem of function allocation will be considered later.

When one or more alternative solutions to the function allocation problem have been obtained, the next phase of systems design is concerned with determining the information flow within the system. This requires a detailed specification of the procedures by which the system will operate. Depending on how the function allocation problem has been solved, this analysis may include a specific consideration of how the human shares his attention among several functions for which he has simultaneous responsibility. From a human factors point of view, this analysis of information flow will dictate the information to be displayed to the human and the information expected from the human.

Information can be displayed to the human in various modalities including visual, auditory and tactile. In designing or choosing a display, one is concerned first that the human will be able to perceive the displayed information and then concerned that the human will interpret the information correctly and thereby produce acceptable decisions. Further, it is often necessary that this process of perception, integration and decision should occur quickly. In some cases, to help achieve these goals, it may be possible to design machine-aided displays which assist for example, in the process of integrating information.

There are numerous devices or controls by which the human can input information to a machine; keyboards, joysticks, trackballs, buttons, switches and levers are all possibilities. In choosing controls it is necessary to consider a number of things including the environment in which the system operates, whether inputs are to be continuous or discrete, forces required, and costs.

Once appropriate displays and controls have been selected, the next phase of systems design is the integration of humans, machines, displays and controls into a workplace. Important considerations include placing the displays and controls where they can be seen, heard and used by the appropriate people. This includes assuring control/display compatibility which means that the movement of display elements in response to control motions should be consistent with normal conventions. For example, turning the volume control on a radio clockwise should result in an increase in volume rather than a decrease. Also part of workplace design involves considering combinations of displays for several similar functions into an integrated single display. A further factor is that any necessary interaction among humans should be facilitated. The comfort and safety of the humans should be assured.

The selection of displays and controls as well as the design of workplaces are discussed in detail in the textbooks; further reading is listed at the end of this chapter.

The final aspects of human factors in systems design involves the empirical evaluation of design alternatives and the development of selection and training procedures for the humans who are to use the system. For military systems and for some industrial systems, selection and training can be quite elaborate and hence quite expensive. Thus considerable research has been devoted (and continues to be) to developing reliable selection procedures and efficient training methods. On the other hand, selection and training in the domain of consumer products allows, at best, only the inclusion of an instruction booklet with the product.

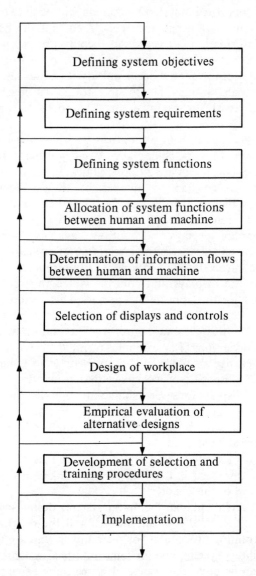

Figure 10.1   The systems design process.

The systems design process is summarized in Figure 10.1. This diagram illustrates the usual iterations between steps, indicating that the systems design process is not really quite as straightforward as the discussion here might lead one to believe. Further, the considerations change somewhat depending on the type of system (e.g. military system compared to a consumer product). Nevertheless, this brief introduction to systems design illustrates how the human factors specialist is involved in the systems design process.

SOME CURRENT ISSUES

As technology changes rapidly, human factors specialists are constantly beset with new issues to resolve. With little hesitation, one can claim that the area where this is most pronounced is that of computer technology. Computers are becoming faster and smaller, and also cheaper. Whether they know it or not, people are increasingly interacting with computers.

Computer technology is offering the systems designer many new alternatives. Some of these alternatives are unique because the computer is not 'just another machine'. In some situations, computers can be programmed to act intelligently and can replace people in tasks once thought to be the domain only of humans. Some of the more exotic examples include proving mathematical theorems (Bledsoe and Bruell 1974) and, to a limited extent, psychiatry (Weizenbaum 1966).

If a computer could be programmed to perform all tasks within a particular environment, human factors issues would not arise since humans would not be required. However, it is often the case that both humans and computers are needed. And, because of the increasing intelligence of computer programs, the human and computer have overlapping abilities. This allows for interesting possibilities in allocating system functions between humans and computers. Instead of the more usual static approach which strictly partitions functions between man and machine, one can consider a dynamic approach where human and computer have overlapping responsibilities such that any particular system function is allocated to the decision maker (human or computer) who, at that moment, is best able to perform that function (Rouse 1977).

While this dynamic approach can, theoretically at least, lead to a more efficient use of system resources and a better control of the workload imposed on the human, it does present practical problems. Humans will have to deal with computers as almost equals. This is quite different from the human's way of viewing conventional machines. Another practical problem is communication between human and computer, especially in the human to computer direction. When two humans work together as equals, they use facial expressions, tone of voice, etc. as additional communication links beyond normal talking or writing. To be an effective and unburdensome partner, the computer needs such additional information.

Several approaches to unobtrusively obtaining such information about the human have been proposed. For example, Enstrom and Rouse (1977) have used a model of human behaviour in tracking tasks analogous to flying an aeroplane or driving a car to infer, as the task is performed, whether or not the human is concentrating solely on the tracking task. Perhaps more promising and applicable to a wider task domain, is the approach of Wickens *et al.* (1976) who are attempting to use event-related brain potentials to communicate the state of the human to the computer.

In combination with improving computer technology, there are many new electronic display alternatives that offer the systems designer a wide variety of options (Sherr 1974; Markin 1976). While many applicable human factors design guidelines are available (e.g. Rouse 1975; Rijnsdorp and Rouse 1977), these new displays have some characteristics which dictate further human factors research.

Besides the straightforward issues of display legibility, there is the more difficult issue of how to utilize these new electronic displays which are very different from conventional electromechanical displays. More specifically, what should be displayed and what format it should have, so as to assure a reasonable transfer of training for those users who are familiar with the electromechanical displays, are questions for further study.

While a reasonable approach to this problem might be to slowly introduce electronic displays, incrementally replacing the electro-mechanical displays, the economics of the situation will not allow this. Electronics in general have become so inexpensive and versatile that systems designers virtually have to use them. As an illustration, one aircraft company is considering replacing most conventional aircraft cockpit displays by nine electronic displays (Bateman 1977). As Bateman points out, this brings up many human factors issues which require investigation. For example, what are the ramifications for the human of not having the usual plethora of conventional displays simultaneously available for viewing, but instead having a few electronic displays on which he (or the computer) can select to display various groupings of information?

The introduction of electronic displays has not been confined to aerospace applications. There has been considerable interest in the industrial area also (Rijnsdorp and Rouse 1977). In fact, applications in the industrial domain present more human factors problems than are found in aerospace applications because of the relatively low educational level of industrial workers and their relatively high reluctance to change, compared with aircraft pilots.

As more and more products of technology are utilized in industry and in the home, one learns all too quickly that machines do not always operate exactly as planned. Quite simply, they fail or break down and therefore, require repair. Thus, a vast maintenance industry has developed with specialists for repairing television sets, furnaces, plumbing, stoves, refrigerators, automobiles, aircraft and computers.

One might even argue that computer technology will eventually evolve to the point where most normal operations of systems will be completely automated and one of the human's main roles will be that of trouble-shooter or problem solver (Rouse 1978a). While some enthusiasts have claimed that even trouble-shooting will become completely automated, designers of such systems have found that this goal may not be realistic (Torrero 1977). Thus, an increasingly important human factors issue will be that of training humans to be trouble-shooters. Two important research directions developing in this area are computer-aided maintenance training (Brown and Burton 1975; Freedy and Crooks 1975) and studies aimed primarily at understanding the human's trouble-shooting abilities (Rasmussen and Jensen 1974; Rouse 1978a, 1978b). Some specific issues include determining what type of information is most useful to the human trouble-shooter and also, what aspects of trouble-shooting the human does not perform very well. Results in this latter area should be useful in designing computer-aided trouble-shooting systems.

An issue of particular interest concerns whether or not humans can be trained to have general trouble-shooting skills rather than skills applicable, for the most part, only to specific types of equipment. Many people are now trained in specific skills and, since technology is changing quickly, they have to be frequently retrained. If general skills could be developed, retraining would be much easier and consequently less expensive. While there is some data suggesting that general skills may not transfer very well among specific tasks (Smith 1973), the issue is important enough to require further research.

Within this brief essay, it is impossible to discuss all the current issues in human factors engineering. For example, other issues that are receiving increasing attention are mental workload and job satisfaction. With respect to mental workload, it is generally agreed that it is important and that both underload and overload are detrimental. However, numerous definitions and measures have been proposed and there is, as yet, no general consensus as to which are most appropriate (Moray 1978). Job satisfaction has become increasingly important to new generations of workers who have come to expect their jobs to provide more than just the means to obtaining the basic needs of food, clothing and shelter.

A perennial issue in almost all fields of research is that of theory versus practice. Practitioners claim that theorists avoid real problems to work on more manageable problems. On the other hand, theoreticians claim that many practitioners do not add anything of general usefulness to the body of human factors knowledge. Since, as noted in the introduction, the human factors area is populated by a very diverse set of individuals, this issue is raised quite frequently. However, it is not one that can be readily resolved and it is evident that both have an important part to play.

CONCLUSIONS

Within this chapter, I have briefly discussed allocation of functions between man and machine as well as the issues surrounding the design of electronic displays and the training of humans to be trouble-shooters. We have also very briefly mentioned mental workload, job satisfaction and the theory versus practice dilemma. Beyond those issues considered here, there are many others of current interest to those working in human factors.

One of the most appropriate ways for one to survey most of the current activities within human factors is to scan the recent issues of the half dozen journals mentioned below. This would certainly give the reader the breadth that this short chapter cannot possibly provide. Such a survey will give a similar impression of human factors to that provided here, namely, that human factors engineering is concerned with interfacing humans with the products of technology so as to assure that systems are appropriately designed for people who use and are affected by them.

With technology increasingly affecting everyone, this is an exciting time to be in the field of human factors engineering. Further, while the current rate of technological progress may not continue, there are a sufficient number of important and difficult issues to assure that human factors engineering will be a vital endeavour for a long time to come.

ACKNOWLEDGEMENT

The author would like to thank his colleagues, Gunnar Johannsen and Christopher Wickens, for their comments on an earlier version of this chapter and their suggestions for its improvement.

REFERENCES

Bateman, L. F. 1977. 'Flight decks for future civil transport aircraft.' *J. Navigation* *30*, 207-19.

Bernotat, R. and Hunt, D. P. 1977. *University curricula in ergonomics.* Meckenheim, Germany: Forschungsinstitut für Anthropotechnik.

Bledsoe, W. W. and Bruell, P. 1974. 'A man-machine theorem proving system.' *Artificial Intelligence 5*, 51-72.

Brown, J. S. and Burton, R. R. 1975. 'Multiple representation of knowledge for tutorial reasoning.' In Bobrow, D. G. and Collins, A. (eds) *Representation and understanding.* New York: Academic Press.

Enstrom, K. D. and Rouse, W. B. 1977. 'Real-time determination of how a human has allocated his attention between control and monitoring tasks.' *IEEE Trans. Systems, Man and Cybernetics SMC-7*, 153-61.

Freedy, A. and Crooks, W. H. 1975. 'Use of an adaptive decision model in computer-assisted training of electronic trouble-shooting.' *Proceedings of Conference on New Concepts in Maintenance Training*, Orlando, Florida. (Proceedings available from Defense Documentation Center, No. AO 17216.)

Johannsen, G., Boller, H. E., Donges, E. and Stein, W. 1977. *Der Mensch im Regelkreis: Lineare Modelle.* München: R. Oldenbourg Verlag.

Kraiss, K-F. and Moraal, J. (eds) 1976. *Introduction to human engineering.* Köln: Verlag TÜV Rheinland.

Markin, J. (ed.) 1976. Special Issue on Flat Panel and Large Screen Displays, *Proc. Soc. Information Display 17*.

McCormick, E. J. 1976. *Human factors engineering.* New York: McGraw-Hill.

McElroy, F. E. (ed.) 1969. *Accident prevention manual for industrial operators.* Chicago: National Safety Council.

Moray, N. (ed.) 1979. *Mental workload.* New York: Plenum Press.

Olishifski, J. B. and McElroy, F. E. (eds) 1971. *Fundamentals of industrial hygiene.* Chicago: National Safety Council.

Rasmussen, J. and Jensen, A. 1974. 'Mental procedures in real-life tasks: a case study of electronic trouble-shooting.' *Ergonomics 17*, 293-307.

Rijnsdorp, J. E. and Rouse, W. B. 1977. 'Design of man-machine interfaces in process control.' In H. R. Van Nauta Lemke and H. B. Verbruggen (eds) *Digital computer applications in process control.* Amsterdam: North-Holland.

Rouse, W. B. 1975. 'Design of man-computer interfaces for on-line interactive systems.' *Proc. IEEE 63*, 847-57.

Rouse, W. B. 1977. 'Human-computer interaction in multi-task situations.' *IEEE Trans. Systems, Man and Cybernetics SMC-7*, 384-92.

Rouse, W. B. 1978a. 'Human problem solving performance in a fault diagnosis task.' *IEEE Trans. Systems, Man and Cybernetics SMC-8*, 258-271.

Rouse, W. B. 1978b. 'A model of human decision making in a fault diagnosis task.' *IEEE Trans. Systems, Man and Cybernetics SMC-8*, 357-361.

Sheridan, T. B. and Ferrell, W. R. 1974. *Man-machine systems.* Cambridge, Massachusetts: MIT Press.

Sherr, S. (ed.) 1974. Special Issue on Computer Graphics, *Proc. Soc. Information Display 15*.

Smith, J. P. 1973. 'The effect of general versus specific heuristics in mathematical problem-solving tasks.' *Dissertation Abstracts International 34*, 2400.

Torrero, E. A. 1977. 'Automatic test equipment: not so easy.' *IEEE Spectrum 14*, Number 4, 29-34.

Van Cott, H. P. and Kinkade, R. G. (eds) 1972. *Human engineering guide to equipment design.* Washington, DC: U.S. Government Printing Office.

Weizenbaum, J. 1966. 'ELIZA – a computer program for the study of natural language communication between man and machine.' *Communications of the Association for Computing Machinery 9*, 36-44.

Wickens, C. D., Israel, J., McCarthy, G., Gopher, D. and Donchin, E. 1976. 'The use of event related potentials in the enhancement of system performance.' *Proc. Twelfth Ann. Conf. on Manual Control, NASA TM X 73, 170*, 124-134.

FURTHER READING

A fairly complete summary of journals and books in human factors engineering is provided by Bernotat and Hunt (1977). Representative textbooks dealing with human information processing from the applied standpoint include Van Cott and Kinkade (1972), McCormick (1976) and Kraiss and Moraal (1976). The research in this area is usually experimental and appears in journals such as *Human Factors, Ergonomics* and *Proceedings of the Society for Information Display*.

Physiologically orientated work in human factors is treated in the textbooks by McElroy (1969) and Olishifski and McElroy (1971); research reports which are mostly experimental are often published in journals such as *Ergonomics* and *Applied Ergonomics*.

Two quite recent textbooks on systems engineering are Sheridan and Ferrell (1974) and Johannsen *et al.* (1977). Research reports are published in *Institute of Electrical and Electronic Engineers: Transactions on Systems, Man and Cybernetics* and *International Journal of Man-Machine Studies*.

Chapter 11

Hemispheric Differences in Cognitive Processes: Evidence from Experimental Psychology

A. J. SIMPSON

INTRODUCTION

The foundations of our knowledge about differences between cognitive processes in the two halves of the brain have been laid by clinical work, whose two main aspects have been investigations of patients suffering from unilateral damage to the cortex (Milner 1971; Newcombe 1974) and studies of cases in which the two hemispheres have been separated by cutting the corpus callosum (Gazzaniga 1970; Nebes 1974). As with all inferences from clinical evidence, it is essential that the clinical results be confirmed and extended by studies of normal, intact subjects. Experimental techniques have been devised to enable such investigations to take place, and evidence provided by these techniques is discussed in this chapter. Existing reviews of studies of normal subjects may be found in Springer (1977) and in Dimond and Beaumont (1974).

A glance at the breadth of research in this area will reveal that a broad survey of recent developments cannot be accomplished in a short chapter. I have chosen, therefore, to survey the general field only briefly, and to review more deeply two topics: the perception of faces and of music. Recent advances in these areas particularly merit review.

VISION

The Tachistoscopic Method

The anatomical basis of work on laterality effects in vision is that
stimuli presented to one side of the fixation point are transmitted to
the contralateral hemisphere of the brain (Figure 11.1). Thus stimuli
presented in the right visual field (RVF) are initially processed by the
left hemisphere, and those in the left visual field (LVF) by the right.
Brief presentation is essential, ideally less than 150 msec (White 1969),
for otherwise eye movements towards the stimulus result in bilateral
registration. Stimulus durations as short as this leave little possibility
for complex material to be processed by the subject, yet most
investigators have used durations within this limit. Longer durations,
however, do not necessarily invalidate the results (Moscovitch,
Scullion and Christie 1976). It is important that the subject should be
unable to predict the side at which the stimulus is to occur (for if
he can fixation is harder to control) and stimuli are therefore
usually presented at random in the LVF and RVF, typically at least
2° from the fixation point.

Qualitative and Quantitative Hypotheses

The result of the procedure described above is the initial registration of
a stimulus in one hemisphere, but in intact subjects material directed
to one hemisphere will very shortly afterwards be shared with the
other, by transmission across the corpus callosum. Why, then, should
any differences be observed between responses to LVF and RVF
stimuli? Two main hypotheses suggest answers. One, qualitative,
proposes that each hemisphere exclusively specializes in particular
types of material, and transmits unsuitable material to the other side.
By this hypothesis, laterality effects are due to the time taken for
material to cross the corpus callosum or to the degradation of the
information during this transmission. The other, quantitative,
hypothesis proposes that both hemispheres can process any
information, but that the hemisphere that initially receives the
information operates on it according to its own predispositions. By
this hypothesis, laterality effects reflect the relative efficiency of the
two hemispheres at processing different sorts of material.

Evidence on this question is far from conclusive, but a number of
experiments point to the following tentative conclusion. For
visuospatial material, both hemispheres are able to function but the

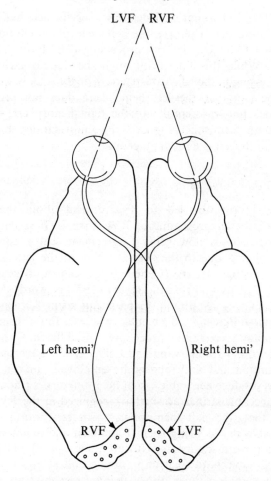

Figure 11.1 Schematic diagram of neural pathways producing representation of left visual field (LVF) and right visual field (RVF) stimuli in the contralateral hemispheres.

right is more efficient than the left; for verbal stimuli, the majority of the evidence suggests that material is processed exclusively in the left hemisphere, if necessary after transmission across the corpus callosum (Geffen, Bradshaw and Wallace 1971; Levy and Bowers 1974; Umiltà, Frost and Hyman 1972). On the basis of a number of her own studies, Springer (1977) has come to the same conclusion. There is some evidence, however, of a quantitative difference between the hemispheres even for verbal processing (Geffen, Bradshaw and

Nettleton 1973). I shall not consider this issue further, but it should be borne in mind that a phrase like 'left hemisphere inferiority' will be used loosely to indicate inferior processing of RVF (or, later, right ear) stimuli. While this inferiority might be due to exclusive but inferior processing in the left hemisphere, it might equally well be due either to the fact that the left hemisphere does not process the material at all, but transfers it into the right hemisphere, or to the fact that both hemispheres share the information, but initial registration in the left is disadvantageous.

Verbal and Visuospatial Material

Although early research led to disagreement about the reasons underlying the better processing of RVF than LVF verbal material (White 1969) there is now general agreement that a considerable component of it is due to the specialization of the left hemisphere for speech, whether letters (Cohen 1972; Geffen, Bradshaw and Nettleton 1972; Umiltà, Frost and Hyman 1972) or words (McKeever 1971) are employed as stimuli. Experiments using letters generally employ 'same-different' judgements, whereas those using words generally employ a recognition procedure. This difference is important, because Axelrod, Tirtadharyana and Leiber (1977) have shown that, when recognition and oral reports are employed, unpronounceable letter strings produce negligible visual field differences (though words and pronounceable strings are better recognized in the RVF). They concluded that the left hemisphere processes words as units (pronounceable strings being treated as units) and is not specialized for processing word fragments. However, the use of oral responses may have led subjects to treat unpronounceable strings in a special, possibly non-verbal, manner. When manual responses are employed within 'same-different' or target monitoring procedures, not-readily-pronounced strings of letters do produce left hemisphere superiority (Umiltà *et al.* 1972).

Complementing the verbal ability of the left hemisphere, evidence demonstrating superior visuospatial processing in the right hemisphere has been assembled by Kimura and Durnford (1974). Findings in this area are less robust, and Fontenot (1973) has drawn attention to many studies in which negligible differences were found. One specific result which seems to be in doubt is that of superior performance by the right hemisphere at spatial localization tasks – those in which the subject has to report the location of a dot briefly presented in one of a number of possible positions. Bryden (1976) reviews several studies which attempted to replicate Kimura's original finding (1969) of a superior 'spatial co-ordinate system' in the right hemisphere, most of which found no clear effect. When he introduced blank trials into the task, Bryden found subjects more inclined to report a dot, although none was present, in the LVF. He argues that this greater tendency to report stimuli in the LVF could have given adventitiously correct localizations in earlier experiments, and proposes that the right hemisphere is uncritical and disposed to 'consider almost any signal as evidence that something is happening in the LVF.' This interesting suggestion is, however, in conflict with Cohen (1973) who suggested on the basis of false positive responses in a 'same-different' task that the *left* hemisphere may be biased towards positive judgements, and Dimond and Beaumont (1971) who obtained more false positives from the left hemisphere in a vigilance task and suggested that the left hemisphere may be more 'motor impulsive' because of its general responsibility for initiating action.

In general, it seems likely that differences between the hemispheres in their tendencies to respond will depend principally on the nature of the task undertaken at any given time. Whatever is the case on that point, the reliability of the spatial localization phenomenon seems open to doubt. Nevertheless, the accumulated evidence from a wide variety of experiments requires that the general hypothesis of superior visuospatial processing in the right hemisphere should be retained. One such class of experiments, dealing with the perception of faces, merits examination in detail.

Perception of Faces

Numerous studies have shown that the perception of faces is faster or more accurate in the right hemisphere. Berlucchi, Brizzolara, Marzi, Rizzolatti and Umiltà (1974) and Rizzolatti, Umiltà and Berlucchi (1971) have shown faster processing of anonymous real faces presented in the LVF, and Geffen, Bradshaw and Wallace (1971) have shown faster processing of LVF 'Identi-Kit' faces. These investigators employed manual responses in target identification or 'same-different' judgement tasks, but even when verbal responses are required in a 'same-different' task (Hilliard 1973; Ellis and Shepherd 1975) the right hemisphere is found to be more accurate, despite the advantage one might expect this procedure to confer upon the left hemisphere. These results are consistent with evidence of an impairment in the ability of patients with right hemisphere damage to recognize faces (Newcombe 1974).

Under some circumstances the right hemisphere is inferior to the left at facial perception. Marzi, Brizzolara, Rizzolatti, Umiltà and Berlucchi (1974) reported that when subjects were required to discriminate (with a manual response) between four faces of *famous* people, faces presented in the RVF produced faster responses. Furthermore the LVF superiority usually obtained with anonymous faces (Rizzolatti *et al.* 1971) can be changed to a RVF superiority if subjects are taught to allocate a name to each face. These results suggest that retrieval of names from the left hemisphere is a more significant factor than visuospatial discrimination by the right.

When a large set of famous faces was employed, Marzi and Berlucchi (1977) again found a RVF superiority, this time for accuracy of recognition. They suggest that their subjects may have adopted a single-feature detection strategy and that this may have biased the task in the left hemisphere's favour, but a plausible alternative is that the face names to be retrieved from memory were more accessible in the left hemisphere. Data supporting the importance of language mechanisms in the recognition of faces have been reported by Berent (1977). Work on clinical patients (Warrington and James 1967) has shown that damage to the right hemisphere affects the perception of both unknown and famous faces. It is unlikely, therefore, that the *perceptual* mechanisms for recognizing familiar and unfamiliar faces are based in different hemispheres.

Another variable affecting facial discrimination is the degree of emotion expressed by the faces. Suberi and McKeever (1977) found that discrimination between four faces was faster in the right hemisphere for both emotional and unemotional faces, but that the laterality effect was considerably more marked for the emotional faces. The authors related this finding to other evidence of right hemisphere involvement in emotion (e.g. Carmon and Nachshon 1973, on the perception of emotional sounds). Also, Tucker, Roth, Arneson and Buckingham (1977) have concluded from eye-movement data that the right hemisphere is more active during stress, but, in contrast, an analysis of EEG records obtained while subjects imagined emotional events led Harman and Ray (1977) to the opposite conclusion – that the left hemisphere is more involved in emotion.

Moscovitch, Scullion and Christie (1976) have explored the parameters determining facial perception in the two hemispheres, using 'Identi-Kit' faces. Visual field differences in response times were absent when two faces were presented together for a 'same-different' judgement, but were present when briefly presented faces were compared with a memorized 'target' face. When Moscovitch *et al.* varied the interval between the occurrence of two faces to be judged for identity, visual field differences appeared only when this interval exceeded about 100 msec. They concluded that both hemispheres can equally well process the rapidly decaying 'iconic' trace while it exists, but following its disappearance the right hemisphere is faster at detecting facial identity. Even with no interval between the faces, Moscovitch *et al.* obtained faster responses to LVF stimuli provided that an abstraction process was required – they used comparisons between photographs and caricatures. (These faces were, incidentally, well known, but since their names were irrelevant to the task of transforming one visual representation into another the right hemisphere proved superior.) The results of these experiments may be summarized by saying that the early, precategorical stages of visual processing (those employed in straightforward visuospatial matching) are equivalent in the two hemispheres, but more complex visuospatial processes result in right hemisphere superiority.

The generality of the first part of this conclusion is dubious, however, for Oscar-Berman, Blumstein and De Luca (1976) have found that retrieval of symbolic material from iconic memory is faster in the right hemisphere. Furthermore, straightforward visuospatial matching does often produce right hemisphere superiority, as for example in an experiment by Gross (1972) in which two matrices of dots were simultaneously presented in a 'same-different' matching task.

The results reviewed in this section support the general conclusion that the right hemisphere is superior at perceiving faces, but indicate that this conclusion must be qualified to take account of a number of factors which affect the degree to which the particular skills of the two hemispheres are required by the task. Ultimately, the best predictor of hemispheric superiority is not the type of material to be processed, but rather the nature of the processes to be employed on the material.

AUDITION

Monaural and Dichotic Presentation

In the visual modality it is possible to present a single stimulus so that it is transmitted initially to just one of the cerebral hemispheres. In audition this cannot be done. Since each ear sends projections to

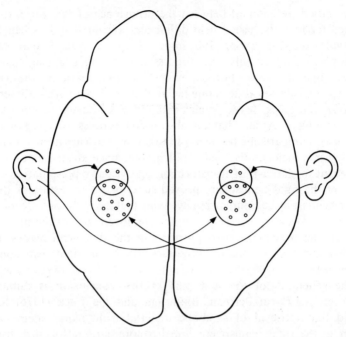

Figure 11.2   Schematic diagram of auditory cortical cells excited by stimulation from the contralateral or ipsilateral ear or both. More cells are excited contralaterally than ipsilaterally.

both hemispheres, a sound presented to one ear will be processed on both sides of the brain. However, since the contralateral pathways appear to excite more cortical cells than the ipsilateral do (Rosenzweig 1951; Vaughn and Ritter 1970) laterality effects might be expected from monaural stimulation. Also, since the contralaterally projected information suppresses the ipsilateral (Rosenzweig 1951; Butler, Keidel and Spreng 1969) dichotic presentation should enhance such effects. Figure 11.2 shows the pathways schematically. Although some researchers (e.g. Kimura 1964) have argued that dichotic presentation is essential if laterality effects are to be obtained, others (e.g. Catlin, VanDerveer and Teicher 1976) have obtained clear effects with monaural stimulation. Kallman (1977) has claimed that the same cerebral mechanisms are revealed by the monaural and dichotic methods.

Perception of Speech

Early work established an effect known as the 'right-ear advantage'

(REA) for verbal material. Kimura (1961, 1964) found that when word pairs or lists of digits were dichotically presented (Figure 11.3b) the right-ear material was more accurately recalled. She concluded that the REA is due to superior perception of speech by the left hemisphere. It is possible, however, that the recall procedure is sensitive to recall order. In an experiment by Freides (1977) subjects tended to recall spontaneously the right-ear material first. When they were instructed to retrieve first from a given side, the ear advantage corresponded to the side specified. On the other hand, Bryden (1963), using similar instructions, found the REA to be independent of recall order. Moreover, Freides' demonstration that subjects prefer to recall right-ear stimuli first, itself suggests that the right-ear material is more accessible in memory and may, therefore, have been more efficiently coded initially.

In recognition tasks biases due to order of report are much less likely to affect the results, yet the REA is still observed. Broadbent and Gregory (1964) employed a task in which four binaural recognition lists were presented shortly after the dichotic memory-list of digits. (The general procedure is shown in Figure 11.3c.) They found that digits presented to the right ear were more accurately recognized.

Experiments on ear differences for speech sounds, as opposed to complete words, generally support the notion of the REA for speech. Shankweiler and Studdert-Kennedy (1967) found that stop consonants (but not vowels) were more accurately perceived in the right ear in a dichotic listening procedure (Figure 11.3b). Superior left hemisphere perception of vowels has been demonstrated by Weiss and House (1973) who obtained such a result by using a low signal-noise ratio. Using a monaural paradigm (Figure 11.3a), Catlin, VanDerveer and Teicher (1976) found that consonant-vowel syllables presented to the right ear produced faster identification of a target syllable than did those in the left ear. Also using monaural stimulation, Kallman (1977) found that the speech target syllable /ga/ was more rapidly identified in the right ear whereas a non-verbal target (a plucked cello note) was more rapidly identified in the left. Another study comparing verbal and non-verbal material is due to Donnenfeld, Rosen, Mackavey and Curcio (1976). They controlled for order of report in a dichotic task and found a significant REA in subjects who heard verbal material (consonant-vowel phonemes) and a similar LEA in subjects who heard non-verbal material (pitch contours lasting for 480 msec).

These last results, which contrast speech and non-speech sounds, are part of a large body of research which demonstrates that the right hemisphere complements the left hemisphere's role in speech perception

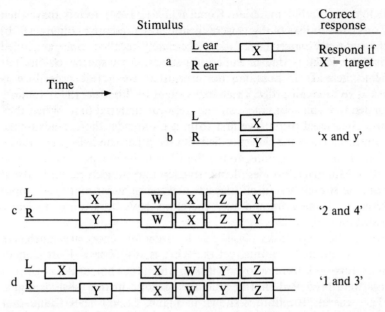

Figure 11.3 Four experimental procedures used in audition: a, monaural target identification (reaction time is measured); b, dichotic presentation with oral report; c, dichotic presentation of test items followed by binaural recognition sequence; d, monaural presentation of test items followed by binaural recognition. In a, the stimulus item is usually presented to the left or right ear at random; in c, and d, the test items occur at random positions in the binaural sequence. Each item (W, X, Y or Z) may be a word, a consonant-vowel syllable, a list of letters or digits, a musical chord or phrase or a series of pulses.

by specializing in the perception of non-verbal sounds, and music in particular.

Perception of Music

Although some work has been done on various non-verbal sounds (e.g. Carmon and Nachshon 1973; King and Kimura 1972) the form of sound that has received most attention is music. Early results indicated a right hemisphere superiority for music. Working with not particularly musical subjects, Kimura (1964) found that solo passages from Baroque concerti were more accurately recognized after presentation to the left ear (in a dichotic listening and binaural recognition procedure, see Figure 11.3c). This result is consistent with clinical evidence for a right hemisphere involvement in the perception of music (Milner 1962). Also using the paradigm illustrated in

Figure 11.3c, Gordon (1970) found that four-note chords played for 2 sec on an electronic organ produced a left-ear advantage in musicians. Whereas the left hemisphere scored at chance level, the right hemisphere performed at significantly above that level. Gordon failed to find, however, an ear advantage when his subjects were asked to recognize 4 sec melodies played on the recorder. Possibly the use of musicians as subjects or the relative importance of rhythm in the dance tunes employed, led to the disappearance of the right hemisphere's advantage. These factors are discussed later in this section.

Evidence which contrasts the right hemisphere's predilection for music with the left's linguistic preference is provided by Heilman, Bowers, Rasbury and Ray (1977). They required subjects to detect a pitch change in one of a short sequence of tones played monaurally twice. When speech was played with the tones, discrimination of right-ear tones was more affected; when music accompanied the tones, the reverse was true, presumably because of interference within the right hemisphere as it attempted to process both the tones and the music. Geffen, Bradshaw and Nettleton (1973) showed that whereas a secondary *verbal* task (dichotic listening to letters) reversed the RVF advantage in a primary visual digit-detection task, a secondary *musical* task (dichotic listening to Bach and Schumann for a wrong note) did not. Presumably the two verbal tasks produced interference within the left hemisphere, whereas the musical task (carried out by the right hemisphere) allowed the left hemisphere to proceed with the primary task undistracted by interference.

These experiments suggest that music is processed in the right hemisphere. Yet music is a far from unitary entity, and is generally considered to consist of three components – melody, harmony and rhythm. Melody and harmony seem to be right hemisphere functions, but what of rhythm? Several investigators (e.g. Cohen 1973; Nachshon and Carmon 1975; Levy-Agresti and Sperry 1968) have suggested that the left hemisphere operates in a sequential fashion, in which case the sequential component of music, rhythm, might be expected to show a left hemisphere advantage. Robinson and Solomon (1974) have also predicted a left hemisphere superiority for rhythm processing, although they argued on the basis of the importance of rhythm in speech. Using the recognition procedure illustrated in Figure 11.3c, where each item to be recognized was a sequence of 50 and 150 msec pulses, Robinson and Solomon found that sequences presented to the right ear were more accurately recognized. A similar result occurred in an experiment by Natale (1977) who also showed that more complex rhythms conferred a greater advantage on the left hemisphere. Gordon (1974) has concluded that melody recognition becomes less of a right hemisphere task as rhythm becomes more important for distinguishing phrases.

An important factor in the perception of music is the type of subject and his strategy. Bever and Chiarello (1974) distinguished between musically naive listeners who focus on 'the overall melodic contour' (i.e. the tune) and musically experienced listeners, who perceive relations between notes. Using constant rhythm musical phrases, they found that naive musicians could not identify excerpts from the phrases, but could tell whether the full phrases had been presented earlier in the experiment, and did this better when they had been presented to the left ear. In contrast, experienced musicians could recognize both excerpts and the full phrases, and in the second task they showed a right-ear advantage. Bever and Chiarello concluded that experienced musicians recognize right-ear melodies better than left because they subject the phrases to analysis (a left hemisphere process) whereas naive musicians do better with the left ear because their holistic strategy is a right hemisphere function. Encouraged by these findings, Gordon (1975) re-examined his non-significant data on melody recognition (mentioned earlier) and found that the size of the recognition score was inversely related to the degree of right hemisphere superiority. Those musicians who had the highest recognition scores tended to display a left hemisphere superiority.

The skilled musician's employment of the left hemisphere for processing music has been related by Johnson (1977) to the general role of the left hemisphere in language. Johnson found that differences between musicians and non-musicians, when recognizing violin melodies presented dichotically for 2 sec, were simply the result of greater use of the left hemisphere by musicians – the two groups did not differ in their left ear scores. He argued that a musician's experience with 'the language of music' leads to the activation of a language mechanism in the left hemisphere which analyzes musical sounds into meaningful sequences of units in a similar manner to its analysis of speech sounds. The left hemisphere superiority displayed by musicians in this experiment may, however, have been partly due to the very short sequences employed, for brief phrases may encourage analysis. Under other circumstances, described below, musicians do not show left hemisphere superiority when processing music.

Even when a left hemisphere advantage does appear, this may not necessarily be due to the analysis of intervals associated with musicianship, as argued by Bever and Chiarello. Johnson, Bowers,

Gamble, Lyons, Presbrey and Vetter (1977), using novel six-beat sequences in the recognition procedure shown in Figure 11.3d, found that musicians and non-musicians were alike in displaying right hemisphere superiority – unless they could transcribe music. Those subjects who possessed this skill showed a left hemisphere superiority for conventional musical phrases, but the reverse for random pitch and rhythm patterns. These results suggest that the left hemisphere superiority of those who could transcribe may not have reflected analysis as such, but rather the allocation of names to the notes and pitch intervals. Analysis would still be possible with random intervals, but assignment of names would be much harder. Musicians unable to transcribe would not be able to allocate names readily, even to conventional intervals, hence their right hemisphere advantage.

Research by Goodglass and Calderon (1977) supports the view that many musicians process music in the right hemisphere. They employed trained musicians in a range of dichotic tasks which involved both verbal and musical processing. When their subjects had to report both dichotically presented digits and dichotic note patterns, an independent and concurrent left hemisphere superiority for the verbal component of the task, and right hemisphere superiority for the tonal part, was found.

One resolution of the question of whether musicians and non-musicians differ in their laterality for music is provided by Gates and Bradshaw (1977), who argue that processing strategy rather than musical training determines hemispheric superiority. They report results in which both trained musicians and non-musicians were more accurate in the left hemisphere at recognizing excerpts from unfamiliar melodies, but were more accurate in the right hemisphere for familiar melodies. Such results are consistent with the notion that unfamiliar melodies are subjected to analysis (a left hemisphere strategy) while familiar melodies are treated holistically (a right hemisphere strategy). It might seem that Gates and Bradshaw's results conflict with those of Johnson *et al.* and those of Goodglass and Calderon, who found the right hemisphere to be generally superior even though the tunes they employed were unfamiliar. An important difference in the Gates and Bradshaw experiment is, however, its use of recognition of excerpts. Such a procedure probably encourages analysis whereas the other two experiments, by requiring subjects to recognize or report complete phrases, may have encouraged an holistic approach.

The conclusion to be drawn with respect to hemispheric superiority for the perception of music is similar to that drawn about the perception of faces. While a general right hemisphere advantage is evident, in any particular situation the best predictor of hemispheric superiority will be the nature of the processes to be employed – in particular whether an analytic or holistic or naming strategy is likely to be induced by the nature of the task or the subject's aptitudes.

FURTHER ISSUES

It has been necessary in this review to ignore a number of important issues (e.g. the development of laterality, the relationship between handedness and hemispheric differences in cognitive processes, and the question of sex differences in laterality) but one further issue which should be mentioned is that of theories of hemispheric differences. Some workers (e.g. Kimura 1964; McKeever 1971) incline towards the view that differences in perceptual processes underlie laterality effects. An alternative view is that different memory processes are involved (Seamon 1974), or that perception and short-term memory interact (Donnenfeld, Rosen, Mackavey and Curcio 1976). Alternatively again, Kinsbourne (1970, 1973) has argued that laterality effects reflect different attentional processes in the two hemispheres.

All these theories apply the verbal/non-verbal distinction to the two hemispheres, but a different theoretical approach is one which emphasizes the type of processing employed by the subject rather than the nature of the material processed. Reference was made to analytic and holistic strategies in the section on music, and this distinction is seen by some researchers as more fundamental than the verbal/non-verbal dichotomy. Stimulated by Levy-Agresti and Sperry's report (1968) of an analytic strategy in the left hemisphere and an holistic strategy in the right hemisphere of commissurotomized patients, workers have attempted to explore this distinction in intact subjects. Patterson and Bradshaw (1975) and Bradshaw, Gates and Patterson (1976) have suggested that when visuospatial material produces the usual right hemisphere superiority, this may be because holistic identity-matching judgements are being made. If the subject has to analyze a visuospatial stimulus into separate components, the left hemisphere often proves to be superior, due to its predisposition for analysis. It seems, therefore, that the simple verbal/non-verbal description of stimuli will not do as a predictor of hemispheric differences, since left hemisphere superiority can be obtained with non-verbal material, but the suggestion that the analytic-holistic dichotomy may be more fundamental than the verbal-visuospatial is almost impossible to test, for whenever analysis is required verbal processes may still be the vehicle on which the analysis rests.

Many studies in the areas of facial and musical perception demonstrate the shortcomings of the unqualified assertion that non-verbal material is processed more efficiently by the right hemisphere. However, while the strategies employed by the hemispheres, rather than the material presented, may be the main determinants of hemispheric superiority, it is likely that the left hemisphere's analytic style of processing cannot be separated from linguistic thinking and the right hemisphere's holistic impression may be equally inseparable from visuospatial or auditory imagery.

REFERENCES

Axelrod, S., Tirtadharyana, H. and Leiber, L. 1977. 'Oral report of words and word approximations presented to the left or right visual field.' *Brain and Language 4*, 508-20.

Berent, S. 1977. 'Functional asymmetry of the human brain in the recognition of faces.' *Neuropsychologia 15*, 829-31.

Berlucchi, G., Brizzolara, D., Marzi, C. A., Rizzolatti, G. and Umiltà, C. 1974. 'Can lateral asymmetries in attention explain interfield differences in visual perception?' *Cortex 10*, 177-85.

Bever, T. G. and Chiarello, R. J. 1974. 'Cerebral dominance in musicians and nonmusicians.' *Science 185*, 537-9.

Bradshaw, J. L., Gates, A. and Patterson, K. 1976. 'Hemispheric differences in processing visual patterns.' *Quart. J. exp. Psychol. 28*, 667-81.

Broadbent, D. E. and Gregory, M. 1964. 'Accuracy of recognition for speech presented to the right and left ears.' *Quart. J. exp. Psychol. 16*, 359-60.

Bryden, M. P. 1963. 'Ear preference in auditory perception.' *J. exp. Psychol. 65*, 103-5.

Bryden, M. P. 1976. 'Response bias and hemispheric differences in dot localisation.' *Perception and Psychophysics 19*, 23-8.

Butler, R. A., Keidel, W. D. and Spreng, M. 1969. 'An investigation of the human cortical evoked potential under conditions of monaural and binaural stimulation.' *Acta Oto-laryngologica 68*, 317-26.

Carmon, A. and Nachshon, I. 1973. 'Ear asymmetry in perception of emotional non-verbal stimuli.' *Acta Psychologica 37*, 351-7.

Catlin, J., VanDerveer, N. J. and Teicher, R. D. 1976. 'Monaural right-ear advantage in a target identification task.' *Brain and Language 3*, 470-81.

Cohen, G. 1972. 'Hemispheric differences in a letter classification task.' *Perception and Psychophysics 11*, 139-42.

Cohen, G. 1973. 'Hemispheric differences in serial versus parallel processing.' *J. exp. Psychol. 97*, 349-56.

Dimond, S. J. and Beaumont, G. 1971. 'Hemisphere function and vigilance.' *Quart. J. exp. Psychol. 23*, 443-448.

Dimond, S. J. and Beaumont, G. 1974. 'Experimental studies of hemisphere function in the human brain.' In S. J. Dimond and J. G. Beaumont (eds) *Hemisphere function in the human brain.* London: Elek Science.

Donnenfeld, H., Rosen, J. J., Mackavey, W. and Curcio, F. 1976. 'Effects of expectancy and order of report on auditory asymmetries.' *Brain and Language 3*, 350-8.

Ellis, H. D. and Shepherd, J. W. 1975. 'Recognition of upright and inverted faces presented in the left and right visual fields.' *Cortex 11*, 3-7.

Fontenot, D. J. 1973. 'Visual field differences in the recognition of verbal and non-verbal stimuli in man.' *J. comp. physiol. Psychol. 85*, 564-9.

Freides, D. 1977. 'Do dichotic listening procedures measure lateralization of information processing or retrieval strategy?' *Perception and Psychophysics 21*, 259-63.

Gates, A. and Bradshaw, J. L. 1977. 'Music perception and cerebral asymmetries.' *Cortex 13*, 390-401.

Gazzaniga, M. S. 1970. *The bisected brain.* New York: Appleton.

Geffen, G., Bradshaw, J. L. and Wallace, G. 1971. 'Interhemispheric effects on reaction time to verbal and non-verbal visual stimuli.' *J. exp. Psychol. 87*, 415-22.

Geffen, G., Bradshaw, J. L. and Nettleton, N. C. 1972. 'Hemispheric asymmetry: verbal and spatial encoding of visual stimuli.' *J. exp. Psychol. 95*, 25-31.

Geffen, G., Bradshaw, J. L. and Nettleton, N. C. 1973. 'Attention and hemispheric differences in reaction time during simultaneous audio-visual tasks.' *Quart. J. exp. Psychol. 25*, 404-12.

Goodglass, H. and Calderon, M. 1977. 'Parallel processing of verbal and musical stimuli in right and left hemispheres.' *Neuropsychologia 15*, 397-407.

Gordon, H. W. 1970. 'Hemispheric asymmetries in the perception of musical chords.' *Cortex 6*, 387-98.

Gordon, H. W. 1974. 'Auditory specialization of the right and left hemispheres.' In M. Kinsbourne and W. L. Smith (eds) *Hemispheric disconnection and cerebral function.* Springfield, Illinois: Thomas.

Gordon, H. W. 1975. 'Hemispheric asymmetry and musical performance.' *Science 189*, 68-9.

Gross, M. 1972. 'Hemispheric specialisation for processing of visually-presented verbal and spatial stimuli.' *Perception and Psychophysics 12*, 537-63.

Harman, D. W. and Ray, W. J. 1977. 'Hemispheric activity during affective verbal stimuli: an EEG study.' *Neuropsychologia 15*, 457-60.

Heilman, K. M., Bowers, D., Rasbury, W. C. and Ray, R. M. 1977. 'Ear asymmetries on a selective attention task.' *Brain and Language 4*, 390-5.

Hilliard, R. D. 1973. 'Hemispheric laterality effects on a facial recognition task in normal subjects.' *Cortex 9*, 246-58.

Johnson, P. R. 1977. 'Dichotically-stimulated ear differences in musicians and non-musicians.' *Cortex 13*, 385-9.

Johnson, R. C., Bowers, J. K., Gamble, M., Lyons, F. M., Presbrey, T. W. and Vetter, R. R. 1977. 'Ability to transcribe music and ear superiority for tone sequences.' *Cortex 13*, 295-9.

Kallman, H. J. 1977. 'Ear asymmetries with monaurally-presented sounds.' *Neuropsychologia 15*, 833-5.

Kimura, D. 1961. 'Cerebral dominance and the perception of verbal stimuli.' *Canad. J. Psychol. 15*, 166-71.

Kimura, D. 1964. 'Left-right differences in the perception of melodies.' *Quart. J. exp. Psychol. 16*, 355-8.

Kimura, D. 1969. 'Spatial localisation in left and right visual fields.' *Canad. J. Psychol. 23*, 445-58.

Kimura, D. and Durnford, M. 1974. 'Normal studies on the function of the right hemisphere in vision.' In S. J. Dimond and J. G. Beaumont (eds) *Hemisphere function in the human brain.* London: Elek Science.

King, F. L. and Kimura, D. 1972. 'Left-ear superiority in dichotic perception of vocal non-verbal sounds.' *Canad. J. Psychol. 26*, 111-16.

Kinsbourne, M. 1970. 'The cerebral basis of lateral asymmetries in attention.' *Acta Psychologica 33*, 193-201.

Kinsbourne, M. 1973. 'The control of attention by interaction between the cerebral hemispheres.' In S. Kornblum (ed.) *Attention and performance IV* New York: Academic Press.

Levy, C. M. and Bowers, D. 1974. 'Hemispheric asymmetry of reaction time in a dichotic discrimination task.' *Cortex 10*, 18-25.

Levy-Agresti, J. and Sperry, R. W. 1968. 'Differential perceptual capacities in major and minor hemispheres.' *Proc. Nat. Acad. Sci. 61*, 1151.

McKeever, W. F. 1971. 'Lateral word recognition: effects of unilateral and bilateral presentation, asynchrony of bilateral presentation, and forced order of report.' *Quart. J. exp. Psychol. 23*, 410-16.

Marzi, C. A. and Berlucchi, G. 1977. 'Right visual field superiority for accuracy of recognition of famous faces in normals.' *Neuropsychologia 15*, 751-6.

Marzi, C. A., Brizzolara, D., Rizzolatti, G., Umiltà, C. and Berlucchi, G. 1974. 'Left hemisphere superiority for the recognition of well known faces.' *Brain Res. 66*, 358.

Milner, B. 1962. 'Laterality effects in audition.' In V. B. Mountcastle (ed.) *Interhemispheric relations and cerebral dominance.* Baltimore: John Hopkins.

Milner, B. 1971. 'Interhemispheric differences in the localization of psychological processes in man.' *Brit. med. Bull. 27*, 272-7.

Moscovitch, M., Scullion, D. and Christie, D. 1976. 'Early versus late stages of processing and their relation to functional hemispheric asymmetries in face recognition.' *J. exp. Psychol: Hum. Percep. and Perform. 2*, 401-16.

Nachshon, I. and Carmon, A. 1975. 'Hand preference in sequential and spatial discrimination tasks.' *Cortex 11*, 123-31.

Natale, M. 1977. 'Perception of non-linguistic auditory rhythms by the speech hemisphere.' *Brain and Language 4*, 32-44.

Nebes, R. D. 1974. 'Hemispheric specialization in commissurotomised man.' *Psychol. Bull. 81*, 1-14.

Newcombe, F. 1974. 'Selective deficits after focal cerebral injury.' In S. J. Dimond and J. G. Beaumont (eds) *Hemisphere function in the human brain.* London: Elek Science.

Oscar-Berman, M., Blumstein, S. and De Luca, D. 1976. 'Iconic recognition of musical symbols in the lateral visual fields.' *Cortex 12*, 241-8.

Patterson, K. and Bradshaw, J. L. 1975. 'Differential hemispheric mediation of nonverbal visual stimuli.' *J. exp. Psychol: Hum. Percep. and Perform. 1*, 246-52.

Rizzolatti, G., Umiltà, C. and Berlucchi, G. 1971. 'Opposite superiorities of the right and left cerebral hemispheres in discriminative reaction time to physiognomical and alphabetical material.' *Brain 94*, 431-42.

Robinson, G. M. and Solomon, D. J. 1974. 'Rhythm is processed by the speech hemisphere.' *J. exp. Psychol. 102*, 508-11.

Rosenzweig, M. R. 1951. 'Representations of the two ears at the auditory cortex.' *Amer. J. Physiol. 167*, 147-58.

Seamon, J. G. 1974. 'Coding and retrieval processes and the hemispheres of the brain.' In S. J. Dimond and J. G. Beaumont (eds) *Hemisphere function in the human brain*. London: Elek Science.

Shankweiler, D. and Studdert-Kennedy, M. 1967. 'Identification of consonants and words presented to the left and right ears.' *Quart. J. exp. Psychol. 19*, 59-63.

Springer, S. P. 1977. 'Tachistoscopic and dichotic-listening investigations of laterality in normal human subjects.' In S. Harnad, R. W. Doty, L. Goldstein, J. Jaynes and G. Krauthamer (eds) *Lateralisation in the nervous system*. New York: Academic Press.

Suberi, M. and McKeever, W. F. 1977. 'Differential right hemispheric memory storage of emotional and non-emotional faces.' *Neuropsychologia 15*, 757-68.

Tucker, D. M., Roth, R. S., Arneson, B. A. and Buckingham, V. 1977. 'Right hemisphere activation during stress.' *Neuropsychologia 15*, 697-700.

Umiltà, C., Frost, N. and Hyman, R. 1972. 'Interhemispheric effects on choice reaction times to one-, two- and three-letter displays.' *J. exp. Psychol. 93*, 198-204.

Vaughn, H. and Ritter, W. 1970. 'The sources of auditory evoked responses recorded from the human scalp.' *EEG clin. Neurophysiol. 28*, 360-7.

Warrington, E. K. and James, M. 1967. 'An experimental investigation of facial recognition in patients with unilateral cerebral lesions.' *Cortex 3*, 317-26.

Weiss, M. and House, A. S. 1973. 'Perception of dichotically presented vowels.' *J. Acoust. Soc. Amer. 53*, 51-8.

White, M. J. 1969. 'Laterality differences in perception: a review.' *Psychol. Bull. 72*, 387-405.

Chapter 12

The Ecology of Primate Psychology

ANDREW WHITEN

INTRODUCTION: PRIMATE PSYCHOLOGY AND ECOLOGY

Tinbergen (1963) has pointed out that when one asks the question *'Why* does this animal behave in this way?' it can mean at least four very different things. The same applies to psychological processes, and we can put it another way by considering four different *answers* to the question of why any psychological process is as it is. First, we may answer that it is the result of immediate external and internal causal factors; in this way the question of why a certain female monkey is soliciting copulation might be answered by reference to such factors as her current sexual receptivity and the presence of a male. Secondly, we may refer to developmental factors in our answer; perhaps the process controlling soliciting depends on the long-term effects of sexual play with peers in infancy. Thirdly, we might answer with respect to the biological function of the process – the consequences of such processes which had led to their selection in competition with other processes in prior evolutionary history. What benefits does the female's behaviour confer? The fourth answer makes reference to phylogenetic relationships; the female may behave in this way because her ancestors had similar psychologies which set certain constraints on what was likely to evolve next. A new species of cat might behave differently simply because it evolved from an ancestor with cat characteristics and not from one with primate characteristics.

The Evolutionary Answers

The four different answers to the question 'why?' are not exclusive; they may be applied simultaneously to the same behaviour or psychological process. However, comparative psychologists studying primates have, by concentrating on laboratory research, a small range of species, and environmental determinants of learned behaviour, almost ignored the last two of the four types of answer – the evolutionary answers.

In short, what has been neglected is the adaptation of an animal to its natural environment which results from an abiding relationship between the animal's ancestors and significant features of that environment. It is that adaptive relationship which I shall refer to as ecological, and whose implications for understanding primate psychology I shall pursue. But two important points must be made before exploring specific implications.

We should not neglect any of the four 'whys'. Dealing with the last two types of answer does not imply ignoring the first two – just the opposite; what it does do is to give meaning to the particular question asked in those categories. Much of the vast research effort focusing on primate learning and cognition studied in the laboratory (see Bessemer and Stollnitz 1971; Jarrard 1971; Medin and Davis 1974; Davis 1974; Wilson 1974; Rogers and Davenport 1975; Rumbaugh 1975; Fouts 1975 for reviews of different areas) could benefit from this perspective.

It seems likely, for example, that chimpanzees who can be made to demonstrate certain linguistic abilities (Premack 1971) did not acquire them because they served a linguistic function; discovering what function they do serve in the chimpanzee's natural ecology, besides its intrinsic interest, would provide insights to guide the sort of question to be asked about their causation and development.

The same argument applies outside the laboratory; studying cognitive processes in the natural environment and taking into account their ecology, is likely to lead to fruitful developmental and causal answers as well as evolutionary ones. Altmann and Altmann (1970), for example, believe that baboon movements are guided by a mental map of important resources, such as water-holes and sleeping-groves, and hazards such as previous leopard attack sites. This must be a funda-mental feature of the baboon's psychological relationship with its world, yet it would be completely missed by any approach which removed the baboon from its natural ecology. Such a mental system would have important developmental implications, notably in what the infant could learn from the combined experience of the group members. It also raises profound causal questions. Even if we were considering only a single baboon, the problem presented to it is one of how to budget the various essential daily activities and organize them sequentially so as to move from safe sleeping-grove to sleeping-grove, taking in perhaps a water-hole and certain fruiting trees and avoiding high risk areas. When and where are decisions made and on what basis?

But we are not dealing with a single baboon; baboon ecology involves a social group and it appears that the causal web may thus be complicated by the added necessity of negotiation between individuals over their different plans. Kummer (1968) describes how younger hamadryas baboon males may make initiations of movement in several directions, but the final decision governing the route of the whole group may come from an old high-ranking male in the middle of the group who eventually clearly adopts one of these 'suggestions'.

We should not neglect learning. There are two qualitatively different processes producing adaptation to the environment. Evolution by natural selection, in which the 'information on the environment' entailed in adaptation is coded and transmitted genetically, and learning during the individual's lifetime, in which the relevant information is coded only psychologically. In order to understand why this second process is not excluded from the definition of adaptation above, which made reference to an abiding relationship between several generations and the environment, it is useful to divide it into individual learning and social learning. Social learning is pervasive in primates; it refers to acquisition through observation of other members of the social group, and for it to be adaptive a continuity in the relationship with the environment across generations is obviously required. Individual learning does not involve such social transfer. But even adaptation through learning on one's own depends on the possession of a mechanism which ensures that the animal learns what *is* adaptive for it, and therefore again on a continuity in certain features of the ecological relationship between psychology and environment across generations.

ECOLOGY OF SOCIAL BEHAVIOUR

The notion of ecology as applied to either behaviour or psychology will for many tend to conjure up the idea that we are dealing with 'basic' biological phenomena such as feeding. I shall therefore focus instead on social behaviour, so as to emphasize that the approach is in no way necessarily restricted to some subset of psychological components.

Ecological Grades and Social Structure

Crook and Gartlan (1966) were the first to propose how aspects of social organization characteristic of different primate groups could be correlated with features of the environment in order to construct different *grades of socio-ecological relationship*. There are nearly 200 species of primates and only a few dozen had by then been subjected to significant field study, but Crook and Gartlan were able to construct five major grades (Table 12.1). The progression through the grades may represent the evolutionary process whereby, starting with primitive forms, types of primate societies evolved to exploit different environments. This does not mean that the advanced forms which evolved most recently, such as the apes, are all in the highest grade, because these forms have not necessarily exploited the environment of type V which is most different from that of the primitive forms.

Grade I contains primitive nocturnal primates which live on insects, a way of life which is associated with a fairly solitary existence. With a change to eating fruit or leaves in grade II we find small social groups and since sociality is one of the fundamental characteristics of all higher primate psychology this was a major evolutionary step. Crook and Gartlan suggest that it was produced by the switch from insect-hunting, where the resources are small and scattered and so cannot be exploited by groups, to a feeding ecology in which groups can more efficiently find and exploit resources which occur in widely spaced yet concentrated patches, such as fruiting trees.

Grade III primates tend to live near the forest fringe and it is suggested that their larger group sizes and the inclusion of several males instead of the single adult male characteristic of grades I and II, may be a protective adaptation to an increased predator threat in such an environment. These changes are taken further in grade IV where species such as baboons living in dry forest fringes and tree savannah may have larger group sizes of up to about two hundred individuals, with several adult males clearly involved in protective behaviour with respect to predators. Such groups tend to wander over a larger home range, avoiding neighbouring groups rather than aggressively defending territorial boundaries. This is probably because their food is at low density, which, coupled with high group size entails a large home

Table 12.1 *Adaptive grades of primates (after Crook and Gartlan 1966)*

	Grade I	*Grade II*	*Grade III*	*Grade IV*	*Grade V*
Examples	Bush babies Some lemurs	Some lemurs Gibbons	Colubus monkeys Gorillas	Macaques Savannah baboons	Hamadryas baboons Gelada baboons
Habitat	Forest	Forest	Forest/ Forest fringe	Forest fringe/ Tree savannah	Grassland/ Arid savannah
Diet	Mostly insects	Fruit/Leaves	Fruit/Fruit and leaves	Vegetarian-omnivore Occasionally carnivorous in baboon and chimpanzee	Vegetarian-omnivore Hamadryas occasionally carnivorous
Diurnal activity	Nocturnal	Crepuscular or diurnal	Diurnal	Diurnal	Diurnal
Size of groups	Usually solitary	Very small groups	Small to occasionally large parties	Medium to large groups	Medium to large, and very variable
Reproductive units	Pairs where known	Small family parties	Multi-male groups	Multi-male groups	One-male groups
Sexual dimorphism and social role differentiation	Slight	Slight	Slight except gorilla	Marked in baboons and macaques	Marked
Population dispersion	Probably territories	Territories with displays and marking	Territories and home ranges	Usually home range	Home range. Group dispersion and congregation

range which has such a long border that it cannot be defended economically.

Grade V species – the patas monkey, and hamadryas and gelada baboons – are vegetarian omnivores inhabiting arid savannah and grassland, and are especially interesting since a terrestrial savannah existence is thought to have characterized the early stages of human evolution (De Vore and Washburn 1963; Jolly 1970; Leakey and Lewin 1977). Large group sizes are maintained and males are active in detection or defence against predators. But there is an important change in sexual relationships. In contrast to the multi-male group structure of grade IV, in which mating is promiscuous with a female in oestrous being mated by several males, all three species assigned to grade V exhibit a harem or one-male unit structure in which one male is permanently associated with one or several females with whom he mates exclusively. It is suggested that this organization adapts individuals of these species to their harsh habitat by reducing the number of males in the group so that the poor food supply is shared among several females rather than by other males who because of their size would consume much food yet contribute nothing to the breeding potential of the group; one male is sufficient to fertilize all the females and perhaps to protect them.

This argument is pursued in explaining the plasticity of structure which is evident in the gelada (Crook 1966). When geladas were faced with a phase of particularly poor feeding conditions the one-male units diverged from the excess males which formed all-male units, foraging separately and thus further reducing competition for scarce resources. Hamadryas baboon social structure changes during a *daily* cycle (Kummer 1968). A group or band consists of a particular combination of one-male units. At night several such bands may aggregate into a troop of several hundred individuals at sleeping cliffs, disbanding again in the morning and travelling as separate groups to different feeding sites. Here the bands split into one-male units to forage. Thus there exists at least a three-level organization (recently a fourth may have been established), each level representing an ecological adaptation to the environment relevant to different activities in the daily cycle. The troops appear to be an adaptation to scarcity of safe sleeping sites, the one-male units to feeding conditions. The function of the intermediate bands is not so obvious but it may represent an optimal compromise between the numbers appropriate for protection between sleeping and feeding sites and the ideal number for exploiting the different feeding locations.

The original Crook and Gartlan scheme was intended as a first attempt only. It is presented here since it does introduce in a fairly clear way the general range of primate social and ecological variety as well as some basic ideas about the way the natural environment can mould a species' social psychology. But the concept has undergone a number of changes in the decade following its formulation. First, the explosion in field studies has complicated the picture and three ways in which it has done so will be outlined.

Phylogenetic inertia. Studies concerning hitherto little researched species, such as the many forest-living primates, have revealed a variety of social structures across grades I-III despite an apparent similarity in habitat. Wilson (1975) emphasizes that if this does represent a failure to find correlations between ecology and social structure one reason may be phylogenetic inertia. Recall that the fourth answer to Tinbergen's 'why?' referred to the phylogenetic constraints placed on an animal's behaviour by its ancestry. Such constraints are not independent of ecology since they themselves are a product of natural selection, but they represent adaptations to the relatively ancient ancestral environment rather than the immediately recent one. Phylogenetic inertia can therefore prevent the establishment of neat socio-ecological grades in at least two ways – first, because one species moving into a similar habitat to that exploited by another species may bring different equipment, whether morphological or psychological. An example of the former which may clarify this is the difference in size between two open-country primates, the little patas monkey and the much larger savannah baboon. The latter seems to exploit its size in defence of the group by, in certain circumstances, direct joint activity by adult males. The smaller patas male is not capable of such direct defence and instead acts as a 'watchdog', alerting his harem to predators and fleeing from them like the females. This difference in the social role of males, profound in itself, may have had further influence on the difference in group size and structure, since the baboons may benefit by living in large groups containing several protective males, whereas the smaller patas one-male group would not gain in the same way. Thus a single phylogenetically conservative feature – male size – may lead to different socio-ecological correlates when faced with similar environmental characteristics.

A second way in which inertia may be responsible for a lack of universal socio-ecological correlations is where the particular relationship between a population and its environment is relatively recent, so that ancestral 'adaptations' are no longer adaptive. It is difficult to know to what extent this may be true for any species overall, but we can see the effect clearly at the edge of a species' habitat. In Ethiopia there is a fairly clear change in ecological conditions along a river at the Awash Falls. Roughly corresponding to this is a change from savannah baboons, living in multi-male groups, to hamadryas baboons, living in hierarchically organized groups of one-male units. But the species and habitat borders are not identical and a few savannah baboon groups are to be found in the typical hamadryas habitat. They exhibit inertia in maintaining their savannah type social organization, yet its imperfect adaptation is evidenced by a lower reproductive rate than their relatives still living in the savannah (Nagel 1971).

Groups of age-graded males. Eisenberg *et al.* (1972) have proposed that other new data, in particular those on the place of males in the social structure, require a reformulation of the grades insofar as they constitute a hypothesis about the evolution of social systems from grade I to V, as opposed to a mere classification. The Crook and Gartlan plan sees the grade V harem structures as an adaptation to arid-country living and representing a modification from the more basic multi-male organization of grades III and IV. Eisenberg *et al.* point out that not only has the one-male structure now been found to be quite common, but the apparent multi-male structure ascribed to some species may in fact not contain several *adult* males, but instead males at several different stages below full maturity. They call this an age-graded male type of group and suggest that it may represent an intermediate between a basic one-male and a specialised multi-male structure, the latter therefore marking the end of an evolutionary progression in the tolerance of males for other males in the group (Table 12.2) rather than a basic pattern as in Crook and Gartlan's plan. This is an important contribution both to our understanding of the nature of certain primate societies and to our stock of hypotheses about the evolutionary development of societies and the way in which it is channelled by changes in ecological relationships. In the Crook and Gartlan scheme it was difficult to see why the explanation for one-male units in grade V – that it reduced male competition with the females – should not apply to all species. In the Eisenberg model it does apply essentially to grades III and IV, which include many arboreal species. The higher tolerance for other adult males in grade V, containing mainly the terrestrial baboons and macaques, may then be explained as a special adaptation to protection against predators in an open environment.

Table 12.2 The evolutionary grades of primates (after Eisenberg, Muckenhirn and Rudran 1972)

Social Organization	1. Solitary	2. Parental family (monogamous)	3. Minimal adult male tolerance (one-male troop)	4. Intermediate tolerance (age-graded male troop)	5. Highest male tolerance (multi-male troop)
Ecologies	A. Insect and fruit B. Leaf	A. Fruit and insect B. Leaf and fruit	A. Arboreal, leaves B. Arboreal, fruit C. Semiterrestrial, fruit	A. Arboreal, leaf B. Arboreal, fruit C. Semiterrestrial, fruit and omnivorous D. Terrestrial, leaves and fruit	A. Arboreal, fruit B. Semiterrestrial, fruit and omnivore

Intraspecific variation. A further complication is the opposite of inertia; new data has also indicated that certain aspects of social structure vary between groups of the *same* species which are to be found in different habitats (Crook 1970; Gartlan 1973). Thus, for example, savannah baboons living in the forest appear to consist of relatively small, changing groupings whereas those inhabiting the savannah tend to form large and more cohesive groups.

Although this is a problem for any scheme which assigns to each species *a* social organization and seeks to relate it to broad ecological grades, it does not show that socio-ecological relationships are un-important; rather, like the complication of hamadryas organization changing through the day to fit varying ecological requirements, it demonstrates a fine tuning of social organization to local ecology. Thus species variations in social structure over both time and space express a flexible but no less adaptive ecological relationship than was embodied in Crook and Gartlan's original idea. Such flexibility seems particularly marked in the psychology of the terrestrial open-country primates and may in itself represent an adaptation to their relatively unstable environment.

Although such complexity appears to be functional then, it does imply that to consider the reality of socio-ecological relationships requires a more accurate approach to specification of the relevant environmental variables over time (from time-of-day through seasonal changes to long-term climatic and habitat changes) and in space (Hladik 1975). With regard to the latter, the relevant variables may not be the general type of food, as implied by the Crook and Gartlan grades, but rather its precise distribution in time and space, which may, for example, vary considerably for different types of fruit eaten by different frugivores, while nevertheless profoundly influencing their social strategy of foraging.

The complexity also implies that each species, and indeed sub-populations of some species, is faced with a unique combination of environmental variables, including the spatio-temporal distribution of food, water, sleeping sites, predators and competitors. These will interact in determining the optimum adaptations, so that primate socio-ecological relationships might be expected to form a multi-dimensional matrix rather than following a linear-grade pattern, and each subpopulation may have to be understood in its own right.

Ecology and Individual Social Psychology

This reasoning can be extended to argue that each *individual* should be considered in its own right: for any primate of a particular sex, age and experience, the ideal ecological relationship may be different from that of another (Goss-Custard *et al.* 1972). Looking at functional aspects of behaviour from the individual point of view makes sense in that there is no evidence that natural selection acts on any entity larger than the individual, such as the social group. From a theoretical standpoint this is not surprising since any psychological trait which benefits the group but not the individual will be weeded out by natural selection operating between that individual and other members of the group. This also means that traits which are adaptive for the individual may be selected for even though they are damaging to the group or species as a whole.

One can argue further that since natural selection permits certain genes to exactly replicate themselves into the next generation, rather than individuals replicating themselves, the appropriate level of analysis of evolutionary processes is that of the gene, rather than of the individual (Dawkins 1976). One could then even go on to analyze the behavioural ecology of the gene, viewing it as an asexually reproducing creature, and indeed search for any of the four answers to Tinbergen's 'Why?'. But because we are interested in those answers with respect to psychology, which we shall take to be a characteristic of individuals and not genes, we shall proceed, given the space available, at the level of the individual.

This affects our discussion of the relationship between psychology and ecology in two ways. First of all, the relationship between social structure and habitat becomes an indirect one. Given that in any particular habitat the most adaptive social organization from the point of view of individual A is different from that of B, the results of their interaction will produce a certain relationship – and the social structure can be thought of as the combination of all such relationships (Hinde 1975) – which is not necessarily adaptively optimal *as a relationship* or aspect of social structure. The conflicting strategies of A and B may each in their own right be directed towards a goal which *is* optimally adaptive, even though the social structure generated by the interaction of these strategies may not be optimal.

A clear example of this is the relationship between males pursuing strategies which are similar – and therefore conflicting – in their goal of fertilizing a particular female. The individual psychological processes may be adaptive, even though their interaction may, for example, introduce aggression which reduces the efficiency of the group as a whole.

There are many other possible relationships of conflict between

individuals in a primate group, and several are reviewed by Clutton-
Brock and Harvey (1976). They underline that in an important sense
social structure is merely a by-product of the interaction between
individual psychologies, and is therefore less likely to be adaptive in
itself than are the latter. But although conflict interactions present
this viewpoint most starkly we must remember that its implications
are still with us when considering strategies which do not conflict.

The second major shift in emphasis when considering the ecology
of social psychology from the individual's point of view is that the
environment with respect to which adaptation takes place is not just
the physical habitat; it includes the behaviour of all the other
individuals of the group, and indeed of other groups with which there
may be interactions. The selection pressures thus exerted by the social
environment on individual social psychology include the conflicts
mentioned above. In the example of the conflict between males, male
behaviour will be moulded by the competitive behaviour of other males,
and one of the evolutionary products of this selection might be, for
example, enhanced male aggression. However we must remember that
such products are optimal compromises between a host of different
selection pressures. If the female in the above example has any
choice in who mates with her, it may be to *her* advantage to select
not so much on the basis of aggression, but on some other
characteristic like paternal tendencies which may benefit her offspring
more. The ecology of any psychological entity such as aggression
is likely to encompass many of such social selective factors as well
as those of the non-social environment.

However the significance of features of both the social and non-
social environments will be different according to the age of the
individual. Natural selection operates at all stages of development
and so will tend to produce what we might think of as a series of
psycho-ecological relationships manifested through the lifetime of the
individual.

This complexity in turn becomes part of the social environment
with respect to which adaptations evolve. Even in a stable physical
environment it should therefore be possible for there to be evolutionary
changes in social psychology, since these can in themselves contribute
to an unstable social environment, which would promote further
changes in social psychology.

Social evolution therefore appears like a never-ending game, each
player being forced into a new move or strategy as the previous one
creates a new selection pressure for it, and indeed game theory has
recently been applied to the analysis of such processes (see Maynard

Smith and Parker (1976) for a specific example and Dawkins (1976) for a more general introduction).

Humphrey (1976) has elaborated on Jolly's (1966) suggestion that primate intelligence may be an adaptation not so much for dealing with the physical environment, but rather for playing this social game in the complexity of a group consisting of known individuals differing in a multitude of characteristics, such as sex, age, status, kinship and temperament. Most important of all, those individuals are likewise exercising their intelligence in social manipulation, creating a spiralling selection pressure for that little bit more intelligence which will outwit the other.

Humphrey goes on to argue that the human intellect evolved as the most extreme expression of this social function and that it may in fact be less appropriate for solving non-social problems than we realize.

There is not space here for any more extended discussion of the relevance of this approach to understanding human psychology. Let me therefore finish by recommending readers interested in following this course specifically to Trivers' (1971) attempt to give a functional answer to the question of why man's psychological system includes such characteristics as gratitude and guilt, and more generally to the works listed below.

The excitement of such work is that it seems to indicate that we are at last starting to grasp the reality and complexity of the ecology of primate psychology.

REFERENCES

Altmann, S. A. and Altmann, J. 1970. *Baboon ecology*. Chicago: Chicago University Press.

Bessemer, D. W. and Stollnitz, F. 1971. 'Retention of discriminations and an analysis of learning set.' In A. M. Schrier and F. Stollnitz (eds) *Behaviour of nonhuman primates 4*. London: Academic Press.

Clutton-Brock, T. H. and Harvey, P. H. 1976. 'Evolutionary rules and primate societies.' In P. P. G. Bateson and R. A. Hinde (eds) *Growing points in ethology*. Cambridge: Cambridge University Press.

Crook, J. H. 1966. 'Gelada baboon herd structure and movement: a comparative report.' *Symp. Zoo. Soc. London, 18*, 237-58.

Crook, J. H. 1970. 'The socio-ecology of primates.' In J. H. Crook (ed.) *Social behaviour in birds and mammals*. London: Academic Press.

Crook, J. H. and Gartlan, J. S. 1966. 'Evolution of primate societies.' *Nature 210*, 1200-3.

Davis, R. T. 1974. 'Monkeys as perceivers'. In L. A. Rosenblum (ed.) *Primate behavior 3*. London: Academic Press.

Dawkins, R. 1976. *The selfish gene*. Oxford: Oxford University Press.

De Vore, I. and Washburn, S. L. 1963. 'Baboon ecology and human evolution.' In F. C. Howell and F. Bourlière (eds) *African ecology and human evolution.* New York: Viking Fund Publications in Anthropology.

Eisenberg, J. F., Muckenhirn, N. A. and Rudran, R. 1972. 'The relation between ecology and social structure in primates.' *Science 16*, 863-74.

Fouts, R. S. 1975. 'Capacities for language in great apes.' In R. H. Tuttle (ed.) *Socioecology and psychology of primates.* The Hague: Mouton.

Gartlan, J. S. 1973. 'Influences of phylogeny and ecology on variations in the group organisation of primates.' In E. W. Menzel (ed.) *Symposia of the fourth international congress of primatology 1*, Basel: Karger.

Goss-Custard, J. D., Dunbar, R. I. M. and Aldrich-Blake, F. P. G. 1972. 'Survival, mating and rearing strategies in the evolution of primate social structure.' *Folia primat. 17*, 1-19.

Hinde, R. A. 1975. 'Interactions, relationships and social structure in non-human primates.' In S. Kondo, M. Kawai, A. Ehara and S. Kawamura (eds) *Proceedings from the symposia of the fifth congress of the international primatological society.* Tokyo: Japan Science Press.

Hladik, C. M. 1975. 'Ecology, diet and social patterning in Old and New World primates.' In R. H. Tuttle (ed.) *Socioecology and psychology of primates.* The Hague: Mouton.

Humphrey, N. K. 1976. 'The social function of intellect.' In P. P. G. Bateson and R. A. Hinde (eds) *Growing points in ethology.* Cambridge: Cambridge University Press.

Jarrard, L. E. (ed.) 1971. *Cognitive processes of non-human primates.* London: Academic Press.

Jolly, A. 1966. 'Lemur social behavior and primate intelligence.' *Science, 153,* 501-6.

Jolly, C. J. 1970. 'The seed-eaters: a new model of hominid differentiation based on a baboon analogy.' *Man, ns 5*, 5-26.

Kummer, H. 1968. *Social organisation of hamadryas baboons: a field study.* Chicago: University of Chicago Press.

Leakey, R. and Lewin, R. 1977. *Origins.* London: MacDonald and Jane's.

Maynard Smith, J. and Parker, G. A. 1976. 'The logic of asymmetric contests.' *Anim. Behav. 24*, 159-75.

Medin, D. L. and Davis, R. T. 1974. 'Memory.' In A. M. Schrier and F. Stollnitz (eds) *Behavior of non-human primates 5.* London: Academic Press.

Nagel, U. 1971. 'Social organisation in a baboon hybrid zone.' *Proc. 3rd Int. Congr. Primatol. 3*, 48-57. Basel: Karger.

Premack, D. 1971. 'On the assessment of language competence in the chimpanzee.' In A. M. Schrier and F. Stollnitz (eds) *Behavior of non-human primates 4.* London: Academic Press.

Rumbaugh, D. R. 1975. 'The learning and symbolizing capacities of apes and monkeys.' In R. H. Tuttle (ed.) *Socioecology and psychology of primates.* The Hague: Mouton.

Rogers, C. M. and Davenport, R. K. 1975. 'Capacities of non-human primates for perceptual integration across modalities.' In R. H. Tuttle (ed.) *Socioecology and psychology of primates.* The Hague: Mouton.

Tinbergen, N. 1963. 'On aims and methods of ethology.' *Z. Tierpsychol. 20,* 410-33.

Trivers, R. L. 1971. 'The evolution of reciprocal altruism.' *Quart. Rev. Biol.* *46*, 35-7.

Wilson, E. O. 1975. *Sociobiology*. London: Belknap Press.

Wilson, M. 1974. 'Identification, discrimination and retention of visual stimuli.' In A. M. Schrier and F. Stollnitz (eds) *Behavior of non-human primates 5*. London: Academic Press.

FURTHER READING ON NON-HUMAN AND HUMAN PRIMATE PSYCHO-ECOLOGY

Fishbein, H. D. 1976. *Evolution, development and children's learning*. Paçific Palisades: Goodyear Publishing.

Jolly, A. 1972. *The evolution of primate behaviour*. London: Macmillan.

Kummer, H. 1971. *Primate societies: group techniques of ecological adaptation*. Chicago: Aldine-Atherton.

Lancaster, J. B. 1975. *Primate behavior and the emergence of human culture*. London: Holt Rinehart and Wilson.

Lee, R. B. and De Vore, I. 1976. *Kalahari hunter gatherers: studies of the Kung Sang and their neighbours*. Cambridge Mass.: Harvard University Press.

Rowell, T. 1972. *Social behaviour of monkeys*. London: Penguin.

Chapter 13

Psychopharmacological studies in relation to disorders of mood and action

SUSAN D. IVERSEN

INTRODUCTION

Psychopharmacology endeavours to explain how drugs, which alter mental states, produce their effects. Brain function is likely to be influenced by any drug taken into the body. If the drug molecules are able to penetrate the blood brain barrier, the effect on the brain is direct, but drug-induced changes in body physiology may also have repercussions indirectly on the central nervous system. Psychopharmacology, however, is concerned principally with drugs which have their prime effect on nervous tissue (in either the central or the peripheral nervous system) and which people take because of these effects. Within this category the following kinds of drugs may be distinguished (although such classifications are somewhat arbitrary):

(1) Drugs which alter the biochemical functioning of neurones, e.g. metabolism and hence the availability of energy or level of protein synthesis. Such drugs will not concern us in this review.
(2) Drugs which alter the transmission of information in nervous tissue. There are several factors which determine the transmission of information in the brain; (i) the biophysical properties of the neurone membrane, (ii) the metabolic characteristics of the neurone, (iii) the topography of connections between neurones and (iv) the nature of the communication mechanism between neurones, whether it be electrical or chemical.

The brain consists of many different areas, inter-connected for specific modes of operation. At a functional level these circuits are of great significance and their disruption results in behavioural disorganization. The existence of *defined* anatomical connections has long been accepted, but the discovery that defined chemical connections also exist in the brain is perhaps the most significant discovery in neurobiology in the last twenty years. We now know that in the brain, as in the peripheral nervous system, communication between neurones is not necessarily electrotonic; it may equally involve chemical messengers. Chemically transmitting synapses in the brain have in general the same morphological and biochemical properties as those in the periphery. A set of criteria has been compiled which should be fulfilled if any substance is to be accepted as a chemical transmitter:

(1) The chemical messenger or neurotransmitter is synthesized within the neurone, stored in terminals and released by nerve impulses.
(2) Specific receptors on the post synaptic membrane form a link in the chain of events resulting in activation of the post synaptic neurone.
(3) The released neurotransmitter is then removed from the synapse by enzymatic degradation or by selective re-uptake processes in the membrane of the presynaptic terminal and re-stored in the vesicles.

A current overview of this organization is presented in Figure 13.1. Space is not available to describe in detail our knowledge of the working of the chemically transmitting synapse. However, it is clear that attention must be paid ultimately to those mechanisms if a full understanding of drug action on brain chemistry and behaviour is to emerge.

So far the following substances have acquired recognized status as putative neurotransmitters: the catecholamines, noradrenaline (NA) and dopamine (DA); the indoleamine, serotonin (5HT); γ-aminobutyric acid (GABA); acetylcholine (ACh); substance P; the aminoacids, glycine, glutamate, aspartate, proline and taurine. The peptides, enkephalin and related endorphins are possible candidates for transmitters.

A major advance in understanding chemical coding in the brain was the realization that the synapses using a given chemical transmitter were not distributed in a random fashion throughout the brain (Iversen and Iversen 1975). Knowledge of the amounts of the endogenous neurotransmitters in brain and of their function at an

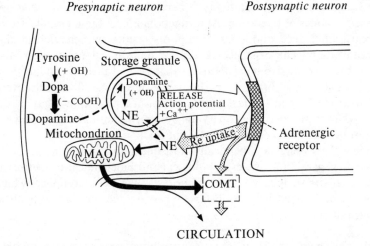

Presynaptic neuron   *Postsynaptic neuron*

CIRCULATION

Figure 13.1 Stylized aminergic synapse illustrating the biosynthetic pathway for dopamine (DA) and noradrenaline (NA) and the various processes available for removal of the released amines from the synaptic cleft. MAO = monoamine oxidase; COMT = catechol-O-methyl transferase.

isolated synapse reveals nothing of this form of organization. In order to appreciate its anatomical distribution, it is necessary to stain the neurotransmitter *in situ* and plot its distribution in the brain. In this endeavour 'lesion' methods (pharmacological depletion or surgical lesions) have played an important role. For example, if X contains high levels of a vesicle-localized neurotransmitter, selective section of the input pathways to X should reveal the site of the cell bodies which form the neurotransmitter-containing terminals. Lesions of those cell bodies should then deplete the neurotransmitter terminals in X. Different histochemical techniques have been devised to make the various CNS transmitters visible. For example, the catecholamines, noradrenaline (NA) and dopamine (DA) form a highly fluorescent compound when brain sections are exposed to formadelyde gas. Appropriate fluorescent microscopy then allows the cell bodies, axon and terminals of amine neurones to be seen (Ungerstedt 1971). In Figure 13.2 the distribution of DA and NA are compared using such a technique and Figure 13.3 provides an up to date picture of the extent of the DA pathways.

The distribution of ACh has been studied by Lewis and Shute (1978) using a staining technique for acetylcholinesterase (AChe), the enzyme in the synaptic region responsible for breaking down ACh. However,

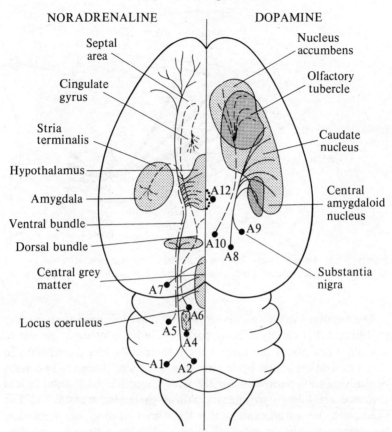

Figure 13.2   Horizontal representation of ascending noradrenaline (NA) and dopamine (DA) pathways in the rat brain. (Modified from Ungerstedt, 1971.)

it is clear AChe occurs at sites other than specific ACh synapses and a more specific means of marking ACh is required. More recently immunofluorescent methods have been developed for staining brain transmitters. Such methods depend on the preparation, in the rabbit, of antibodies to the naturally occurring, endogenous transmitter (antigen). When injected into the experimental animal, the antibody is taken up by the endogenous receptor for that transmitter and being fluorescent its distribution can be plotted. This method has made it possible to visualize the peptide hormone substance P in rat brain and to begin defining the distribution of the novel morphine-like (enkephalin, endorphin) transmitters in brain.

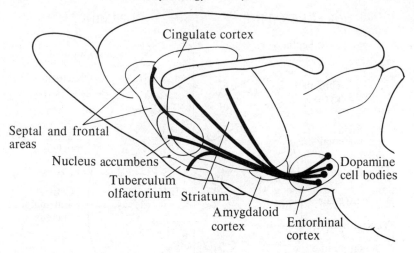

Figure 13.3 Lateral view of the forebrain innervation patterns of the nigrostriatal and mesolimbic/cortical dopamine pathways (supplied by Ungerstedt).

The discovery that particular transmitters are localized anatomically to different, but clearly defined, pathways in brain made it feasible to ask questions about the role of these chemically coded pathways in the organization of the brain. Broadly speaking, there are two ways of studying such pathways. Firstly, with drugs, which on independent evidence are known to interact with a particular transmitter. For example, *in vitro* studies show that the stimulant drug, amphetamine, has several actions on catecholamine containing neurones, including the ability to release endogenous NA and DA from their storage sites in the nerve terminals. Amphetamine enters the brain readily after intraperitoneal injection and thus it is reasonable to suppose that the behavioural effects of the drug are partly explained by its interaction with catecholamine transmitters. Unfortunately amphetamine is distributed throughout the brain and it is not possible to ascribe the effect to an action at a particular site. The direct application of drugs to the brain through small implanted cannulae circumvents this problem and is a method being widely adopted. Some drugs act to block chemical neurotransmission (antagonist) rather than to mimic it (agonist), as in the case of amphetamine. For example, the neuroleptic drugs used to control the psychotic symptoms of schizophrenia act by blocking catecholamine receptors, particularly DA receptors. If applied locally to DA terminal regions, neuroleptic drugs block the effect of amphetamine-released catecholamines and thereby abolish the observed stimulant effects of amphetamine on behaviour.

An alternative approach to studying the role of transmitter pathways involves the use of lesion techniques. *Selective* damage to a particular pathway should disrupt any function dependent on it. The problem then is to develop selective lesion techniques. Electrolytic lesions are not specific and destroy nervous tissue whether it contains high levels of a particular transmitter or not. Efforts have been made to develop selective chemical toxins for making lesions. 6 hydroxydopamine (6-OHDA), a drug closely related chemically to NA and DA was synthesized and found to destroy catecholamine-containing neurones when injected into the ventricle or directly into brain structures. Injected intraperitoneally it will also destroy the peripheral autonomic nervous system. A similar drug 5,7 dihydroxy-tryptamine destroys 5HT neurones.

Biological psychiatry concerns itself with hypotheses relating mental illness to endogenous disorders of brain whether they be due to genetical, neuropathological, developmental or sociological influences. Critics of the discipline object to and find unacceptable popular claims of this kind. Such generalizations are indeed dangerous and unlikely to prove to be the case for all forms of mental illness. However, there have been some notable achievements in recent years in the search for biological bases of abnormal behaviour and in their treatment with drugs. It is the purpose of this chapter to review some of these.

Drugs are taken to alter psychological states, most commonly to reverse deviations from the accepted norm. Broadly speaking, the following psychological states may be identified, which can be modulated in a relatively selective manner by drugs:

(1) Mood.
(2) Action.
(3) Sleep and waking.
(4) Arousal and attention.
(5) Memory.
(6) Feeding (Excessive water intake or sexual activity are relatively uncommon but theoretically at least may be controlled pharmacologically).

We shall confine ourselves to discussing examples from categories (1) and (2). Excellent reviews on 3, 4, 5 and 6 may be found in the *Handbook of Psychopharmacology 8*, Iversen, Iversen and Snyder (eds) (1977).

PSYCHOPHARMACOLOGICAL MODELS IN RELATION TO MOOD DISORDERS

Anxiety

Clinical anxiety states are alleviated by minor tranquillisers, the so called anxiolytic drugs. Meprobromate, a potent muscle relaxant, was the first drug introduced to treat such disorders specifically. Until recently, barbiturate drugs were also prescribed frequently for the relief of anxiety and the associated disruption of sleeping patterns. The inherent danger with barbiturates of addiction or death by overdose made the development of the benzodiazepine minor tranquillisers particularly valuable.

Behavioural models. There are well defined animal tests for identifying anti-anxiety drugs. The Geller-Seifter punishment procedure is one that is specific and reliable (Iversen and Iversen 1975). Punishment is defined as the presentation of a stimulus which decreases the probability of responding. A rat is trained, in the presence of a blue light, to press a lever for reward (food) which is presented on a variable interval schedule (food available irregularly but on average every few minutes). These schedules result in high, sustained rates of lever pressing. When the performance level has been reached, orange light periods alternate with blue. Reinforcement continues to be available during the blue periods but in the presence of the orange light, although the same reinforcement schedule is in operation, every lever response is followed by an electric shock to the rat's feet. Thus conflict exists when the orange light is on; the desire to press for food coupled with the anticipation of the highly noxious electric shock associated with lever pressing in these conditions. Behaviour is modified rapidly, so that lever pressing occurs during the blue periods but is suppressed in the presence of the orange light. Animals treated with minor tranquillisers or barbiturates do not show response suppression in the presence of the shock conditions but continue to press for food despite the presentation of shock. Such results are illustrated in Figure 13.4 where pigeons were trained on an alternating signalled schedule (Kelleher and Morse 1964). In orange light, key pecks (30) resulted in the presentation of reward and five rewards were given before the light changed to white. In this sector the reinforcement schedule (FR30) was the same but the first ten pecks on each FR resulted in a shock. Total suppression of responding was observed despite perfectly normal responding in the alternating orange light (reinforcement only) conditions. After treatment with 10 mg/kg of the barbiturate

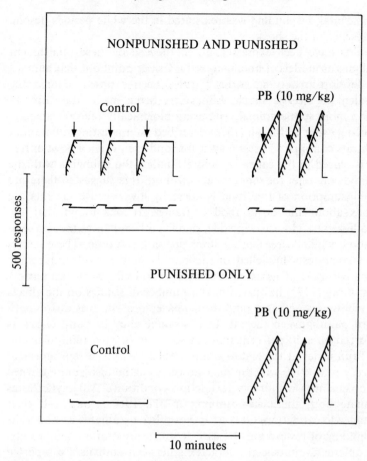

Figure 13.4 Effects of pentobarbital (PB) on key pecking suppressed by punishment. Each frame shows a complete control session followed by a complete drug session. The drug was given intramuscularly 15 minutes before the beginning of the drug sessions. Upper: in non-punishment components (event record displaced upward), a 30-response, fixed-ratio schedule of food presentation was in effect in the presence of an orange light. The termination of each non-punishment component is indicated by a small arrow. In punishment components (event record displaced downward), a 30-response, fixed-ratio schedule was in effect in the presence of a white light; each of the first ten responses of each ratio produced a 30-msec electric shock of 6 ma, 60 Hz, delivered through gold wire electrodes implanted around the pubis bones of the bird. The termination of each punishment component is indicated by the resetting of the pen to the bottom of the record. Lower: the punishment procedure was in effect throughout each session in the presence of a white light. Note that under both procedures pentobarbital attenuates the suppression of responding by punishment. (From Kelleher and Morse, 1964.)

pentobarbital, responding was reinstated in the white periods despite the presence of the shock.

Doubts have been expressed about the use of these punishment paradigms as models of human anxiety. Critics point out that humans who develop anxiety states have rarely been exposed to anything equivalent to electric shock. Efforts are being made, therefore, to develop more subtle animal tests using biologically relevant anxiety-producing events. Morgan (1974) described an interesting situation in which rats continue to press a lever for food even when a bowl of free food is placed in the cage. The more familiar the animal is with the free food container the more is eaten from it. It is suggested therefore that consumption of free food is normally low because the rats are anxious about the novel food container. It was found that the benzodiazepine, chlordiazepoxide, significantly enhances the intake of free food, while decreasing the lever pressing response. These results suggest that tests modelled on neophobia may provide interesting alternative ways of assessing the behavioural effects of anti-anxiety drugs. Gray (1977) has performed a number of studies on the effects of barbiturates, ethanol and benzodiazepines on frustrative non-reward paradigms in the rat. In a straight alley learning task rats reinforced on a 50 per cent random schedule (partial reinforcement, PRF) run faster at the end of training than rats given reinforcement on every trial. PRF rats are also slower to extinguish running when reinforcement is withdrawn (extinction condition). Anxiolytic drugs attenuate both the faster running in the PRF group and their resistance to extinction. Gray describes other paradigms in which the withholding of reward may be used to create frustration and anxiety. In a different vein, social interactions between animals are reported to be influenced by anxiety-producing stimuli. It has been observed that the social interaction between two male rats is severely reduced if they are placed in an unfamiliar environment or one with bright lights. The reduction in social behaviour is correlated with changes in independent measures of anxiety (defaecation, exploration and freezing), suggesting that the rats become anxious in the changed environment. This is supported by the observation that chronic chlordiazepoxide treatment reverses environmentally-induced suppression of social behaviour.

Where in the brain do minor-tranquillisers act to relieve anxiety? Do these drugs have any specific effects on neuropharmacological substrates? Answers are being provided to both these questions.

Neuropsychological theories of anxiety. Basing his work on the paradigm of partial reinforcement described earlier, Gray (1977) has developed the theory that a neuronal circuit focused on the hippocampus is essential for the expression of anxiety. The electrical activity in the hippocampus (the theta rhythm) is controlled or 'driven' by a cholinergic input from the medial septal nuclei. Recordings were made from the hippocampus in freely moving rats behaving in a non-reward situation and correlations were found between the response to frustrative non-reward and a particular frequency band of theta rhythm (7.7Hz). Gray proposes that when rats behave in anxiety-provoking situations this brain mechanism is activated. Anxiolytic drugs attenuate the response to frustrative non-reward and in acute recording experiments it was shown that barbiturates, benzodiazepines and other anxiolytic compounds raise the threshold of septal stimulation required to induce the 7.7 Hz theta rhythm and, by implication, the response of the animal to anxiety provoking conditions.

Whether this same brain mechanism operates to mediate the suppressive behavioural effects of punishment presented on the Geller Seifter paradigm remains to be established. If non-reward and punishment are mediated by the same brain mechanism this will provide strong support for learning theorists who view all forms of response suppression within a unitary framework. However, in addition to partial reinforcement and punishment, there are other ways of suppressing behavioural responses. For example, extinction and time out conditions. Much work remains to be done to prove that the mechanism described by Gray in relation to frustrative non-reward mediates all forms of response suppression. Preliminary evidence suggests that different forms of response inhibition may have dissociable although related neuropharmacological profiles.

Neuropharmacological theories of anxiety. In recent studies Gray (1977) has explored neuropharmacological substrates in relation to the septo-hippocampal system mediating frustrative non-reward. He found that lesions to both the ascending 5HT and the dorsal NA pathway which innervates the hippocampus, or drugs which interfere with 5HT or NA neurotransmission, modify septal driving of the 7.7 Hz theta rhythm. Lesions to the dorsal NA bundle with the neurotoxin, 6-hydroxydopamine, raise the threshold of septally driven theta rhythm in the 7.7 Hz band. The model emerging from this work is of a septo-hippocampal substrate modulated by 5HT and NA innervations.

Similar experiments have been performed using Geller-Seifter punishment schedules as the behavioural measure of response suppression. 5HT and NA have both been implicated in the mediation of this form of behaviour adding support to the contention that there is a similar neuropharmacological basis for all forms of response suppression. However, a number of studies suggests that 5HT systems play the central role in the suppression induced by punishment and the ability of benzodiazepine drugs to reinstate responding. *In vitro* neuropharmacological experiments demonstrate that benzodiazepines reduce brain turnover of both NA (Fuxe *et al.* 1975) and 5HT (Stein *et al.* 1975). However, when chronic doses are used, it has been found that the biochemical effect on NA substrates quickly develops tolerance whereas the depressant effect on 5HT mechanisms is sustained. These observations have been correlated with the clinical observation that benzodiazepines initially cause sedation in patients. This effect is short-lived, whereas the anxiolytic effect is maintained on chronic treatment. It has been suggested, therefore, that the effect of these drugs on NA systems correlates with the sedation whereas the anxiolytic effect is mediated by the effect on 5HT substrates (Stein *et al.* 1975, 1977). There is direct support for the first suggestion from experiments with rats responding on a Geller-Seifter paradigm, where it has been shown that the suppression of responding in the punishment periods is reversed by intraventricular injection of noradrenaline. If raised NA enhances response output, then one would predict that lowered NA associated with benzodiazepine treatment would depress behaviour.

It seems very likely, therefore, that the reduction in brain 5HT is responsible for the benzodiazepine-induced release of punished responding. Thus inhibition of 5HT synthesis or blockade of 5HT receptors should mimic the behavioural releasing effects of benzodiazepines on punishment paradigms, and raising brain 5HT should intensify behavioural inhibitory mechanisms. Both of these predictions have been verified in independent studies (Stein *et al.* 1977). Using the neurotoxin, 5,6 dihydroxytryptamine, Tye *et al.* (1977) found that bilateral lesions to the 5HT pathways at the level of the medial forebrain bundle resulted in a release of punished responding equivalent in magnitude to that induced by benzodiazepines. 6-OHDA lesions to the dorsal NA bundle did not result in release of punished responding, although Mason and Iversen (1977) have found that such lesions impede the suppression of responding by extinction and non-reward in a successive visual discrimination task.

More recently, the interaction between benzodiazepines and other brain neurotransmitter systems has been investigated. In addition to their effect on 5HT and NA, these drugs also bind potently to glycine and GABA (γ-aminobutyric acid) receptors (Snyder *et al.* 1977) and block the reduction of cGMP in cerebellar neurones induced by GABA-minergic drugs (Costa *et al.* 1977). GABA antagonists (e.g. isoniazid) increase cerebellar cyclic-guanosine monophosphate (cGMP) and this effect is blocked by diazepam in doses as low as 0.52 μmole/kg, intra-peritoneal Stein *et al.* (1975) suggest that GABA neurones intereact with 5HT systems to induce presynaptic inhibition and thus reduce the release of serotonin.

Prior to the introduction of the benzodiazepines, barbiturates were used as anxiolytic agents. As we have seen, barbiturates like benzodiazepines have a potent releasing effect on punished and non-rewarded responding. However, there is reason to believe that these two drug groups have different neuropharmacological profiles. Barbiturates and benzodiazepines have sedative properties and both intereact strongly with GABA receptors, which may provide the basis of the sedative actions. However, whereas with the barbiturates the anxiolytic action appears to correlate with the sedative effect, benzodiazepines produce their potent anxiolytic action at non-sedative doses. This makes them invaluable clinically, avoiding the hazard of death of overdose associated with the more strongly sedative barbiturates. Benzodiazepines but not barbiturates also bind to glycine receptors, and it has been suggested that these receptors play a role in the more specific anxiolytic actions of this class of drugs. The interaction between glycarine and benzodiazepine receptors and the other neurotransmitter systems implicated in the response to anxiety remains to be explored. Few attempts have been made to measure transmitter levels in anxious patients. However, a number of workers have stressed the importance of genetic factors in determining the sensitivity to stress and the correlations between physiological variables and the tendency to develop anxiety states (Eysenck 1957; Lacey 1967).

Depression

There are many different views on the diagnostic classification of depressive syndromes. Thus in considering animal models, one is faced initially with the task of defining what kind of depression one is trying to model. Akiskal and McKinney (1975) refer to primary depression as '. . . an affective disorder with no pre-existing major psychiatric syndromes . . .', and secondary depression as '. . . superimposed on pre-existing non-affective psychiatric illness or parallel-like threatening experiences'. Endogenous and reactive are other adjectives which have been applied to these forms of the illness. For many years disquiet has been expressed on the use of the term 'reactive' (Davison and Neale 1974). van Praag (1977) has recently provided a cogent overview of these opinions and suggests that the terms 'vital' and 'personal' be used to refer to primary and secondary depression. He emphasizes that both forms of depression can commonly be related to adverse environmental events and are thus both potentially reactive illnesses. In vital depression other potential aetiological factors have to be recognized including endogenous, psychosociogenic and idiopathic conditions.

It is with vital depression we shall concern ourselves and particularly with the unipolar illness rather than with the manic-depressive, or bipolar, form of the illness.

A very large number of theories of depression have been expounded over the years ranging from the psychoanalytic to the existential view. Particular theories tend to align themselves most clearly with recognized subcategories of depression. A few examples will illustrate this point.

Bowlby (1969), working within the psychoanalytic framework, noted that a very high percentage of patients depressed in adulthood had experienced loss of a love object (usually the mother) during childhood. Observation of children in such a situation, commonly institutionalized children, revealed that an obvious and pathological set of behavioural symptoms appeared during the acute separation phase and that these persisted. Rutter (1972) has provided an excellent reassessment of these results. The development of anaclytic depression, as the syndrome is described, consists of three phases: (i) protest stage when the infant is extremely active and vocal; (ii) hypoactive phase with the demeanour of depression which has been termed the 'despair' phase; (iii) the permanent state which emerges with abnormal motor behaviours including head banging, self-clasping, rocking and sucking. Without questioning the importance of these observations or Bowlby's theory, one may ask if it is reasonable to suppose that all depressions are associated with some form of social deprivation in childhood. Experiments on monkeys have confirmed the nature of this syndrome and its permanence. Monkeys tested years after the separation experience and after long periods of rehabilitation in a social colony, still show these behavioural deficits to an obvious degree. Harlow and his co-workers (Harlow and Harlow 1969) pursued these studies and found that isolated monkeys when adult showed: (i) inadequate social and even non-social play; (ii) avoidance of physical contact; (iii) absence of normal heterosexual behaviour; (iv) inability to inhibit antisocial aggression when not too terrified to aggress.

More recently, considerable interest has been aroused by Seligman's (1975) experimental work on learned helplessness. Dogs were placed in a chamber and shocked each time a buzzer sounded. More than sixty shocks were administered before the task was changed to an active avoidance task. Now, when the buzzer sounded it was possible for the dog to leap a hurdle in order to avoid the imminent shock; of the 150 dogs tested, two thirds showed a strange behaviour, termed 'learned helplessness'. They were quite unable to move but remained immobile as the shocks were presented. Seligman suggests that these animals are showing something akin to reactive depression, marked by profound immobility and a failure to modify their behaviour in the changed circumstances. Although clearly most relevant to what van Praag (1977) would call 'personal' depression, Seligman pleads for the general relevance of the paradigm. 'While reactive depressions are at the primary focus of the learned helplessness model of depression, I will suggest that endogenous depressions have much in common psychologically with reactive depressions.' By reactive in this context, Seligman is clearly referring to what we would call personal or secondary depressions.

What, one may ask, are the criteria for an animal model of a psychiatric condition? McKinney (1974) suggests the following: (i) similarity of inducing conditions; (ii) similarity of behavioural states produced; (iii) common underlying neurobiological mechanisms; (iv) reversal by clinically effective treatment techniques.

In the case of anxiety criteria (i) or (iv) are clearly met and although there could be argument about (ii) and (iii) at least one could make a plausible case for relevance of the animal modelling. Turning to depression, the situation is far less satisfactory. Several predisposing or inducing factors have been recognized in clinical depression. Should a relevant model take account of them all? If so, then none of the models discussed to date is adequate. Object separation models emphasize loss of a love object whereas learned helplessness involves the inescapable presentation of stressful stimuli. These manipulations certainly result in behavioural disruption and the emergence of some behavioural signs cardinal to the clinical depressed state, e.g. immobility, inability to programme purposeful behaviour and so on. But it is doubtful if any produce the wide spectrum of changes characteristic of the clinical state. Finally, when we come to criterion (iv) the picture is even less encouraging. One may argue that a partial model is acceptable, if the abnormal behaviour is normalized by treatments effective in the clinical condition. Unfortunately, there is no model of depressed behaviour, even loosely resembling the clinical state, which responds selectively to anti-depressant drugs.

Why, one may ask, is it so difficult to design an animal model of depression? In models we tend to focus on one feature of the aetiology and manipulate it in an effort to produce the desired imbalance in behaviour. The aetiology of depression is so diversified that variation of one factor may be insufficient to mimic the clinical situation. It is clearly difficult but not impossible to manipulate several inducing factors simultaneously but this is a novel approach not yet attempted.

Neuropharmacological theories of depression. Two major classes of antidepressant drug have been developed; the tricyclic compounds like imipramine and desmethylimipramine and the monoamine oxidase inhibitors like pargyline and iproniazid. The latter are not commonly used now as they cause cardiovascular side effects in some circumstances. *In vitro* pharmacological experiments demonstrated that both groups of antidepressants act at the aminergic synapse to increase functional levels of transmitter in the synapse. The tricyclic compounds inhibit re-uptake from synaptic cleft of released NA and 5HT. Dopamine uptake mechanisms are hardly affected. Monoamine oxidase (MAO) inhibitors prevent the enzymatic degradation of amines and likewise enhance their availability in the synaptic cleft. It is generally accepted that these properties underlie the antidepressant action of these drugs. Reasoning one step further, it has been proposed that deficiencies in NA and 5HT mechanisms may exist in depressed patients. What is the direct evidence for such a view? Coppen *et al.* (1973) reported that in a group of patients with vital depressions the free tryptophan levels were lowered in plasma. 5HT is synthesized from tryptophan and so also is B vitamin nicotinic acid (BVNA) which is involved in protein synthesis in the neurones. In stressful conditions, corticosteroid hormone is released and is known to induce the synthesis of enzymes necessary for the production of BVNA. Stress would therefore increase the demand for tryptophan and if an individual for some unrelated reason (e.g. genetic) had low tryptophan levels, the added stimulus could push the deficiency to serious levels. Unfortunately other investigators have failed to replicate Coppen's result and it can only be said that a subgroup of depressed patients have severely deficient 5HT metabolism. This is borne out by a study of Åsberg *et al.* (1976) in which cerebral spinal fluid levels of the 5HT metabolite, 5-hydroxyindoleacetic acid (5HIAA) were measured and used as an index of 5HT turnover in brain. In two separate groups of patients they found a bimodal distribution of 5HIAA levels, despite the fact that there was no difference in the severity of depression in the two parts of the distribution. However, within the subgroup showing the lowest levels of 5HIAA a negative correlation was found between the severity of the depression and the absolute level of the metabolite. By contrast, the patients in the higher mode of the 5HIAA distribution, showed lowered levels of NA metabolites and their depression correlated in severity with the magnitude of the inferred reduction in NA functions. Schildkraut (1975) has also reported decreased NA and normetanephrine excretion in vital depressions. Lowered DA levels may also be a feature of depression, and may account for the psychomotor retardation, i.e. slowness and fatigue, which can be alleviated with L-dopa therapy.

It is becoming increasingly clear that in dealing with vital depressions, several subgroups have to be recognized as far as neuropharmacological correlates are concerned. This is not surprising in view of the wide range of aetiological factors recognized in this disease state. The different subgroups also respond in different ways to drugs. For example, Coppen *et al.* (1967) report that administration of tryptophan produces dramatic improvement in the subgroup of depressive patients with low free plasma tryptophan, who do not respond to tricyclic therapy. However, even when recovery has occurred, such patients continue to give evidence of low 5HT activity suggesting to Coppen that the 5HT disorder reflects a constitutional abnormality making the individual more prone to depression. In the patients who show the catecholamine deficiency, treatment with tricyclic drugs is invariably successful and the metabolite levels become normal, suggesting that the lowered NA function may be central to the depressed condition. Using animal models there is some evidence that shock-induced stress indeed does increase turnover of brain NA, (Thierry *et al.* 1968) and if sufficiently intense may ultimately reduce endogenous levels of brain NA. More recently, Glazer and Weiss (1976) in reinvestigating the learned helplessness paradigm have also found transitory changes in catecholamine substrates in the brain, which they believe correlate with the short lasting behavioural immobility induced in such situations. Benzodiazepines will counteract stress-induced increases in NA turnover in most part of the brain (Fuxe *et al.* 1975).

PSYCHOPHARMACOLOGICAL MODELS OF ACTION

Action is defined variously as 'extension of energy . . . management of the body or thing done'. Action is the final product of brain function and evidence from many sources suggests that forebrain DA pathways play an essential role in the translation of intention into action. The study of the drugs which depress or enhance action have played an important role in understanding these mechanisms. Many drugs (probably all if given in sufficient dosage) produce non specific effects on action, which is hardly surprising as many areas of the central nervous system are involved in the production of organized behaviour. However, the effects of stimulant drugs have been selected for discussion because there is good evidence that their ability to increase both the quantity and quality of action depends on specific CNS effects. The d-isomer of amphetamine is the most commonly studied stimulant, although there is every reason to suppose that related compounds act in a similar manner to stimulate behaviour. D-amphetamine (but not the l-isomer) stimulates behaviour in all species in a dose-dependent fashion. In the rat, low doses of amphetamine stimulate locomotor activity. The rat moves rapidly and frequently in the cage, often showing associated exploratory behaviours like rearing and sniffing in interesting parts of the apparatus. The measurement of this behaviour is improved if the apparatus enhances these tendencies. For example, many investigators have used apparatus with holes cut in the floor. The investigatory responses to these holes can be automatically recorded with photocell devices. In such a situation low doses of amphetamine increase locomotion and head dipping into the holes. However, when the dose of amphetamine is raised, the behaviour, while still obviously stimulated, becomes stereotyped and unpurposeful. The animal remains in one position repeating, in a highly abnormal fashion, some small element of its normal motor repertoire. Rats sniff and lick one spot in the cage or poke their noses repeatedly through one hole in the holeboard, cats show stereotyped postural and staring behaviours, monkeys bite and show 'examining' stereotypies like picking the skin in one part of the body. Human amphetamine addicts also show stereotyped behaviour (Rylander 1971) '. . . women sort out their handbags again and again or tidy up their flat whether it needs tidying or not.'

The performance of trained motor acts are modified in a similar manner by varying doses of amphetamine. Rats trained to press a lever for food, press more frequently under low doses of amphetamine. This is particularly well demonstrated if animals are responding on schedules of reinforcement which generate low rates of ongoing behaviour. For example, if reinforcement is programmed on a fixed interval schedule, say, to be available every minute, animals respond in a characteristic scalloped pattern between reinforcements. Immediately following reinforcement, responding occurs at a very low rate but accelerates as the time of the next reinforcement approaches. Amphetamine acts to increase greatly the low levels of responding in the early segments of the fixed interval. When higher doses induce stereotypy, conditioned behaviour of this kind is severely disrupted because the rat is engaged in repetitive behaviour away from the response panel. However, experimental situations can be contrived in which the response most likely to be stereotyped is the required response. In such a case even high doses of amphetamine may improve performance.

We know that the forebrain pathways must be intact if amphetamine is to produce these behavioural effects. Coupled with the fact that *in vitro* pharmacological studies show that amphetamine releases stored DA from the terminals of the neurones, it is generally agreed that amphetamine releases brain DA to produce these behavioural effects. If the synthesis of brain catecholamines is inhibited with α-methyl-p-tyrosine, amphetamine-induced behaviours are blocked. Likewise lesions to the origin of the DA pathways in the midbrain block these stimulatory effects. More recently using a selective lesion technique, we have found that the enhancement of purposeful behaviour induced by low doses of amphetamine is mediated by the non-striatal DA pathways (meso-limbic and meso-cortical) whereas the induction of stereotyped behaviour involves the nigro-striatal DA projection (Kelly *et al*. 1975). Thus it has been proposed that the release of DA in two different forebrain areas is essential on the one hand for the initiation of purposeful behaviour and on the other for its selection and production. In the absence of these pathways the animal can neither decide what to do, nor do it; or in other words the translation of an intention into action is no longer possible.

Just as many drugs stimulate action, many depress behaviour. Hypnotic drugs, like the barbiturates and ethanol if given in increasing dosage, abolish behaviour and induce sleep. Such drugs depress all aspects of cognitive function. Another group of depressant drugs, the neuroleptics or major tranquillisers also block action but in a more selective manner. Both unconditioned and conditioned responses are reduced by neuroleptic drugs. We know from neuropharmacological studies that neuroleptics act by blocking the receptors on the neurone sensitive to the transmitters NA and DA. More recently developed neuroleptics block DA receptors selectively. If DA release increases motor behaviour one would expect the blockade of DA action to decrease responding. Furthermore, one would expect neuroleptic drugs to prevent the action of stimulant drugs like amphetamine, and indeed the classical screening tests for neuroleptic drugs involve their ability to block amphetamine-induced stimulation of conditioned and unconditioned behaviour. Low doses of the potent neuroleptics completely abolish the locomotor exploration and stereotypy induced by amphetamine. This blockade of action is selective for it has been shown that although the neuroleptic treatment presents the animal behaving, learning still proceeds. In one study (Iversen 1977) rats were exposed to a learning task in which they had to move on a signal in order to avoid shock. When trained under the influence of a neuroleptic, avoidance responding was not possible and yet when re-tested after the drug effects had worn off, it was clear that the animals had been learning about the shock situation even though they had been prevented from responding.

These experimental results have generated much interest. First, because abuse of amphetamine in human addicts leads to a form of psychotic behaviour which has many of the properties of paranoid schizophrenia (Angrist and Gershon 1970) and secondly, because neuroleptic drugs provide the most effective treatment for paranoid schizophrenia (and amphetamine psychosis). It is possible that amphetamine-induced behaviours provide useful models of human psychotic behaviour. Schizophrenic symptoms in man are attenuated by dopamine receptor blocking drugs, which suggests that heightened DA activity may be associated in some way with the clinical condition. Preliminary biochemical study of postmortem brain tissue from schizophrenic patients suggests that brain levels of DA are increased in certain limbic areas including the amygdala (Bird *et al.* 1977). Referring back to the role of DA pathways in the control of animal behaviour one might suggest that whereas lesions to the DA pathways prevent the normal correlation of intention and action, heightened DA activity might be expected to facilitate abnormally such interactions. In man action involves thought and language as well as overt motor responses and schizophrenia is characterized more by cognitive disorder than by overactivity or stereotypy. However stereotyped behaviour has been documented in schizophrenic patients and the time would appear ripe for a behavioural re-evaluation of the similarity and difference in schizophrenic and stimulant-induced behaviour.

The other striking parallel between animal experiments on the DA pathways and clinical material is found in Parkinson's Disease. Animals with massive lesions to the origin of the DA pathway in the hind brain are devoid of behaviour, including feeding, which accounts for their rapid death (Ungerstedt 1971). Parkinson's disease is associated with a progressive degeneration of the nigro-striatal DA pathway and after death it can be shown that striatal levels of DA are severely reduced (Hornykiewicz 1973).

This condition is characterized by a progressive loss of the ability to act. The initiation of voluntary movement involved in standing up or beginning to walk is severely impaired, so also is the ability to perform the integrated response sequences required, for example, in shaving or eating with a knife and fork. In the later stages of the disease Sacks (1974) has commented upon the additional loss of motivation or what I would call intention. Magda B. for example was described as, '. . . profoundly incapacitated, unable to speak and almost unable to initiate any voluntary motion . . . Added to the motor problems were a striking apathy and apparent incapacity for emotional response . . .' It is likely that in these severe cases non-striatal DA pathways to the limbic and cortical areas are also involved.

The rational development of a drug (L-dopa) to overcome this selective loss of forebrain DA is one of the greatest achievements of modern neuropharmacology. L-dopa, the natural biochemical precursor for DA synthesis is given to patients orally. Functional levels of DA are thereby re-instated and a marked improvement is seen in the ability to initiate and sequence complex motor acts. As the DA neurones are presumed to have degenerated, it is not known where or how this compensatory DA mechanism operates.

Leaving aside the mechanism, the complete reversal of akinesia in some patients is remarkable. So also is the observation in some 'burned-out' Parkinson patients of a return, albeit short lived, of emotional responsiveness to the environment and motivation. Of Magda B., Sacks (1974) writes 'she was able to rise to her feet and stand unaided . . . to walk twenty steps . . . to adjust her position in chair or bed . . . to feed herself . . . At least as dramatic as the motor improvement . . . was the recovery of emotional responsiveness in this patient who had been so withdrawn and apathetic for so many years. With continued improvements of her voice, Mrs B. became quite talkative and showed an intelligence, a charm and a humour which had been almost totally concealed by her disease . . .' In her improvement she was able to describe her feelings when she had been severely incapacitated and commented 'I ceased to have any moods . . . I ceased to care about anything. Nothing moved me – not even the death of my parents. I forgot what it felt like to be happy or unhappy. Was it good or bad? It was neither. It was nothing.'

Unfortunately long-term L-dopa therapy creates problems of its own and the research continues for other pharmacological agents with which to manipulate and normalize DA function. The use of animal models and behavioural pharmacology have come to play a central role in such endeavours.

REFERENCES

Akiskal, H. S. and McKinney, W. T. 1975. 'A review of recent research in depression.' *Arch. gen. Psychiat. 32*, 285-305.

Angrist, B. M. and Gershon, S. 1970. 'The phenomenology of experimentally induced amphetamine psychosis – preliminary observations.' *Biol. Psychiat. 2*, 95-107.

Åsberg, M., Toren, P. and Träskman, L. 1976. '"Serotonin depression" – a biochemical subgroup within the affective disorders.' *Science, 191*, 478-80.

Bird, E. D., Spokes, E. G., Barnes, J., MacKay, A. V. P., Iversen, L. L. and Shephard, P. M. 1977. 'Increased brain dopamine and reduced glutamic acid decarboxylase and choline acetyl transferase activity in schizophrenia and related psychoses.' *Lancet II*, 1157.

Bowlby, J. 1969. *Attachment and loss*. London: Hogarth Press.

Coppen, A., Brooksbank, B. W. L. and Peet, M. 1973. 'Total and free tryptophan concentration in the plasma of depressive patients.' *Lancet II*, 60-3.

Coppen, A., Shaw, D. M., Herzberg, B. and Maggs, R. 1967. 'Tryptophan in treatment of depression.' *Lancet II*, 1178-80.

Costa, E., Guidotti, A. and Mao, C. C. 1977. 'Evidence for GABA involvement in the action of benzodiazepines: studies on rat cerebellum.' In *Mechanisms of action of benzodiazepines*, E. Costa and Greengard, P. (eds), 113-30. New York: Raven Press.

Davison, G. C. and Neale, J. M. 1974. *Abnormal psychology: an experimental-clinical approach*. London: Wiley.

Eysenck, H. J. 1957. *Dynamics of anxiety and hysteria*. London: Routledge and Kegan Paul.

Fuxe, K., Agnati, L. F., Bolme, P., Hökfelt, T., Lidbrink, P., Ljungdahl, A., Perez de la Mova, M. and Ögren, S-O. 1975. 'The possible involvement of GABA mechanisms in the action of benzodiazepines on control catecholamine neurons.' In *Mechanism of action of benzodiazepines*. E. Costa and P. Greengard (eds), 45-61. New York: Raven Press.

Glazer, H. I. and Weiss, J. M. 1976. 'Long-term and transitory interference effect.' *J. exp. Psychol: An. Beh. Processes 2*, 191-201 and Long-term interference effect: an alternative to "Learned Helplessness."' *Ibid. 2*, 202-13.

Gray, J. A. 1977. 'Drug effects on fear and frustration: possible limbic site of action of minor tranquillisers.' In *Handbook of psychopharmacology 8*, Iversen, L. L., Iversen, S. D. and Snyder, S. H. (eds), 433-529. New York: Plenum Press.

Harlow, H. F. and Harlow, M. K. 1969. 'Effects of various mother-infant relationships on rhesus monkey behaviour.' In *Determinants of infant behaviour 4*, B. M. Foss (ed.). London: Methuen.

Hornykiewicz, O. 1973. 'Dopamine in the basal ganglia.' *Brit. med. bull. 29*, 172-8.

Iversen, L. L., Iversen, S. D. and Snyder, S. H. 1975-78. *Handbook of psychopharmacology 1-14*. New York: Plenum Press.

Iversen, S. D. 1977. 'Brain dopamine and behaviour.' In *Handbook of psychopharmacology 8*, Iversen, L. L., Iversen, S. D. and Snyder, S. H. (eds), 333-84. New York: Plenum Press.

Iversen, S. D. and Iversen, L. L. 1975. *Behavioural pharmacology*. New York and Oxford: Oxford University Press.

Kelleher, R. T. and Morse, W. H. 1964. 'Escape behaviour and punished behaviour.' *Fed. Proc. 23*, 808-17.

Kelly, P. H., Seviour, P. W. and Iversen, S. D. 1975. 'Amphetamine and apomorphine responses in the rat following 6-OHDA lesions to the nucleus accumbens septi and corpus striatum.' *Brain Res. 94*, 507-22.

Lacey, J. I. 1967. 'Somatic response patterning in stress: some revisions of activation theory.' In *Psychological stress*. M. H. Appleby and R. Trambull (eds). New York: McGraw-Hill.

Lewis, P. R. and Shute, C. C. D. 1978. 'Cholinergic pathways in CNS.' In Iversen, L. L., Iversen, S. D. and Snyder, S. H. *Handbook of psychopharmacology 9*. New York: Plenum Press.

Mason, S. T. and Iversen, S. D. 1977. 'Effects of selective forebrain noradrenaline loss on behavioural inhibition in the rat.' *J. comp. physiol. 91*, 165-73.

McKinney, W. T. 1974. 'Animal models in psychiatry.' *Perspectives Biol. and Med. 17*, 529-41.

Morgan, M. J. 1974. 'Resistance to satiation.' *Anim. Behav. 22*, 449-66.

Rutter, M. 1972. *Maternal deprivation reassessed*. Harmondsworth: Penguin.

Rylander, G. 1971. Stereotype behaviour in man following amphetamine abuse. In: The correlation of adverse effects in Man with Observations in Animals. Ed. S. B. de C. Baker. pp. 28-31. Excerpta Medica, Amsterdam.

Sacks, D. W. 1974. *Awakenings*. Garden City, New York: Doubleday.

Schildkraut, J. J. 1975. 'Depression and biogenic amines.' In *American Handbook of Psychiatry VI*, D. Hamburg (ed.). New York: Basic Books.

Seligman, M. E. P. 1975. *Helplessness*. San Francisco: W. H. Freeman.

Snyder, S. H., Enna, J. J. and Young, A. B. 1977. 'Brain mechanism associated with therapeutic actions of benzodiazepines: focus on neurotransmitters.' *Amer. J. Psychiat. 134*, 662-5.

Stein, L., Wise, C. D. and Belluzzi, J. D. 1975. 'Effects of benzodiazepines on central serotonergic mechanisms.' In *Mechanism of action of benzodiazepines*. E. Costa and Greengard, P. (eds), 29-44. New York: Raven Press.

Stein, L., Belluzzi, J. D. and Wise, D. C. D. 1977. 'Benzodiazepines: behavioural and neurochemical mechanisms.' *Amer. J. Psychiat. 134*, 665-9.

Thierry, A. M., Javoy, F., Glowinski, J. and Kety, S. S. 1968. 'Effects of stress on the metabolism of norepinephrine dopamine and serotonin in the central nervous system of the rat. I: Modifications of norepinephrine turnover.' *J. Pharm. exp. Ther. 163*, 163-71.

Tye, N. C., Everitt, B. J., and Iversen, S. D. 1977. '5-Hydroxytryptamine and punishment.' *Nature 268*, 741-3.

Ungerstedt, U. 1971. 'On the anatomy, pharmacology and function of the nigro-striatal dopamine system.' *Acta. Physiol. Scand. Suppl.* 367.

van Praag, H. M. 1977. *Depression and schizophrenia.* New York: Spectrum Publications Inc.

Chapter 14

Current Topics in Neuropsychology

HERBERT KOHN

This chapter presents a brief survey of three areas in neuropsychology:
localization of function (including cerebral asymmetry and its
development), task strategy, and technology. Localization of higher
cognitive functions has been found to exist in man. However, it
is less anatomically specific as compared to the localization of
primary sensory and motor functions. As a more specific case of
localization, cerebral asymmetry is discussed. Although innate
differences in anatomy and electrophysiology are present perinatally,
there is some plasticity in the functions that the left and right
hemispheres may develop early in life. A basic assumption of research
on localization is that all individuals approach a given task in the
same way. However, recent evidence questions the validity of the
assumption. Different strategies may be employed in arriving at the
same goal and hence different brain loci may mediate what appears
to be the same behaviour. This issue confounds the assessment of
localization of function. Finally, a section on technology is presented
which shows the methods presently available for assessing central
nervous system physiology during task performance.

LOCALIZATION AND DEVELOPMENT OF
HEMISPHERIC ASYMMETRY

Almost 200 years ago the Austrian neuroanatomist Gall proposed
that higher cognitive functions were carried out in the outer few
millimeters of brain tissue called the cortex. He further suggested that

various personality characteristics and cognitive capacities were located in specific sites of this mantle. He was not the first to make such claims but he was the first to have sufficient effect to provoke the French Academy to respond. An effort was made to quiet the stir created by Gall, but enquiry into this position continued. The decade 1860-70 saw the localization of motor speech by Broca, the proposals of Hughlings Jackson on motor representation in the brain and finally the confirmation of those proposals by Fritsch and Hitzig.

The remainder of the nineteenth century further reinforced this position. Wernicke showed, through clinical case studies, that when the left posterior temporal region and/or parietal areas adjacent to the sylvian fissure were damaged, the reception of speech was impaired. The left angular gyrus was implicated in patients showing reading disorders, and many combinations of language disorder were correlated with particular lesions of the left hemisphere (Nielsen 1946).

Despite the evidence for localization, many continued to champion the idea that the brain acted as a whole. Franz (see Young 1970), pairing the techniques of ablation and problem solving, found that regardless of where the locus of lesion occurred, cats with brain insults needed more trials to learn than normal controls. Additionally, his experiments showed that increasing the size of lesions increased the learning impairment. These findings were later elaborated in the rat by Lashley (who had been Franz's student) and they resulted in Lashley's proposal of the laws of equipotentiality and mass action (1929). These were essentially a formal statement of Franz's earlier work on the effects on performance of size and locus of lesion. The anti-localization group did not totally deny the findings of its opponents. Instead, they ultimately evolved a more refined position in that they admitted localization for some functions, including language, the various senses and motor control.

A major force contributing to the appeal of Lashley's view was the explosion in the size of the brain-damaged population. The first World War produced a wide array of brain insults in soldiers and the flu pandemic of 1918-1920 produced many cases of generalized encephalopathy. Goldstein and Scheerer (1941) in an elaborate study, demonstrated that a common symptom in patients, regardless of locus and size of injury, was an impairment in the capacity to think abstractly and a concomitant increase in the degree of concreteness. Many examples of this change in behaviour are reported for both language (e.g. proverb interpretation) and non-language (e.g. block sorting behaviour). For example, when given a proverb such as 'People who live in glass houses shouldn't throw stones', a brain-damaged patient may respond by pointing out that glass will break when it is hit by a stone. Analogously, when given blocks varying in size, colour and shape and asked to sort them in as many ways as possible, such patients will attend to a single dimension such as colour and fail to use the other properties. In combination, the findings of Franz in animals and Goldstein in men were taken to support the notion that the brain functions in a global, wholistic way for higher cognitive processes.

This interpretation was challenged by the findings from non-human primates (see Pribram 1958) which demonstrated that local lesions to frontal cortex resulted in an impairment in particular types of learning. This suggested that a comparable localization of function might be found in man for higher cognitive processes. The studies of brain-injured soldiers from World War II produced support for the localization position. It also highlighted a different aspect of localization, namely, cerebral asymmetry (differential functioning of the two cerebral hemispheres). Specifically, right hemisphere lesions resulted in impairment of the perception of space while left hemisphere lesions resulted in the well-known findings of impairment of language performance (Semmes, Weinstein, Ghent and Teuber 1960).

While localization of function was clearly present, aside from primary sensory (e.g. vision) and motor cortex, it was not so specific as to be confined to specific gyri. Penfield and Roberts (1959) showed that motor aspects of speech, elicited by focal electrical stimulation of the cortex, were spread more widely than the classic area of Broca and included a mesial representation at the longitudinal fissure. These observations have been extended and replicated using more refined electrical parameters of stimulation. Mohr (1976) approached this problem through anatomical studies. He demonstrated that motor speech impairment went beyond the area described by Broca and encompassed both banks of the sylvian fissure, posteriorly, in an ovoid shape that was related to the arterial blood supply. This area was similar to that mapped by electrical stimulation techniques.

An analogous lack of strict specificity was documented for functions in the right hemispheres by Hecaen and Ajuriaguerra (1964) and Benton (1969). In combination, these studies demonstrated that there was a wide variability in the organization of function and anatomy of the brain from individual to individual in the non-sensory and motor cortices.

The differential functioning of the two hemispheres raises questions as to whether cerebral asymmetry is present at birth. Wada, Clarke and Hamm (1975) added greatly to our study of this issue through their research on 100 adult and 100 infant brains. Their findings show that regardless of age, the classical Broca's area is smaller in the left than in the right hemisphere while the posterior portion of the sylvian fissure is larger. The inborn presence of asymmetry is further supported by electrophysiological data. In a study using event-related potentials (ERPs = changes in brain activity with stimulation), Molfese (1977) reported a marked asymmetry in the amplitude of ERPs in the mid-temporal region of the scalp to verbal versus non-verbal stimuli in infants under ten months of age. Larger amplitudes to verbal stimuli were seen on the left as opposed to the right. In contrast, musical sounds provoked larger potentials on the right. Molfese went one step further and utilized stimuli ('gae', 'ae') which had either bandwidth characteristics of speech or narrower bandwidths. In this study, the subjects were neonates under 24 hours of age. Potentials evoked by the speech bandwidth stimuli showed larger amplitudes over the left hemisphere while the narrow bandwidth stimuli produced larger potentials over the right hemisphere. Comparable findings in behavioural studies were obtained by Turkewitz and Hammer (Turkewitz 1977) who showed a difference in head turning to the human voice among infants who were 24 hours old. The neonates turned right to the bilateral presentation of the human voice and left to bilateral white noise. The above research clearly demonstrated that the left hemisphere is anatomically and physiologically organized to carry out processes involved in language functions.

The areas of the brain associated with language are traditionally described as association cortex; the areas associated with sensory and motor functioning are described as primary cortex. Both types of cortex appear to depend upon environmental influences for their functional and physiological development. For example, cats raised in visual environments lacking variation in line orientation show impairment of discrimination for the absent orientations (Hirsch and Spinelli 1970; Blakemore and Cooper 1970). These studies show electrophysiological responsivity of single cells and behavioural discrimination to be, in part, a function of the environment. Comparable findings have been obtained in man in that those who suffer from astigmatism which is corrected only late in life continue to display relatively poorer discrimination for the affected orientations (Mitchell, Freeman, Millodot and Hagerstrom 1973). Russian research (Novikova 1973) has also demonstrated that congenital or very early absence of pattern vision in humans results in a failure in the development of the normal occipital alpha rhythm. Further, the normal alpha rhythm develops only with maturation of the nervous system. It is poorly organized in infancy and does not reach its highest level of organization until adolescence (Lindsley 1940).

The complex interplay among anatomical localization, maturational changes and environmental influences may be seen by examining cases where hemispherectomies (surgical removal of one cerebral hemisphere) are performed. Those who undergo left hemispherectomies in infancy do show impairments in speech as one would expect from the localization position. However, the impairments are subtle suggesting that the right hemisphere has plasticity of function for speech. However, the language performance is adequate, but not optimum. For example, syntactic comprehension is not as effective when only the right hemisphere is available (Dennis and Kohn 1975). Further Dennis and Whitaker (1976) have demonstrated that the understanding of grammatical structure is more rapidly achieved when the single hemisphere is the left one rather than the right one.

Detailed studies of the development of cerebral asymmetry have recently been undertaken. For purposes of simplicity, only one paradigm, dichotic listening, will be explored here. (However, other paradigms such as visual half-field of presentation, McKeever and Huling 1970, and tactile capacity, Witelson 1974, have been studied.) The discussion will be further limited to findings in righthanded individuals. (It has been shown that among left handers, the familiar pattern of handedness is a significant factor in the development of hemispheric asymmetries, Hecaen and Saquet 1971.) Dichotic listening is a task in which two different auditory stimuli are simultaneously presented, one to each ear. The person is then to indicate the stimulus heard. It has been found, that in the case of verbal stimuli, the right ear shows an advantage. This has been related to the predominance of the contralateral auditory pathway and hence left hemisphere superiority in a language task (Kimura 1961). Since performance on this task follows a developmental course, it has been possible to utilize dichotic listening as an assessment of the growth of lateralization of function. Kimura (1963) has demonstrated a right ear superiority as early as age four. In a more recent study, Piazza (1977) has found such ear superiority in the 3-year-old.

As in the discussion above, we find evidence that lateralization is affected by biological and environmental variables. Bryden (1970) assessed the effect of sex on development of ear superiority. He did not report specific ages but did indicate that he used second, fourth and sixth graders; thus, the lowest likely age in his study was six years. No statistically significant difference was reported between boys and girls but, on the basis of curves shown, he reported earlier superiority in girls; boys and girls showed equal preference for the right ear stimulus by Grade 6 – roughly ten to twelve years of age. Bakker, Teunissen and Bosch (1976) reported no difference between boys and girls seven through eleven years of age in a dichotic listening task and hence agreed with the statistical findings of Bryden.

In a study of social class as a variable in the development of dichotic listening skills, Geffner and Dorman (1976) found no ear advantage between 4-year-olds of varying social class background, but they did report a difference between boys and girls with a left ear advantage for boys. Borowy and Goebel (1976) studied the effects of sex, socioeconomic class and race on the development of dichotic listening. They utilized 5, 7, 9 and 11-year-olds, varying the factors above. Sex differences were not found. Race differences were only measured between lower class children as a middle class black population was not included. Again no differences due to race were found. Socioeconomic class did show a significant difference for degree of right ear superiority with a lag of two years for the lower class children. Similar results were obtained by Geffner and Hochberg (1971). Taken together, these studies may be interpreted as indicating that hemispheric lateralization is significantly affected by two main variables, age related maturation and socioeconomic class. This latter is extremely complex since it includes such variables as nutrition, mother-infant interaction, stability of social environment, etc. Each surely deserves attention on an individual basis but the problems inherent in measuring such variables have yet to be solved.

In the discussion to this point, the left hemisphere has been characterized as the language processor and the right hemisphere as a spatial processor. Recent formulations about cerebral asymmetry have reoriented this conceptualization. Specifically, the left hemisphere is deemed not simply to process language but rather it employs a mode of operation that enables it to process information containing analytic, sequential properties. Since language is a prime representative of a skill involving such analytic properties, it has been the prime means for entry into the study of left hemisphere functioning. By contrast, the right hemisphere is now deemed to employ a mode of operations that enables it to process Gestalt-type information (Bogen 1969; Galin 1977). Since spatial skills are a prime representative of skills involving Gestalt-type information, it has been the major behaviour for entry into the study of the right hemisphere functioning. This approach, which views hemisphere functioning in terms of *modes of information processing*, holds the promise for opening up the range of cognitive behaviours that may be related to localized brain function.

STRATEGY

The studies cited above have shown evidence that behaviour is differentially affected by the two hemispheres. However, behaviour is not totally determined by this biological substrate. The set, attitude or plan that one brings to a task affects the way in which either hemisphere will function. Concepts, such as 'set' or 'attitude' have until recently been ignored in neuropsychology but they have been dealt with in experimental psychology. For ease of exposition here, the term 'strategy' will be employed to subsume the behaviours represented by concepts such as set, expectancy, self instruction, etc. The psychological literature is replete with descriptions of the variations in strategy that are employed by individuals facing identical problems. Witelson and Harris (1977) in their recent studies in neuropsychology have adopted the concept of strategy as being necessary for understanding the results of clinical studies in man where variable behavioural deficits occur with similar lesions and conversely where similar deficits occur with variable lesions. An excellent example of differences in strategy has been described by Drake (1970). On the basis of speed and correctness of response, two groups of normal children were constituted; one were 'reflectives' who were slower and more often correct, the other were 'impulsives' who were faster and less often correct. When faced with the task of matching a figure to one of a number of alternatives (see Matching Familiar Figures Test in Kagan 1966), these two groups of children showed markedly different eye movements. The 'impulsive' child, or rapid responder, was shown, by studying eye movements to engage in a kind of global scanning of the field. In contrast, the 'reflective' child or slow responder repeatedly fixated the standard and the choice figures.

The use of different strategies may be a factor in the power of some paradigms to demonstrate cerebral asymmetry. Kershner, Thomae and Callaway (1977) carried out a visual half field experiment with 5 to 6-year-olds, both male and female. While carefully controlling for eye fixation, they presented verbal stimuli, i.e. numbers to the right or left visual fields. The fixation point was either a number from one to nine or a non-verbal stimulus such as an asterisk-like figure. Furthermore, with a number fixation point, a verbal report was requested, while with the non-verbal fixation point, a manual response was used. The hypothesis was that a verbal response and numeral fixation point would prime the left hemisphere with a resultant superiority for the stimuli in the right visual field. Conversely, the manual indication and non-language fixation point would prime the right hemisphere with resultant superiority for number recognition in the left visual field. The results unequivocally supported the hypothesis; in fact, the degree of superiority under the two conditions was almost identical. Thus, when the right hemisphere is engaged by appropriate cueing (i.e. a strategy is fostered), it can process verbal information that is traditionally thought to be handled by the left hemisphere.

Bever and Chiarello (1974) have shown that later-life experiences may affect choice of strategy. Their subjects were fifteen to thirty years of age and differed in the following ways. One group consisted of those who were relatively untrained in music (formal training of less than three years taken at least five years prior to the study). The second group were those who were well trained musically (at least four years of study) and were currently active musically. All the stimuli were presented to one ear only and consisted of twelve to eighteen note melodies which were later repeated. Half the subjects were presented with stimuli on the left and half on the right. The hypothesis was that music may be processed by the left hemisphere if it is treated in an analytic fashion. The findings were as predicted. The musically well-trained and active subjects showed a right ear superiority while the relatively musically naïve subjects showed a left ear superiority. Another task these subjects had to perform was to decide if a two-tone sequence was part of the longer melodies. The relatively untrained group was unable to do this task which suggests they did not have an available strategy.

This study indicates that the mere presence of a biological substrate need not result in the manifestation of a particular strategy, but rather that certain strategies can be taught or learned if the substrate is present. The bond between strategy and localization may rest upon the inherent capacity of a piece of tissue to process input in particular ways. Through experience, one begins to recognize which of several possible strategies is the most appropriate for solving any particular task. This results in the ability to shift input to appropriate processors. Certainly the practised musicians in the Bever and Chiarello study appear to use their left hemispheres in ways other than the un-practised group. This suggests that caution should be exercised in determining localization of function on any given task if the strategy used in attempting to solve the task is unknown. This notion helps us to understand the great variability that may be shown on any task among individuals with similar lesions. Untangling the web of the relations between strategy and localization can only be accomplished through studying CNS function in human beings engaged in real behaviour. Some possible technological developments applicable to the study of living man are discussed in the next section.

TECHNOLOGY

Fritsch and Hitzig made their initial observations while attending to head wounds of soldiers in the battlefield. There they noted that, on occasion, touching the cortex resulted in movement of the soldiers' limbs. This observation prompted them to explore this phenomenon by using the relatively new technology of electrical stimulation with animals. Soon after Caton (1875) successfully recorded electrical changes in the brain in response to sensory stimuli. Indeed, before the turn of the century, the auditory cortex of the cat was mapped by this technique (Brazier 1961).

A period of fifty years passed, however, before these techniques, (of electrical recording and stimulation), were utilized to further the understanding of human neuropsychology. Beginning with Penfield's publications, a monumental number of studies was published on the results of electrical stimulation of the brain. For the most part they, of necessity, offered only confirmatory information with regard to the localization of language, motor and sensory functions. Penfield (1975) emphasized that such studies were, on ethical grounds, constrained to the needs of therapeutic intervention. Recording from electrodes implanted within the brain was subject to the same ethical considerations and hence, it too, had a limited, though important impact on human neuropsychology.

Neuroanatomical study of the brains of patients who had suffered insult provided the context for the theoretical development of brain-behaviour relations in man, but testable hypotheses were not readily generated and many gaps in our knowledge could not be filled by the use of this technique. Electroencephalography (EEG) offered new promise in this regard and Berger in fact (see translation by Gloor 1969) demonstrated that definable changes in the electrical activity of the brain acccompanied behavioural change. When a subject was engaged in visual activity the basic frequency of the EEG became faster than 8-12 Hz (alpha activity) and its voltage decreased, while at rest higher amplitudes and alpha activity were present. A wide variety of behaviours (e.g. personality variables) were studied with respect to changes in EEG activity (e.g. percent time alpha). However, there was little, if any, furtherance of our insight into the brain-behaviour relationships. The critics of these efforts (e.g. Lindsley 1952) addressed the major problems of this research. They pointed out that the behavioural variables could not be operationally defined and the electrographic activity could not be interpreted. Thus, no meaning could be attached to the relationship between such measures as percent time alpha rhythm and such diffuse personality measures as introversion/extroversion.

With the development of theoretical perspectives and concise operational definitions, it became possible to demonstrate meaningful relationships between EEG activity and behaviour. Galin and Orenstein (1972) showed that total power in the EEG, primarily alpha activity, varies between homologous sites over the two hemispheres depending on the task performed by the individual during the recording. Thus, when engaged in a language task, subjects showed less power over the left hemisphere and when engaged in a visual task less power over the right hemisphere. Such findings were reminiscent of Berger's earlier observations referred to above.

A variety of more sophisticated techniques was produced in an attempt to assess the pattern of the spatial distribution of EEG activity at various scalp sites over time. A most direct method was the toposcope of Walter and Shipton (1951) which had one small oscilloscope for each scalp recording site. As the EEG changed, these scopes altered the displays. Rémond (1960) attempted to produce such displays via computer printout of space-time maps, which he termed the chronoscope. In each case, the outputs were not readily quantifiable and were so visually complex as to defy analysis.

More recently, coherence analysis (Brazier 1972) which is a technique of correlating the frequency components of EEG activity at two or more loci over time, has been utilized to discern brain organization during various activities. When this technique has been employed in the waking state with depth electrodes in limbic system structures, it has been shown that theta (4-7 Hz) rhythms in the amygdala are seen 7 milliseconds later in the dorsal medial thalamus. In sleep, some relationships between structures such as amygdala and hippocampus are not present but they do survive barbiturate anaesthesia. Coherence techniques have limited applicability in scalp recordings as the EEG is too broad a summation of cortical activity. The scalp recording represents a volume conducted signal primarily from the cortical mantle and one is not readily able to predict what sites and time periods to analyze.

An alternative scalp technique exists, the recording of potentials which are time locked to a specific event. These are termed event-related potentials, ERP, and were previously discussed with regard to studies by Molfese. The requirements here are the occurrence of a sensory stimulus or motor event. As these potentials are typically less than 10 microvolts and background EEG amplitudes are of similar or larger voltages, signal to noise ratio must be reduced. This is accomplished by repeated stimulus presentations with the addition of voltages occurring at constant sampling times following the stimulus onset (for example, every two milliseconds for a period of one second). That activity, unrelated to the event, will be 'random' and hence cancel itself out (at least in theory). As we have seen from the studies of Molfese, this can be a powerful technique. Its value is even more significant than it might appear in terms of understanding the mechanism. Fox and O'Brien (1965) have shown that if one studies the discharges of a single cell to thousands of stimulus presentations, the temporal distribution of such discharges summed over these trials looks very much like the ERP recorded over the same anatomical locus with a gross electrode. In other words, a population of cells over tens of trials represents the activity of a single cell over thousands of trials to the same event. This is important in the sense that the ERP clearly is not an epiphenomenon.

In order to use the ERP technique in neuropsychological studies, one must be aware of its inherent properties. The early waves up to 100 milliseconds appear to be a function of thalamo-cortical 'primary' projections. A middle range of latencies up to 200 milliseconds varies with changes in the physical parameters of stimuli and subject variables such as attention and level of arousal. Potentials beyond this latency vary with such factors as the probability of stimulus occurrence, the relevance of the stimulus to the task and other task conditions (Desmedt and Robertson 1977; Donchin, Kutas and McCarthy 1977). For example, Donchin and Cohen (1967) showed changes in the late latency potential when two stimuli were presented, a necker cube and a light flash. The necker cube was continuously present and the subject's task was to count necker cube reversals or light flashes. The late potentials to the light flash were markedly reduced when counting reversals. In other words, when the flashes were irrelevant, the response declined.

The obvious limitation of this technique is that it is limited to events that are fixed in time and of short duration. Continuing behaviours, such as listening to music, cannot be studied. There are potentials such as the contingent negative variation (CNV) which can have durations of tens of seconds. This potential is a function of the pairing of two stimuli (e.g. a light is presented, followed some seconds later by a second light) and it can be prolonged by increasing the duration between the stimuli. The CNV is the electrical change of baseline between the stimuli. With careful development of paradigms, it might be possible to show differences in such potentials depending on locus of recording and the task requirements. Rubin and McAdam (1972) have shown that the degree of subjects' certainty about their responses is correlated with CNV amplitude. Butler and Glass (1974) have reported an increase in asymmetry of CNV when the second stimulus was numerical; larger potentials with shorter latency were seen over the dominant hemisphere. In all the above, a knowledge of anatomy related to function, and the judicious use of recording sites is essential.

Electrical activity is but one possible measure of physiological function of the brain. There are at least two more recent developments. One of these is the development of deoxy-d-glucose which can be radioactively tagged and is taken up by cells as glucose but not metabolized. Thus one can study intensive neuronal activity by emissions from this uptake. Little data are presently available that are relevant to neuropsychology, but the possibilities are very promising. A somewhat older technique using radioactive materials to study regional cerebral blood flow (rCBF) in the brain has proved to be very valuable in neuropsychology. The principle in these studies is that removal of a radioactive tracer from tissue is a function of blood flow and with increased neural activity local blood flow will increase. Two techniques of administration have been developed, intracarotid injection (Lassen and Ingvar 1961) and inhalation (Mallet and Veall 1963). In either case, detectors are located over the scalp, the number of which is presently limited only by physical size and available funds. The cost, complexity and potential morbidity of the injection technique has limited the number of studies but important findings have been reported. Risberg and Ingvar (1973) have shown modest changes in flow over the left hemisphere for digit span, feature detection and Raven's matrices. The latter two tasks showed different loci of rCBF change compared to digit span. Ingvar and Schwartz (1974) demonstrated dominant hemisphere differences in rCBF during speech and reading. The findings were striking in that speech showed parietal and temporal lobe increases whereas reading showed only temporal increases. Using the inhalation technique, Risberg *et al.* (1975) showed that differences between the hemispheres occurred with different tasks. While doing Miller Analogies, the left parietal and occipital rCBF increased over homologous areas on the right. During a spatial task, right frontal and parietal areas showed increased flow when contrasted to these sites in the left hemisphere. Jacquy *et al.* (1977) have shown that both imagined fist clenching and actual squeezing are accompanied by rCBF changes and that short and long reaction times show different rates of flow. Expanded use of this technique and combined use of electrophysiology and rCBF techniques will surely be of significant value in elucidating the neural mechanisms of human behaviour. Many types of inquiry about the relationship of man's behaviour to the function of his nervous system have been held back because so much of the research has been dominated by the animal model. The principal concerns of human neuropsychology – higher cognitive functions, language, lateralizations – can best, if not only, be studied in man. These non-invasive methods offer promising tools which remain to be fully exploited.

This glimpse into some current problems and technical advances in human neuropsychology will hopefully whet the appetite for more intensive investigation. With reference to the study of neural substrates, Donchin, Kutas and McCarthy (1977) have stated the problem concisely, 'The crux . . . is the selection of a task which will activate the appropriate processor.' From the point of view of the researcher less concerned with the neural substrate, Klein, Moscovitch and Vigna (1976) have summarized the goals for understanding localization and asymmetry, 'The problem, now, is not to choose the most likely candidate, but rather to understand how different variables, such as stimulus type, encoding processes and cognitive strategies determine the relative contribution of each of these mechanisms in producing perceptual asymmetries in different situations.' Careful reading will show the complementarity of these statements.

I would like to thank Dr. Marion Blank for her interest and help in the preparation of this paper.

REFERENCES

Bakker, D. J., Teunissen, J. and Bosch, J. 1976. 'Development of laterality reading patterns.' In R. M. Knights and D. J. Bakker (eds) *Neuropsychology of learning disorders*. Baltimore: University Park Press.

Benton, A. L. 1969. 'Constructional apraxia, some unanswered questions.' In A. L. Benton (ed.) *Contributions to clinical neuropsychology*. Chicago: Aldine.

Bever, T. G. and Chiarello, R. J. 1974. 'Cerebral dominance in musicians and non-musicians.' *Science 185*, 537-89.

Blakemore, C. and Cooper, G. F. 1970. 'Development of the brain depends on visual environment.' *Nature 228*, 477-8.

Bogen, J. 1969. 'The other side of the brain II. An appositional mind.' *Bull. L. A. Neurol. Soc. 34*, 135-62.

Borowy, T. and Goebel, T. 1976. 'Cerebral lateralization of speech: the effects of age, sex, race and socioeconomic class.' *Neuropsychologia 14*, 363-70.

Brazier, M. A. B. 1961. *A history of the electrical activity of the brain*. London: Pitman.

Brazier, M. A. B. 1972. 'Direct recordings from within the human brain using long-indwelling electrodes.' In G. G. Somjen (ed.) *Neurophysiology studied in man*. Amsterdam: Excerpta Medica.

Bryden, M. P. 1970. 'Laterality effects in dichotic listening.' *Neuropsychologia 8*, 443-50.

Butler, S. A. and Glass, A. 1974. 'Asymmetries in the CNV over left and right hemispheres while subjects await numeric information.' *Biol. Psychol. 2*, 1-16.

Dennis, M. and Kohn, B. 1975. 'Comprehension of syntax in infantile hemiplegics after cerebral hemidecortication.' *Brain and Language 2*, 472-82.

Dennis, M. and Whitaker, H. A. 1976. 'Language acquisition following hemidecortication.' *Brain and Language 3*, 404-33.

Desmedt, J. E. and Robertson, D. 1977. 'Search for right hemisphere asymmetries in event-related potentials to somatosensory cueing signals.' In J. E. Desmedt (ed.) *Language and hemispheric specialization in man: cerebral event-related potentials*. New York: S. Karger.

Donchin, E., Kutas, M. and McCarthy, G. 1977. 'Electroencephalographic investigations of hemispheric specialization.' In J. E. Desmedt (ed.) *Language and hemispheric specialization in man: cerebral event-related potentials*. New York: S. Karger.

Donchin, E. and Cohen, L. 1967. 'Average evoked potentials and intramodality selective attention.' *Electroenceph. clin. Neurophysiol. 22*, 537-46.

Drake, D. 1970. 'Perceptual correlates of impulsive and reflective behavior.' *Developmental Psychology 2*, 202-14.

Fox, S. S. and O'Brien, J. H. 1965. 'Duplication of evoked potential waveform by curve of probability of firing of single cells.' *Science 147*, 888-90.

Galin, D. 1977. 'Lateral specialization in psychiatric issues.' *Ann. N. Y. Acad. Sci. 299*, 397-411.

Galin, D. and Orenstein, R. 1972. 'Lateral specialization of cognitive mode: an EEG study.' *Psychophysiology 9*, 412-18.

Geffner, D. S. and Dorman, M. F. 1976. 'Hemispheric specialization for speech perception in 4-year-old children from low and middle socioeconomic classes.' *Cortex 12*, 71-3.

Geffner, D. and Hochberg, I. 1971. 'Ear laterality performance of children from low and middle socioeconomic levels on a verbal dichotic listening task. *Cortex 7*, 193-203.

Gloor, P. 1969. 'Hans Berger – on the electroencephalogram of man.' *Electro-enceph. clin. Neurophysiol*. Suppl. 28.

Goldstein, K. and Scheerer, M. 1941. 'Abstract and concrete behavior: an experimental study with special tests.' *Psychol. Monographs 53*, 1-51.

Hecaen, H. and Ajuriaguerra, J. 1964. *Left handedness, manual superiority and cerebral dominance*. New York: Grune and Stratton.

Hecaen, H. and Saquet, J. 1971. 'Cerebral dominance in left handed subjects.' *Cortex 7*, 19-48.

Hirsch, H. V. B. and Spinelli, D. N. 1970. 'Visual experience modifies distribution of horizontally and vertically oriented receptive fields in cats.' *Science 168*, 869-71.

Ingvar, D. H. and Schwartz, M. S. 1974. 'Bloodflow patterns induced in the dominant hemisphere by speech and reading.' *Brain 97*, 273-88.

Jacquy, J., Piraux, A., Joquet, P., Lhoas, J. P. and Noel, G. 1977. 'Regional cerebral bloodflow during voluntary movements of the hand.' *Neuropsychobiology 3*, 240-9.

Kagan, J. 1966. 'Reflection – Impulsivity: the generality and dynamics of conceptual tempo.' *J. abn. Psych. 71*, 17-24.

Kershner, J., Thomae, R. and Callaway, R. 1977. 'Non-verbal fixation control in young children induces a left-field advantage in digit recall.' *Neuropsychologia 15*, 569-76.

Kimura, D. 1961. 'Cerebral dominance and the perception of verbal stimuli.' *Can. J. Psychol. 15*, 166-71.

Kimura, D. 1963. 'Speech lateralization in young children as determined by an auditory test.' *J. comp. physiol. Psychol. 56*, 899-902.

Klein, D., Moscovitch, M. and Vigna, C. 1976. 'Attentional mechanisms and perceptual asymmetries in tachistoscopic recognition of words and faces.' *Neuropsychologia 14*, 55-66.

Lashley, K. S. 1929. *Brain mechanisms and intelligence.* Chicago: University of Chicago Press.

Lassen, N. A. and Ingvar, P. H. 1961. 'The bloodflow of the cerebral cortex determined by radioactive Krypton-85.' *Experientia 17*, 42-3.

Lindsley, D. B. 1940. 'The ontogenetic development of brain potentials in human subjects.' *Yearbook Nat. Soc. Study Educ. 39*, 127-30.

Lindsley, D. B. 1952. 'Psychological phenomena and the electroencephalogram.' *EEG clin. Neurophysiol. 4*, 443-56.

Mallet, B. L. and Veall, M. 1963. 'Investigations of cerebral bloodflow in hypertension using radioactive xenon, inhalation and extracranial recording.' *Lancet* 1081.

McKeever, W. F. and Huling, M. 1970. 'Left cerebral hemisphere superiority in tachistoscopic word recognition performance.' *Percep. and Mot. Skills 30*, 763-6.

Mitchell, D. E., Freeman, R. D., Millodot, M. and Hagerstrom, G. 1973. 'Meridonal amblyopia: evidence for modification of the human visual system by early visual experience.' *Vision Research 13*, 535-8.

Mohr, J. P. 1976. 'Broca's area and Broca's aphasia.' In H. Whitaker and H. A. Whitaker (eds) *Studies in neurolinguistics, I.* New York: Academic Press.

Molfese, D. L. 1977. 'The ontogeny of cerebral asymmetry in man: auditory evoked potentials to linguistic and non-linguistic stimuli in infants and children.' In J. E. Desmedt (ed.) *Language and hemispheric specialization in man: cerebral event-related potentials.* New York: S. Karger.

Nielsen, J. M. 1946. *Agnosia, apraxia, aphasia: their value in cerebral localization.* New York: Hoeber.

Novikova, L. A. 1973. *Blindness and the electrical activity of the brain.* New York: American Foundation for the Blind.

Penfield, W. 1975. *The mystery of the mind*. Princeton, N. J.: Princeton University Press.

Penfield, W. and Roberts, L. 1959. *Speech and brain mechanisms*. Princeton, N. J.: Princeton University Press.

Piazza, D. M. 1977. 'Cerebral lateralization in young children as measured by dichotic listening and fingertapping tasks.' *Neuropsychologia 15*, 417-25.

Pribram, K. H. 1958. 'Neocortical function in behavior.' In H. F. Harlow and C. N. Woolsey (eds) *Biological and biochemical bases of behavior*. Madison, Wisc.: University Wisconsin Press.

Rémond, A. 1960. 'Recherche des renseignments significatifs dans les enregistrements electrophysiologiques et mecanisation possible.' *Actualities Neurophysiologiques*, 167-210.

Risberg, J., Halsey, J. H., Wills, E. L. and Wilson, E. M. 1975. 'Hemispheric specialization in normal man studied by bilateral measurements of the regional cerebral bloodflow.' *Brain 98*, 511-24.

Risberg, J. and Ingvar, D. H. 1973. 'Patterns of activation in the grey matter of the dominant hemisphere during memorizing and reading.' *Brain 96*, 737-56.

Rubin, E. H. and McAdam, D. W. 1972. 'Slow potential concomitants of the retrieval process.' *Electroenceph. clin. Neurophysiol. 32*, 84-6.

Semmes, J., Weinstein, J., Ghent, L. H. and Teuber, H. L. 1960. *Somatosensory changes after penetrating brain wounds in man*. Cambridge, Mass.: Harvard University Press.

Turkewitz, G. 1977. 'The development of lateral differentiation in the human infant.' *Ann. N.Y. Acad. Sci. 299*, 399-417.

Wada, J. A., Clarke, R. and Hamm, A. 1975. 'Cerebral hemispheric asymmetry in humans.' *Arch. Neurol. 32*, 239-46.

Walter, W. G. and Shipton, H. W. 1951. 'A new toposcopic display system.' *Electroenceph. clin. Neurophysiol. 11*, 374-5.

Witelson, S. F. 1974. 'Hemispheric specialization for linguistic and non-linguistic and actual perception using a dichotomous stimulation technique.' *Cortex 10*, 3-17.

Witelson, S. F. and Harris, L. J. 1977. 'The analysis of cognitive process in children through the study of hemisphere specialization in different perceptual systems.' Presented at Int. Neuropsychological Soc. 5th Annual Meeting, Albuquerque.

Young, R. M. 1970. *Mind, brain and adaptation in the 19th century*. Oxford: Clarendon Press.

Chapter 15

Motor Control

GEORGE E. STELMACH

Superficially, co-ordinating the appropriate muscular commands for a specified movement might appear to be a relatively simple task. Yet, the successful completion of a refined motor act requires a high degree of temporal precision among the motor commands for protagonist and antagonist muscle groups. How is one able to fulfil these complex demands of co-ordinated movement? The earliest and, until recently, the favoured position was that information from peripheral receptors was necessary and sufficient, for motor control and motor skill learning, (James 1890; Mott and Sherrington 1895; Adams 1971). This position, however, has recently been challenged by those who argue that skilled motor acts can be carried out in the absence of feedback (Kelso 1977). This alternative view contends that movement is regulated by a central, rather than peripheral source.

Thus, questions and controversies concerning how individuals control their limbs during the execution of a movement have stimulated neurophysiological and psychological inquiry for some time. This chapter summarizes the peripheral (closed-loop) and central (open-loop) points of view by reviewing the supporting evidence for each. The primary question throughout is how the two theories accommodate the basic requirements of co-ordinated movement. Other reviews of the theoretical positions and their implications for motor control are presented by Glencross (1977), Kelso and Stelmach (1976) and Schmidt (1977).

The paper is organized into four sections. The first section defines and distinguishes closed-loop and open-loop concepts. The second section considers the mechanisms underlying the two models. The third and fourth sections review the important findings supporting the closed and open-loop models.

CLOSED-LOOP AND OPEN-LOOP MODELS DEFINED

Two major classes of explanation for motor control can be distinguished; open-loop models and closed-loop models. The closed-loop position maintains that peripheral receptors and sensory feedback form the cornerstone for error detection and error correction. Such a system postulates an internal referent or standard that specifies the desired value of the motor output. Subsequently, response produced information is fed back and evaluated against the referent to determine any error. This system is self regulating and uses the error detection process to minimize deviations from the movements specified by the internal referent.

Closed-loop theories have held a dominant position in the explanation of skilled motor behaviour for many years. While closed-loop theory originated in engineering, it has seen many variations in motor behaviour (Anokhin 1969; Fairbanks 1955; Chase 1965; Sokolov 1969). All of these theorists propose that feedback is used as the agent that initiates error detection and correction. The closed-loop tradition has been carried forward recently by Adams (1971) who postulates that feedback from the periphery establishes an internal memory representation that guides and controls movement.

In contrast, the open-loop view proposes that higher centres of the central nervous system dictate the information for a pattern of movement and that outflow information (efference) is sufficient for the control of co-ordinated movement. It has no feedback or mechanisms for error regulation. One of the earliest supporters of this position was Lashley (1917). Working with rats, Lashley and his co-workers demonstrated that there was no reduction in accuracy of maze running when proprioceptive afferents were severed (Lashley and Ball 1929) or when lesions were made in the rat's cerebellum (McCarthy and Lashley 1926). Although these findings have been viewed as controversial, they are often cited as evidence for the existence of some wholly central mechanism as the determinant of a motor sequence. The open-loop position typically uses a motor programme as a centrally stored plan for the movement sequence, and the plan controls the movement during its course. The implication is that feedback is unnecessary for the regulation of movement. The central control position has been out of the mainstream for many years, however, evidence that motor responses are often pre-programmed in advance is becoming more frequent, and has attracted a strong following among those working on motor control (Klapp 1975; Keele 1968; Kelso 1977; Schmidt 1976).

THE LOCUS OF MOTOR CONTROL

Closed-loop

Since closed-loop theories are based on error data, the sensory receptors must collect information about the motor act and relay it to some central processing centre. These receptors are referred to as proprioceptors and they provide information about joint, tendon and muscle activity. Peripheral mechanisms generally identified as providing afferent information about the position of a limb in space are joint receptors and muscle spindles. While both have been identified, there has been much controversy concerning the relative importance of the information provided by each mechanism. Bell (1826) believed that muscles played the primary role in movement detection. In contrast Duchenne (1883) favoured the joint capsule hypothesis (see Kelso and Stelmach 1976). A little over twenty years later Sherrington's (1906) work emphasized the muscle spindle conception. With the development of sophisticated physiological techniques the role of the muscle spindles is now more fully appreciated. For a more detailed account of the physiology and structural properties of the receptors in the joints, tendons and muscles see Skoglund (1956) and Matthews (1972).

Joint receptors. Joint receptors are mechanoreceptors which respond to the mechanical forces of tension, pressure, stretch and torque. These receptors can be classified into three major types; golgi tendon organs, pacinian corpuscles and ruffini endings (Kelso and Stelmach 1976). It is believed that the golgi tendon organs signal direction and joint position. The pacinian corpuscles signal movement acceleration and possibly detect very short movements. The ruffini endings signal the speed and direction of movements. These endings appear to be affected by muscular tension at the joint, therefore they may also signal resistance to movement and perhaps discriminate between active and passive movements. Other results indicate that joint receptor activity increases greatly when the limb approaches maximum extension or flexion, whereas activity at mid-angles is less. For further details regarding the function of joint receptors the reader is directed to reviews by Skoglund (1973), Smith (1969) and Howard and Templeton (1966).

On the behavioural side there are also data that implicate joint receptors as a basis of motor control. Rather than attempting to identify specific neuronal structures or pathways in the central nervous system, behavioural studies have been concerned to discover the movement cues that are utilized in positioning (Marteniuk and Roy 1972; Stelmach and McCracken 1978). The most common finding is that location movements, where joint position is held constant, is a dominant mode of control. In summary, there is neurophysiological and behavioural evidence that velocity, direction and position information may be transmitted from joint receptors. Thus, the movement information provided by joint receptors fits well with the closed-loop control formulation.

Muscle receptors. While the role of joint receptors has been known for several years, the precise contribution of muscle spindles to motor control has been more elusive. Afferent fibres from the spindles are characterized as either primary or secondary endings. The primary endings are fast responding axons, while the secondary endings are slow responding axons. Both types of endings, however, fire at steady rates, which are monotonically related to the stretch of the muscle (Goodwin 1976).

It is generally believed that the muscle spindle serves as a receptor to detect changes in muscle length and as such to function in a peripheral feedback loop. The firing of the spindle afferents increases when the spindle's sensory portions are stretched by external forces lengthening the main muscle, or by increasing the firing of gamma intrafusal fibres. The controversial issue, however, is whether this information can be used to identify the position of a limb. It has been shown by Vallbo (1974), using static contraction, where joint angle is constant, that there is an increased rate of firing from spindle endings. Therefore, if spindle activity is an estimate of joint angle, the central nervous system must correct for the effects of the fusimotor expectation. Goodwin (1976) has similarly pointed out that joint afferents in golgi tendon organs lie parallel in series with load bearing elements in the muscle. Their discharge can only be used to estimate length if their tension transducing properties and the length/tension relationship characteristics of the extrafusal muscle fibres are both known. Nevertheless, strong support for muscle spindle involvement comes from a study by Shambes (1969) who, using a local anaesthetic, blocked gamma afferents in postural muscles of the lower leg. She found increased body sway in standing positions and consistent timing errors with leg movements. Similarly, Smith, Roberts and Atkins (1972) showed that anaesthetizing the gamma system in the triceps resulted in large overshooting of movements directed at touching the nose. Further support comes from Goodwin, McCloskey and Matthews (1972) in their studies on muscle tendon vibration.

The major findings from these studies indicate that when the muscle spindles have been vibrated there is a misperception in movement pattern. Thus, as with the data on joint receptors, these findings suggest that muscle spindles play an important role in the perception of limb movement.

Open-loop

It is well known that when voluntary movement is made there is an efferent discharge by the higher centres that is transmitted to the muscles. It is this discharge that is crucial to the central control model. Open-loop theorists maintain that all the specifications of a co-ordinated movement are contained in the discharge from a centre in the nervous system. Through the years Lashley's original ideas on central control have been extended. Now we think of this as a centrally stored, prestructured set of motor commands that direct rapid co-ordinated acts without sensory information. Many names have been given to describe central control, a 'Victrola record' (Hunter 1930), a 'score' (Weiss 1950), a 'memory drum' (Henry 1960) and more recently a 'motor program' (Keele 1968). Despite these different labels, the position advocated has remained essentially the same. The centralist position maintains that the efferent command determines which muscles contract, the order of contractions, the force of contraction and the duration of contraction, all without the involvement of sensory feedback.

One view of how the efferent command controls movement is seen in von Holst's (1954) hypothesis which claims that when a motor response is initiated, information from the efferent command is given to the musculature preparing the motor system for the receipt of sensory information. This feedforward concept has been extended by Sperry *et al.* (1969) and Teuber (1964). While currently viewed as the corollary discharge hypothesis, this explanation sees the motor programme as providing information about the movement-to-be to sensory centres of the brain. There a comparison with an image representation of the desired movement and any mismatch or error is determined. Further, agreement seems to be emerging that some feedforward mechanism is necessary in order to distinguish between sensory information from active as opposed to passive movements. MacNeilage (1970), working on speech production, has postulated an alternative view in which proprioceptive information about the anticipated goal contacts the perceptual process where it is converted into an abstract code. Once this is achieved the movement is carried out. Thus, it is not a pattern of musculature that is essential for the movement, rather it is the final goal (target) that determines the motor act. In response to criticisms about storage problems associated with the motor programme idea Schmidt (1976) has suggested that the programme does not have a one to one representation with the movements produced. Instead the programme is seen as being general in nature so that it could produce a number of similar movements within a given class. To illustrate this he uses the analogy of a computer program that can calculate means and variances, but needs to have the number of bits of data specified before computation can begin. Common to all the open-loop theories is the notion that when voluntary movements are made, the efferent command dictates the precise characteristics of the motor act.

Case for Closed-loop Control

Determining whether a system is open or closed-loop requires some method for determining whether feedback is involved in the control of movement. The major test of feedback utilization is whether changes in the feedback can be shown to produce predictable (corrective) changes in some observable aspect of the motor response (Schmidt 1976). A number of investigations have used this rationale and focused on the auditory, kinaesthetic and/or visual modalities.

There are a number of experimental studies which suggest that auditory feedback plays a role in the perception of movement requiring temporal regulation. If the acoustic signals associated with a movement sequence are made to lag by approximately 200 ms behind each of the responses that causes them, performance is usually slowed or disrupted (Glencross 1977). This observation has been reported for a wide variety of motor skills, ranging from handclapping (Kalmus, Denes and Fry 1955), Morse code production (Yates 1963), to speech (Fairbanks 1955). Given that delaying feedback has an effect on performance it is reasonable to infer that subjects monitor feedback associated with movement. In the case of delayed auditory feedback the principal changes that occur in speech include a lengthening of phrase utterances, repetition of syllables, omissions, substitutions and mispronunciation (Glencross 1977).

Mechanical vibration to tendons also provides support for the closed-loop position. Goodwin, McCloskey and Matthews (1972) found that when vibration was applied to the arm over a tendon or muscle belly, it produced an illusion of joint rotation. It was reported that applying vibrations to the biceps brachii produced a sensation of extension, in contrast vibrations of the triceps produced a sensation of flexion. Additionally, when the movements were resisted, the subject reported a strong sensation of movement in the opposite direction. The effects of vibrations are specific. Eklund (1972) and Craske (1977) have both shown that illusions of position and movement occur only if the muscle tendon is vibrated. These findings suggest that muscle spindles play an important role in movement perception. Moreover, such illusions of movement and misjudgement can be demonstrated under a variety of conditions (Goodwin 1976) but are best demonstrated by vibrating the flexor and extensor muscles of the thumb.

If the sensory afferents operate in a closed-loop manner, it should be possible to demonstrate movement misperception with other techniques. In a frequently quoted study, Gelfan and Carter (1967) claim that in patients with exposed tendons which could be directly pulled, only distal pulling produced a sensation of movement. Subsequently, Matthews and Simmonds (1974) repeated the experiment with more refined techniques and found that subjects reported marked sensations of movement in both directions. Joint afferents have also been shown to be important by Grigg (1976) who observed poor movement accuracy following prosthetic replacement.

Further support for the importance of kinaesthetic feedback comes from Nielson (1972) who had subjects track unpredictable movements of one limb by another limb and showed that it was possible to track the accuracy of kinaesthetic feedback and determine the latencies in correction. Good tracking performance was found for frequencies of movement below 2 Hz; at higher frequencies the movements appeared much more reflexive or automated.

Perturbations in visual feedback have been shown to affect the speed and accuracy of movements (Kohler 1964; Pick, Warren and Hay 1961; Stratton 1896). Visual distortion by prismatic displacement which has been extensively studied provides a good example. The movement of a hand from the left to a target on the right, while viewing the target through prisms which displace the image to the right, will lead to overshooting of the target to the right because of the distortion of target position. However, if the hand is moved slowly enough, the error which is induced can be detected visually, and corrections can be made in order to compensate for the initially incorrect command to the motor system. With practice under prism displacement, movement accuracy can be regained, a change well known as adaptation (Craske 1977). In a similiar study, Held (1967) used prisms to displace visual targets and found the usual misperception of movement. However, the most interesting finding was that recalibration occurred with movement, presumably the afferent feedback played some role in detecting and correcting the distortion effect. This position is supported by Warren and Cleaves (1971) who varied the discrepancy between the seen and felt position of the limb using prismatic displacement techniques. Visual biasing was reduced when the sources of information became more discrepant.

The normal relationship between vision and the movement of a hand can also be distorted temporarily by delaying the subject's sight of the moving hand. This technique of delayed visual feedback, which was developed by Smith (1962), induces disturbances of movement similar in some respects to those found with prism displacement and is also subject to adaptation effects (Smith and Bowen 1976). When taken together these studies show that manipulating sensory information produces marked changes in motor performance and as such supports a closed-loop position. The implication is that feedback is necessary for the regulation of movement and thus error detection and error correction are linked to response produced feedback.

The Case for Open-loop Control

Sensory reduction studies. The strongest support for open-loop control comes from deafferentation or other procedures involving sensory reduction in which the muscle and joint receptors ascending to the motor centres of the brain are severed. If co-ordinated movements can still be made then there is a prima facia case for the central control of movement.

While realizing the obvious danger of generalizing to humans, there is some rather provocative evidence from work with insects and on the development of song in birds which supports an open-loop model. Wilson (1961) investigated the reduction of sensory information on the pattern of flight action of locust wings. Even after the removal of all or part of the wing, the sequencing of rapid wing movements remained unaffected. Such a finding would not be expected if proprioceptive feedback were an important influence on wing action. Further, it was shown that flight action was started by loss of ground contact, by pinching the abdomen, and by stimulating wind sensitive hairs on the head.

Studies on the development of song in birds offers some additional insight into how co-ordinated motor acts are controlled (Marler and Hamilton 1966). The vocal system of birds can be affected by severing the hypoglossal nerve which innervates the vocal system bilaterally. When Nottebohm (1970) severed the nerve on one side or the other, paralysing certain muscles, parts of the song dropped out. The remaining elements of the song however occurred in the proper time sequence, which Keele (1973) interpreted as evidence that neither the missing kinaesthetic feedback nor the missing auditory stimulation from the eliminated segment was necessary for triggering the remaining elements.

Earlier, McCarthy and Lashley (1926) and Lashley and Ball (1929) reported similar evidence from studies with rats. The learning of a complex maze was examined before and after deafferentation or experimentally produced brain lesions. Lashley and his colleagues found that maze performance was maintained following deafferentation, again supporting the central organization of movement control. Fentress (1973) presented further supporting evidence from work with mice. In normal grooming behaviour mice bring their forelimbs in front of the face, and, as the paws move toward the mouth, the tongue projects outward making contact with the paws. In a second sequence, one forelimb crosses over the eye and the eye closes just before contact. Fentress (1973) amputated the forelimbs of the mice one day after birth and made observations on grooming over a one month period. During this month of observation the portions of the limb remaining after amputation went through the same grooming motions as normal mice. Furthermore, the tongue licked and the eye closed at the appropriate point in the sequence even though no contact was made between the paw and the face.

Taub and Berman (1968) provide further evidence from their work on rhesus monkeys. Afferent feedback from one of the monkey's arms was eliminated surgically by severing the dorsal roots of the nerve entering the spinal cord. Following deafferentation Taub and Berman reported that the monkeys were able to use their forelimbs in a rhythmical manner, and in co-ordination with the hind limbs. The monkeys were able to climb wire cages and showed the usual range of normal behaviour patterns. This early work has been criticized on the basis that vision could have acted as a mediator in correcting movement patterns. Therefore Taub, Perrella and Barro (1972) performed a similar experiment on infant monkeys, but this time blocked both the proprioceptive feedback and visual feedback shortly after birth. These monkeys subsequently learned to walk, indicating that certain types of movement are not dependent on normal afferent or visual feedback (Taub 1976).

Since these deafferentation techniques are irreversible, similar data for humans are extremely rare. One such instance is a study by Lashley (1917) who examined positioning accuracy in a patient who had a deafferent leg from a gunshot wound. In spite of not being able to perceive passive movement, the patient could duplicate his own active movements well. He never made a mistake in detecting the direction of voluntary movement and could reproduce the extent of a movement as well as a control subject. Further evidence on humans is reported by Phillips (1969) who reviewed evidence on patients whose dorsal roots were severed in order to control pain or relieve spasticity. While the evidence is sketchy on the consequences of such surgery, the patients whose upper limbs were deafferented could make blind movements as directed.

It has become more common in recent years to use the technique of nerve compression block (Laszlo 1966) in the search for the locus of motor control in humans. While the technique is not as direct as deafferentation and has been the subject of much controversy (Kelso, Stelmach and Wanamaker 1974), it does provide insight into the contribution of joint receptors to motor control. A modified technique used by Kelso (1977) temporarily rendered joint and cutaneous receptors in the hand insentient via inflation of a child's sphygomanometer cuff. Briefly, a blood pressure cuff is placed around the wrist of a subject, and is then inflated to a point where the blood flow to the limb is stopped. After a period of time, the limb becomes insensitive to sensory stimulation. In this study, which bears upon the open-loop issue, Kelso used positioning responses where precision was important. After eliminating sensory sensitivity, Kelso asked his subjects to make finger movements to a location defined by the subject or to a location defined by the experimenter. The theoretical difference between movement conditions is that when the subject defined the movement, organization of the motor outflow was possible, while in the experimenter-defined condition this organization was not possible. When these movement conditions were compared, in the cuff and no cuff conditions, it became clear that when subjects were allowed to organize their movements the reduction in peripheral feedback did not impair movement accuracy, whereas the constrained movements were markedly impaired. This finding indicates that when prior knowledge about movement is available movement reproduction is less dependent on peripheral information.

The deafferentation studies have been criticized by some (Bossom and Ommaya 1968; Adams 1976; Keele and Summers 1976) on the grounds that some dorsal root fibres may remain intact. Recent physiological research (Coggeshall, Coulter and Willis 1974; Applebaum *et al.* 1976), using electron microscope examinations, has established the existence of very fine unmyelinated fibres in the ventral root whose cell bodies arise in the dorsal root ganglion. As reported by Adams (1977), these studies show that about thirty per cent of the nerve fibres in the ventral root carry sensory information and most of these can be stimulated despite cutting the dorsal roots. Thus, it is possible that only a few fibres are sufficient to mediate co-ordinated performance after recovery from surgery. Since none of these studies used evoked potentials to check on the completeness of the deafferentation procedures this criticism is valid. Kelso (1978), however, maintains that unmyelinated sensory fibres have conduction times that are too slow to regulate movement.

It is also possible that the deafferented limbs could have produced affects on non-deafferented parts of the body through vibration, changes in visual field and the monitoring of sensory feedback. In other words, feedback from other parts could mediate a response in deafferented segments. An additional criticism against afferent reduction techniques which has been made by Bossom (1974), and elaborated by Keele and Summers (1976), centres on the quality of the responses made after either elimination or reduction techniques have been used. Bossom emphasized that there is a considerable loss of elegance of movement control. As reported by Keele and Summers (1976), monkeys can extend their arms, then their wrists and curl their fingers around a food object even when the arm is hidden from view. However, in these movements, it is reported that the thumb is not used and the movements appear clumsy. Keele and Summers (1976) argue that it is possible that the more gross rhythmic movements involved in skills like walking can be sequenced without feedback, but that manipulative skills are dependent on feedback. This suggests that feedback may be necessary only for finer corrections. Support for this idea also comes from Kelso's (1977) study using nerve compression block. Despite the fact that subjects could accurately reproduce simple movements when they were self defined under sensory reduction conditions they appeared temporarily disorganized and disjointed. Such findings give some credence to Adams' (1976) view that perhaps what deafferentation and related studies have shown is that skilled responding is possible without proprioceptive feedback, not that open-loop control has been proven. Nevertheless, the deafferentation and related methods have presented convincing evidence that movements can be made with varying degrees of precision in the absence of peripheral feedback. Perhaps the review by Brooks (1974) summarizes the deafferentation studies best by showing that continuous, well learned movements seem relatively impervious to peripheral feedback manipulations and that discontinuous exploratory type movements are modified by augmented sensory information.

Rapid movements. When movements are of extremely short duration, such as 10-70 ms, it is difficult to argue that sensory feedback can modify the response during its execution. Convincing evidence in this regard comes from studies examining the characteristics of rapid eye movements. The time duration for a one degree eye saccade has been estimated at 10-20 ms and for a 20 degree eye saccade at approximately 60-70 ms (Yarbus 1967). An open-loop control model would imply that the perceptual system obtains knowledge of eye position and eye movement via the monitoring of efferent commands to the extra-ocular muscles. In other words, the central nervous system knows where the eye will be directed before it is ever moved.

Convincing evidence favouring the central programming hypothesis was presented in a study by Festinger and Canon (1965). Performance on a spatial localization task was compared under two experimental conditions. One group localized the visual target using a saccadic eye movement, whereas, a second group localized the visual target by tracking it to its final location. The results revealed that when eye tracking movements were permitted, target localization was more accurate when the target suddenly appeared at its final location. The most interesting interpretation is that saccadic movements are brought about in response to the efferent command generated for the known target position. On the other hand, with tracking movements the eyes follow the target without knowing its final location, thus the efferent signals cannot be directed to the target.

McLaughlin (1967) extended these results showing that the central programme could be modified irrespective of the subject's awareness. He found that when a target, toward which the subject was shifting his gaze, was displaced one degree toward the mid-point, the eye made an overshoot. With repeated presentations the central command adjusted its output so that the discrepancy was reduced. The target was then returned to its original location and the subjects subsequently undershot the target.

In a later study, Festinger and Easton (1974) induced a misperception of movement paths by using a movement illusion. Through the systematic monitoring of eye movements, retinal information was compared with the perception of the movement path of a light. Festinger and Easton postulated that a discrepancy between the two types of information would reflect the informational content of the monitored efferent commands available to the perceptual system. The results indicated that the physical path orientation was always correct. It was thus argued that the efferent command contained the necessary directional information.

Further evidence for open-loop control has been presented by Bizzi, Kalil and Morrosso (1972). In this study, monkeys were trained to predict or anticipate the onset of a visual stimulus. When the events were predictable the head began to move well before (approximately 175 ms) the eye saccade. These results are very clear in suggesting some form of central programming. Kelso (1977) interpreted this finding as indicating that a central feedforward signal was used and that such a signal must contain information about the anticipated consequences of a motor act. Thus, there is evidence that very rapid movements can be made independently of feedback, and such findings accord well with a central programming notion where prestructured commands which control the prescribed movement are utilized.

Reaction time studies. Closed-loop control systems maintain that instantaneous modifications to correct or minimize response errors are made on the basis of the sensory consequences of the actual movement. This assertion points to another difference between open and closed-loop control, namely how quickly individuals can react to changes in environmental stimuli.

Keele and Posner (1968) required subjects to perform an alternate tapping task, where they varied the time duration between taps; 150, 250, 350 or 450 ms. On half of the experimental trials the termination of visual information coincided with the initiation of movement. A comparison of visual and non-visual conditions revealed that the visual information only facilitated tapping accuracy in the longer durations. The conclusion from this experiment was that the minimum time to process visual feedback and use it for movement correction was approximately 200 ms.

Similarly, Chernikoff and Taylor (1952) examined kinaesthetic reaction time. Subjects rested their arm on a horizontal platform and periodically the support was removed. The subject's task was to re-establish the horizontal position as quickly as possible. Reaction times to make the necessary adjustments were approximately 120 ms. In a second experiment, reaction times to counteract the force applied to a joy stick was measured. Estimates of reaction time were increased slightly in this instance to approximately 130 ms.

An insightful experiment concerning reactions to environmental changes was reported by Henry and Harrison (1961). Subjects responded to a light by initiating a rapid, horizontal arm movement toward the centre of the body. At varying intervals following the start light (100, 190 or 350 ms), a second light was presented, which cued subjects to reverse the direction of the original movement. Changes in direction occurred approximately 200 ms after the second light. Moreover, Gottsdanker (1973) used a step tracking task in which subjects made rapid hand movements to either of two targets defined by lights; 6.2 mm or 15.9 mm. On predetermined trials, after the target light had been on for 50 ms, the alternate light appeared and subjects were required to reverse their movements and go to the second target as fast as possible. In general, the time required for switching was of the order of 120 ms.

While these data argue against the closed-loop view where feedback is the agent which initiates error detection and correction, they may be misleading. Recent research has begun to produce evidence that feedback time is perhaps more rapid than previously thought. Fuchs and Kornhuber (1969) have shown that extraocular muscles of the cat can be regulated by feedback in only 10 ms. Similarly, Evarts (1973) has reported that the time from motor stimulation to electromyographic response was only 30-40 ms. These recent findings weaken the impact of the reaction time studies.

SUMMARY

Although an understanding of how movement is controlled has interested psychologists and physiologists for many years our knowledge of the mechanisms involved is still very limited. The experimental evidence generally gives support to both central and peripheral control theories. It seems clear therefore that it is neither simply open or closed-loop, at times we operate under both systems. Evidence supporting this position comes from Bizzi *et al.* (1972, 1976), Kelso (1977) and Pew (1966). In these studies it was shown that with constrained or unpractised conditions, performance was very much affected by a reduction in peripheral feedback. On the other hand, in preselected and well practised conditions, the subject's performance seems unaffected by a loss of peripheral feedback. This work emphasizes the integration of both central and sensory processes in motor behaviour. Thus a major challenge for research on motor control is the manner in which open-loop and closed-loop processes interact.

'It is misleading to assume that sensory feedback, important though it may be, is always necessary to elicit further motor output. Equally unrealistic is the notion that neural networks within the CNS generate stored movement patterns in total independence of peripheral feedback. Both peripheral and central approaches, if accepted in isolation of each other, leave too many questions unanswered.' Kelso and Stelmach (1976), p. 35.

Now that we have moved beyond the question of whether movement is controlled by either an open-loop *or* a closed-loop system, the primary question of interest concerns the receptor and effector mechanisms that mediate control. Future research needs to identify precisely which mechanisms are responsible for control and under what environmental conditions they operate. The research on the role of joint and muscle receptors is still confusing, although broad agreement about their particular contributions to motor control is emerging. Similarly, central control theorists have provided some impressive evidence that the control of skilled movement at times is determined by a prestructured motor command, however, more work needs to be done to define precisely the conditions under which this form of control operates.

The exciting aspect for the future is that research on motor control has become truly interdisciplinary. Behavioural and neurophysiological data are equally contributing in an important way to our understanding of motor control.

REFERENCES

Adams, J. A. 1971. 'A closed-loop theory of motor learning.' *J. Mot. Behav. 3*, 111-50.
Adams, J. A. 1976. 'Issues for a closed-loop theory of motor learning.' In Stelmach, G. E. (ed.) *Motor control: issues and trends.* New York: Academic Press.
Adams, J. A. 1977. 'Feedback theory of how joint receptors regulate the timing and positioning of a limb.' *Psychol. Rev. 84*, 504-23.
Anokhin, P. K. 1969. 'Cybernetics and the integrative activity of the brain.' In Cole, M. and Maltzman, I. (eds) *A handbook of contemporary Soviet psychology.* New York: Basic Books.
Applebaum, M. L., Fazen, P., Stubbs, W. S. and Sykes, R. W. 1976. 'Unmyelinated fibers in the sacral 3 and caudal 1 ventral roots of the cat.' *J. Physiol. 256*, 557-72.
Bell, C. 1826. 'On the nervous circle which connects the voluntary muscles with the brain.' *Philosophical Trans. 116*, 163-73.
Bizzi, E., Kalil, R. E. and Morrosso, P. 1972. 'Two modes of active eye-head co-ordination in monkeys.' *Brain Res. 40*, 45-8.

Bizzi, E., Polit, A. and Morrosso, P. 1976. 'Mechanisms underlying achievement of final head position.' *J. Neurophysiol. 39*, 435-44.

Bossom, J. 1974. 'Movement without proprioception.' *Brain Res. 71*, 285-96.

Bossom, J. and Ommaya, A. K. 1968. 'Visuo-motor adaptation in monkeys with bilateral dorsal rhizotomy.' *Brain 91*, 161-72.

Brooks, V. B. 1974. 'Some examples of programmed limb movements.' *Brain Res. 71*, 299-308.

Chase, R. A. 1965. 'An information-flow model of the organization of motor activity: Part I. Transduction, transmission and central control of sensory information.' *J. Nerv. Ment. Dis. 140*, 239-51.

Chernikoff, R. and Taylor, F. V. 1952. 'Reaction time to kinesthetic stimulation resulting from sudden arm displacement.' *J. exp. Psychol. 43*, 1-8.

Coggeshall, R. A., Coulter, J. D. and Willis, W. D. 1974. 'Unmyelinated axons in the ventral roots of the cat lumbosacral enlargement.' *J. comp. Neurol. 153*, 39-58.

Craske, B. 1977. 'Perception of impossible limb positions induced by tendon vibration.' *Science 196*, 71-3.

Duchenne, G. B. 1883. *Selections from the clinical works of Dr Duchenne*. London: New Sydenham Society.

Eklund, G. 1972. 'Position sense and state of contraction: the effect of vibration.' *J. neurol. neurosurg. Psychiat. 35*, 606-11.

Evarts, E. V. 1973. 'Motor cortex reflexes associated with learned movements.' *Science 179*, 501-4.

Fairbanks, G. 1955. 'Selective vocal effects of delayed auditory feedback.' *J. Speech Hearing Disord. 20*, 333-46.

Fentress, J. C. 1973. 'Development of grooming in mice with amputated forelimbs.' *Science 179*, 704-5.

Festinger, L. and Canon, L. K. 1965. 'Information about spatial location based on knowledge about efference.' *Psychol. Rev. 72*, 373-84.

Festinger, L. and Easton, A. M. 1974. 'Inferences about the efferent system based on a perceptual illusion produced by eye movements.' *Psychol. Rev. 81*, 44-58.

Fuchs, A. F. and Kornhuber, H. H. 1969. 'Extraocular muscle afferents to the cerebellum of the cat.' *J. Physiol. 200*, 713-22.

Gelfan, S. and Carter, S. 1967. 'Muscle sense in man.' *Exp. Neurol. 18*, 469-73.

Glencross, D. J. 1977. 'Control of skilled movement.' *Psychol. Bull. 84*, 14-29.

Goodwin, G. M. 1976. 'The sense of limb position and movements.' In Keogh, J. and Hutton, R. S. (eds) *Exercise and sport sciences reviews 4*. Santa Barbara: Journal Publishing Affiliates.

Goodwin, G. M., McCloskey, D. I. and Matthews, P. B. C. 1972. 'The contribution of muscle afferents to kinaesthesia shown by vibration induced illusions of movement and by the effects of paralyzing joint afferents.' *Brain 95*, 705-48.

Gottsdanker, R. 1973. 'Psychological refractoriness and the organization of step-tracking responses.' *Percep. and Psychophys. 14*, 60-70.

Grigg, P. 1976. 'Response of joint afferent neurons in cat medial articular nerve to active and passive movements of the knee.' *Brain Res. 118*, 482-5.

Held, P. 1967. 'Plasticity in sensory-motor systems.' *Sci. Amer. 213*, 84-94.

Henry, F. M. 1960. 'Increased response latency for complicated movements and a "memory drum" theory of neuromotor reaction.' *Res. Quart. 31*, 448-57.

Henry, F. M. and Harrison, J. S. 1961. 'Refractoriness of a fast movement.' *Percep. and Mot. Skills 13*, 351-4.

Howard, I. P. and Templeton, W. B. 1966. *Human spatial orientation.* New York: Wiley.

Hunter, W. S. 1930. 'A consideration of Lashley's theory of the equipotentiality of cerebral action.' *J. genet. Psychol. 3*, 455-68.

James, W. 1890. *The principles of Psychology 1.* New York: Holt.

Kalmus, H., Denes, F. and Fry, D. B. 1955. 'Effect of delayed acoustic feedback on some nonvocal activities.' *Nature 175*, 1078.

Keele, S. W. 1968. 'Movement control in skilled motor performance.' *Psychol. Bull. 70*, 387-403.

Keele, S. W. 1973. *Attention and human performance.* Pacific Palisades, California: Goodyear Publishing Company.

Keele, S. W. and Posner, M. I. 1968. 'Processing of feedback in rapid movements.' *J. exp. Psychol. 77*, 353-63.

Keele, S. W. and Summers, J. 1976. 'The structure of motor programs.' In Stelmach, G. E. (ed.) *Motor control: issues and trends.* New York: Academic Press.

Kelso, J. A. S. 1977. 'Motor control mechanisms underlying human movement reproduction.' *J. exp. Psychol.: Hum. Percep. and Perform. 3*, 529-43.

Kelso, J. A. S. 1978. 'Joint receptors do not provide a satisfactory basis for motor timing and positioning.' *Psychol. Rev. 85*, 474-481.

Kelso, J. A. S. and Stelmach, G. E. 1976. 'Central and peripheral mechanisms in motor control.' In Stelmach, G. E. (ed.) *Motor control: issues and trends.* New York: Academic Press.

Kelso, J. A. S., Stelmach, G. E. and Wanamaker, W. M. 1974. 'Behavioural and neurological parameters of the nerve compression block.' *J. Mot. Behav. 6*, 179-90.

Klapp, S. 1975. 'Feedback versus motor programming in the control of aimed movements.' *J. exp. Psychol.: Hum. Percep. and Perform. 1*, 147-53.

Kohler, W. 1964. *Gestalt psychology.* New York: Liveright.

Lashley, K. S. 1917. 'The accuracy of movement in the absence of excitation from the moving organ.' *Amer. J. Physiol. 43*, 169-99.

Lashley, K. S. and Ball, J. 1929. 'Spinal conduction and kinaesthetic sensitivity in the maze habit.' *J. comp. Psychol. 9*, 71-106.

Laszlo, J. I. 1966. 'The performance of a simple motor task with kinaesthetic sense loss.' *Quart. J. exp. Psychol. 18*, 1-8.

MacNeilage, P. F. 1970. 'Motor control of serial ordering of speech.' *Psychol. Rev. 77*, 182-96.

Marler, P. R. and Hamilton, W. S. III 1966. *Mechanisms of animal behavior.* New York: Wiley.

Marteniuk, R. G. and Roy, E. A. 1972. 'The codability of kinesthetic location and distance information.' *Acta Psychol. 36*, 471-9.

Matthews, P. B. C. 1972. *Mammalian muscle receptors and their central actions.* London: Arnold.

Matthews, P. B. C. and Simmonds, A. 1974. 'Sensations of finger movement elicited by pulling upon flexor tendons in man.' *J. Physiol. 239*, 27-8.

McCarthy, D. A. and Lashley, K. S. 1926. 'The survival of the maze habit after cerebral injuries.' *J. comp. Psychol. 6*, 423-33.

McLaughlin, S. 1967. 'Parametric adjustments in saccadic eye movements.' *Percep. and Psychophys. 2*, 359-62.

Mott, F. W. and Sherrington, C. S. 1895. 'Experiments upon the influence of sensory nerves upon movement and nutrition of the limbs.' *Proc. Roy. Soc. 57*, 481-8.

Nielson, P. D. 1972. 'Speed of response or bandwidth of voluntary system controlling elbow position in man.' *Med. and Biol. Eng. 10*, 450-9.

Nottebohm, F. 1970. 'Ontogeny of bird song.' *Science 167*, 950-6.

Pew, R. W. 1966. 'Acquisition of hierarchical control over the temporal organization of a skill.' *J. exp. Psychol. 71*, 764-71.

Phillips, C. G. 1969. 'Motor apparatus of the baboon's hand.' *Proc. Roy. Soc. B. 173*, 141-74.

Pick, H. L., Warren, D. H. and Hay, J. C. 1961. 'Sensory conflict in judgements of spatial direction.' *Percep. and Psychophys. 6*, 203-5.

Schmidt, R. A. 1976. 'The schema as a solution to some persistent problems in motor learning theory.' In Stelmach, G. E. (ed.) *Motor control: issues and trends*. New York: Academic Press.

Schmidt, R. A. 1977. 'Control processes in motor skills.' In Keogh, J. and Hutton, R. S. (eds) *Exercise and sport sciences reviews 4*. Santa Barbara: Journal Publishing Affiliates.

Shambes, G. M. 1969. 'Influence of the fusimotor system on stance and volitional movement in normal man.' *Amer. J. phys. Med. 48*, 225-36.

Sherrington, C. S. 1906. *The integrative action of the nervous system*. New Haven: Yale University Press.

Skoglund, S. 1956. 'Anatomical and physiological studies of knee joint innervation in the cat.' *Acta Physiol. Scand. Monog. Suppl. 124*, 1-99.

Skoglund, S. 1973. 'Joint receptors and kinaesthesis.' In Iqqo, A. (ed.) *Handbook of sensory physiology: somatosensory system 2*. Berlin, Heidelberg, New York: Springer-Verlag.

Smith, J. L. 1969. 'Kinesthesis: a model for movement feedback.' In Brown, R. C. and Cratty, B. J. (eds) *New perspectives of man in action*. Englewood Cliffs, N. J.: Prentice-Hall.

Smith, J. L., Roberts, E. M. and Atkins, E. 1972. 'Fusimotor neuron block and voluntary arm movement in man.' *Amer. J. phys. Med. 51*, 225-39.

Smith, K. U. 1962. *Delayed sensory feedback and behavior*. Philadelphia: Saunders.

Smith, W. M. and Bowen, K. R. 1976. 'The effects of delayed visual feedback upon performance.' Unpublished manuscript.

Sokolov, E. N. 1969. 'The modelling properties of the nervous system.' In Cole, M. and Maltzman, I. (eds) *A handbook of contemporary Soviet psychology*. New York: Basic Books.

Sperry, R. V., Gazzaniga, M. S. and Bogen, J. E. 1969. 'Interhemispheric relations: the neocortical commisures; syndromes of hemispheric disconnection.' In Venken, P. J. and Bruyen, G. W. (eds) *Handbook of clinical neurology 4*. Amsterdam: North Holland.

Stelmach, G. E. and McCracken, H. D. 1978. 'Storage codes of movement information.' In Requin, J. (ed.) *Attention and performance VII*. New York: Erlbaum. In press.

Stratton, G. M. 1896. 'Some preliminary experiments in vision without inversion of the retinal image.' *Psychol. Rev. 3*, 611-17.

Taub, E. 1976. 'Movement in nonhuman primates deprived of somato-sensory feedback'. In Keogh, J. and Hutton, R. S. (eds) *Exercise and sport sciences reviews 4*. Santa Barbara: Journal Publishing Affiliates.

Taub, E. and Berman, A. J. 1968. 'Movement and learning in the absence of sensory feedback.' In Freedman, S. J. (ed.) *The neuropsychology of spatially oriented behavior*. Homewood, Illinois: Dorsey.

Taub, E., Perrella, P. and Barro, G. 1972. 'Behavioral development in monkeys following bilateral forelimb deafferentation on the first day of life.' *Trans. Amer. Neurol. Assoc. 97*, 101-4.

Teuber, H-L. 1964. Comment on E. H. Lenneberg's paper, 'Speech as a motor skill with special reference to nonphasic disorders.' In *Acquisition of Language, Monogr. Soc. Res. Child Develop. 29*, 131-8.

Vallbo, A. B. 1974. 'Afferent discharge from human muscle spindles in non-contracting muscles.' *Acta Physiol. Scand. 90*, 303-18.

von Holst, E. 1954. 'Relations between the central nervous system and the peripheral organs.' *Brit. J. Anim. Behav. 2*, 89-94.

Warren, D. H. and Cleaves, W. T. 1971. 'Visual proprioceptive interaction under large amounts of conflict.' *J. exp. Psychol. 90*, 206-14.

Weiss, P. 1950. 'Experimental analysis of co-ordination by the disarrangement of central-peripheral relations.' *Symp. Soc. exp. Biol. 4*, 92-111.

Wilson, D. M. 1961. 'The central nervous control of flight in a locust.' *J. exp. Biol. 38*, 471-90.

Yarbus, A. L. 1967. *Eye movements and vision*. New York: Plenum Press.

Yates, A. J. 1963. 'Recent empirical and theoretical approaches to the experimental manipulations of speech in normal subjects and in stammerers.' *Behav. Res. Ther. 1*, 95-119.

Author Index

Subject Index

Table of Contents of
Psychology Survey, No. 1

Occupational psychology, Peter Warr, Director, MRC Social and Applied Psychology Unit, Department of Psychology, University of Sheffield

Environmental psychology, Charles Mercer, Lecturer in Psychology, University of Wales Institute of Science and Technology

Table of Contents of
Psychology Survey, No. 3